Beyond the Tyranny of Testing

Beyond the Tyranny of Testing

Relational Evaluation in Education

KENNETH J. GERGEN, PHD
Senior Research Professor
Swarthmore College
Swarthmore, PA, USA

and

SCHERTO R. GILL, DPHIL
Executive Secretary/Senior Fellow
GHFP Research Institute
Brighton, East Sussex, UK

OXFORD
UNIVERSITY PRESS

OXFORD
UNIVERSITY PRESS

Oxford University Press is a department of the University of Oxford. It furthers
the University's objective of excellence in research, scholarship, and education
by publishing worldwide. Oxford is a registered trade mark of Oxford University
Press in the UK and certain other countries.

Published in the United States of America by Oxford University Press
198 Madison Avenue, New York, NY 10016, United States of America.

Library of Congress Cataloging-in-Publication Data
Names: Gergen, Kenneth J., author. | Gill, Scherto R., author.
Title: Beyond the tyranny of testing : relational evaluation in education /
by Kenneth J. Gergen and Scherto R. Gill.
Description: New York, NY : Oxford University Press, [2020] |
Includes bibliographical references and index.
Identifiers: LCCN 2020005783 (print) | LCCN 2020005784 (ebook) |
ISBN 9780190872762 (hardback) | ISBN 9780190872779 (epub) |
ISBN 9780197529225 (online)
Subjects: LCSH: Educational tests and measurements.
Classification: LCC LB3051 .G43 2020 (print) | LCC LB3051 (ebook) |
DDC 371.26—dc23
LC record available at https://lccn.loc.gov/2020005783
LC ebook record available at https://lccn.loc.gov/2020005784

1 3 5 7 9 8 6 4 2

Printed by Sheridan Books, Inc., United States of America

Contents

Preface

Agitation over the state of public education has never been more widespread and intense than now. Its expression is carried in teeming numbers of articles, reports, and books from educators, teachers, school leaders, researchers, and government panels. Myriad journals and websites pressing for change are coupled with critiques shared on social media. For example, more than 17 million viewers have watched a single TED Talk by Ken Robinson on the way that schools are killing creativity. All lend fire to public demonstrations by teachers, students, and parents alike. And to this ferment still other voices point to the irrelevance of our educational practices in a world of rapid and unpredictable change. While the global flows in information, ideas, values, and innovation continue to accelerate, our educational systems remain lodged in the assumptions of an earlier century. There is now common agreement that our educational traditions are rapidly becoming dysfunctional and irrelevant. Change seems imperative—but what changes and in which direction?

It is just such questions that sparked our own dialogue. Both of us were born into families of educators, moving from preschool to graduate school and thence to professions in education. We swim in the swirling waters of agitation. We found ourselves especially drawn to the widespread critiques of educational assessment, the attempt to test, measure, and compare students, teachers, schools, regions, and nations against some standard. It is not simply the problematic validity and constraining focus of such measures, nor the ways in which they foster cookie-cutter standardization. As is widely voiced, test performance is becoming the very purpose of education. The tail now wags the dog. For students this means that curiosity, creativity, and potential passion and engagement in learning are replaced by boredom, stress, anxiety, and alienation from each other and from school. To be sure, evaluation (rather than assessment) is an essential part of learning, but as we began to ask, how can we separate and protect this invaluable process from the testing-based assessment? The question seemed sufficiently focused that we might make progress. However, what appeared to be a circumscribed question soon thrust us into combat with more general educational foundations. As we realized, the testing/assessment tradition is an essential element in the long-standing vision of schools as systematically organized institutions for educating the young. Much like a factory, such systems are designed to generate products rather than educated persons. This view of education requires assessment to ensure both the proper functioning of the system, which includes teachers, leaders, schools as institutions, and the quality of its products. Thus, to abandon assessment demands nothing less than locating a compelling alternative to this factory approach to education.

For us, the alternative was already presaged by John Dewey's views on education as a social good. Many educators have since added significant dimensions to this orientation. However, most accounts have remained closely wedded to an individualist conception of social life, which, in brief, suggests that the social world is made up of independent individuals. So long as this view prevails, it will be difficult to shake off the shrouds of performance measurement as the basis for educational assessment. Our offering, then, is more radical: we argue that it is out of *relational process* that individuals emerge and exist. Here, we focus especially on the co-creation of meaning, the way in which our conceptions of the self and the world, our beliefs and values, and our intentions and passions emerge from relational processes. More generally, then, we suggest that schools are not so much like factories as they are myriad conversations in motion. If we strive for vitalized learning and the well-being of the participants, we must nourish the relational process.

With this vision in the forefront, we then set out to articulate a relational orientation to educational evaluation. Central to this orientation is a view of evaluation as collaborative inquiry. Abandoned are traditions in which one person or group sits in judgment on voiceless others. Favored are continuously formative and multi-voiced dialogues specifically aimed at enhancing and sustaining an engagement in learning while contributing to the enrichment of the relational process itself. Ideally, relational approaches to evaluation should include all relevant stakeholders in an extended learning community.

Of course, many could fault such visions as unrealistic. In fact, we would not have embarked on this conceptual journey with a suitcase of ideas alone. We traveled with energizing provisions from educators and schools around the world. Discontent with the measurement-based assessment tradition has served as a goad to innovation. Abundant alternatives to testing have thus been developed, and many of these make a stellar contribution to both learning and the process of relating. We thus devote major chapters of the book to relationally enriching practices of evaluation in primary and secondary schools, in teacher evaluation, and the evaluation of schools.

We recognized very early that our attempt to re-envision evaluation was not mere tinkering, and we were buoyed by these many relevant innovations. However, we were not prepared for the next turn in the road. Yes, we could see that we had fellow travelers across the educational sphere. Relationally sensitive innovations in pedagogy and in curriculum design were especially apparent. Developments in dialogic learning, collaborative classrooms, group-based projects, and emergent curricula, for example, seemed quite at one with a relational orientation to evaluation. However, while excitement in these developments abounds, we began to see how performance assessment persistently obstructs their flowering. Dialogue, collaboration, and participatory action virtually defy measurement and standardization. In this light, we could see the true transformative implications of relational evaluation. In replacing assessment, the floodgates of innovation are opened.

As this narrative took shape, the imagination soared. Are we reaching the point at which a major transformation of education is in sight? Discontent with our educational traditions is rampant; educators everywhere realize that the production model must be replaced by a collaborative orientation. Students, teachers, and school leaders must all participate in co-creating the learning process. Thinkers concerned with the new world of rapid and complex change understand very well that schools must also participate in the global dialogues through which our future is shaped. We can only hope that this small volume can add vital energy to such a transformation.

Finally, we must share the fact that the process of writing this book together has furnished a living workshop in the potentials of relational process. We began this effort with mutual respect, trust, and a shared vision. At the same time, we carried the challenge of multiple differences in gender, age, cultural background, geographical location, intellectual history, fields of study, profession, institutional constraint, and more. If our vision was to be realized, we needed to learn from each other, both in content and logics. Wherever there is learning, there is also evaluation. And thus, through our

ongoing dialogues, we also learned more about how to grapple with conflicting perspectives and incorporate, synthesize, create, and ultimately
arrive in spaces of surprise to both of us. This very process of mutual exploration—with all its tensions and transformations—deeply affirmed the relational vision of evaluation articulated in this book.

—Kenneth J. Gergen and Scherto R. Gill
September 2019

1

Beyond the Tyranny of Testing

"Exams are so stressful."

"It's unfair labeling."

"They make me feel like a failure."

"They only measure your ability to answer exam questions."

"Grades don't represent what I have learned."

"I think I would have loved my school and education if there were
no exams."

—Students commenting on exams

The opening quotes are among the comments of teen-aged students
interviewed about their experience of exams and testing in British secondary
education.[1] Unanimously they spoke of exams as impediments to their engagement in learning. Of course, it is easy to disregard such comments as so
much whining. Isn't the purpose of education to ensure that young people
enter adult life with the knowledge and skills necessary to live productive
and fulfilling lives? Aren't exams indispensable indicators of student performance? Don't test scores provide valuable pointers for students, teachers, and
parents about where each student stands in relation to the attainment of their
peers? Exams and grades are as essential to the educational processes as birth
pains to becoming a mother. By the same token, we need national tests to
inform us not only about the adequacy of specific teachers and schools, but
also the functioning of the national system in comparison to others. From
the individual student to the nation as a whole, assessment is the route to
improvement.

On face value, this logic is quite compelling, but closer attention gives
reason for pause. At the outset, how do we know that exams and tests actually
fulfill these objectives? Given the prevailing penchant for evidence-based
practices, is there evidence that such forms of assessment are meaningful
in any of these ways? Is it possible that they are in fact dysfunctional,

Beyond the Tyranny of Testing. Kenneth J. Gergen and Scherto R. Gill, Oxford University Press (2020). © Oxford
University Press. DOI: 10.1093/oso/9780190872762.001.0001.

as suggested by our young people? Where are the comparisons with alternatives? Moreover, is imparting knowledge and skills the only aim of education? Is it possible that there are other aspirations at stake and that the full process of learning and human development is thwarted by practices of assessment? We shall have much to say about the corrosive impact of such practices as this book unfolds.

Our primary aim, however, is to propose and illustrate a meaningful and also viable alternative to the assessment-driven orientation. We call this alternative a *relational approach to evaluation* or relational evaluation for two primary reasons. First is the attempt to replace current assessment practices with evaluative processes that build and enrich the relationships at the heart of education. We focus here on evaluative practices that enhance learning in and through relationships, not only for the student, but also for all stakeholders—teachers, parents, and community included. Second, in stressing relational processes in evaluation, we give the idea of *valuing* a prominent place. We shift the emphasis from measuring individuals according to predetermined standards to bringing forth what is valuable in the learning experience and in life itself. This is also to reduce the gravity toward grading or comparative ranking—of students, teachers, schools, or nations. Instead we accentuate strengths and potentials for growth, development, and becoming. Our major aim is to give voice and visualization to a relational orientation to evaluation. As we shall see, this shift in evaluation may serve as a touchstone for a major transformation in the educational system.

In this chapter, we draw critical attention to the tyranny of the assessment tradition, including practices of examining, grading, and high-stakes testing of students. To begin, we identify the roots of our contemporary vision of schooling and the place of assessment in the educational process. Although this vision draws on long revered assumptions, subsequent discussion will illuminate major flaws. As we shall see, not only do performance tests lack validity, they also have damaging effects on students' learning and well-being. We will further explore related problems created by national or high-stakes testing practices. We should add that the critical scholarship on some of these topics is voluminous, particularly in the case of challenges to high-stakes testing. Our attempt here is simply to bring together and underscore some of the major issues and critiques, thus establishing the profound need for an alternative to existing assumptions and practices.

At the same time, we must recognize that the assessment tradition derives its credibility largely from the more general vision of education as a

production site. Like a well-functioning factory, schools are directed to produce high-quality products at a minimal cost. Assessment thus functions to
ensure the quality of the product. If changes in our forms of evaluation are
to occur, an alternative vision of education is essential. Thus, in Chapter 2,
we introduce a relational perspective that places human relationships at
the center of education. As proposed, it is together that we co-create the
meaning of our world, what we take to be knowledge, reason, and value. The
learning process—including what is learned, how, and why—depends on the
quality of relationship. Personal well-being cannot be separated from relational well-being. With this framework in place, in Chapter 3, we link this
relational perspective with evaluation. Here we outline the deeper rationale
and components of evaluation from a relational perspective. In the four
chapters that follow, we explore a range of relationally sensitive practices.
Such practices apply not only to primary and secondary schools (Chapters 4
and 5), but to evaluating teachers (Chapter 6) and schools (Chapter 7) as
well. These proposals will raise many questions, and these are addressed in
Chapter 8. Here we also take into account cultural conditions bearing on the
need and potential for a relational transformation in education more generally. Chapter 9 expands on the possibilities of transformation by focusing on
opportunities and challenges in specific arenas of relationship.

The Factory Metaphor and the Reign of Assessment

There were times in Western history when education was centered on the holistic growth of the student. There were hopes for enriching moral wisdom,
inspiring curiosity, and kindling an appreciation of accumulated cultural
accomplishments.[2] Yet, whatever remained of such ideals at the turn of the
twentieth century was largely obliterated by the century's end. Prompted by
the needs of booming industries and the desire for more inclusive democracy, it was a century of concerted attempts to make education available and
mandatory for all. Grappling with such masses presented a challenge for educational organization. How could the large numbers of students, in diverse
settings and from varied subcultures, be forged into a uniform entity? How
were the schools to be financed, accountability to be established, teachers to
be trained, quality to be assured, and so forth?
    A Prussian model of systematized education provided a prototype for
most of the West. With the offerings of such prominent educational figures

as Horace Mann and Ellwood Patterson Cubberly, the contours of the system became clear. Foremost were the needs for centralized planning, the implementation of common standards, the linking of education to socioeconomic needs, efficient functioning, and accountability. The goal of accountability was to be realized through various forms of objective assessment. With the development of measurement theory and standardized performance tests, assessment practices seemed an objective, economical, and systematic route to success.

Testing and grading students was the first and most obvious means of assuring that the system functioned properly. Here was a means of quality control at the local level, with a strong appeal to ideals of fairness to all. Concerns with the normal curve, grading on the curve, and grade inflation remain focal even today. However, localized assessment could not provide the information necessary to properly manage the performance of teachers, schools, or the nation's educational system. This need was fulfilled through the development of standardized tests. Such tests subject large populations of students to the same questions to be answered in the same amount of time. Aggregated scores of students in a given classroom can be used to judge the efficacy of the teacher, scores within a school can be used to judge the school as a whole, scores within communities can signal parents where they may find "good schools," and, on a national level, judgments can be made of national deficiencies and progress. Standardized tests at the international level can signal a nation's standing in what is now a global competition. As many see it, this vision of controlled production is identical to the design of large factories competing for market position and profit.

It is also important to note the close association between the testing tradition and standardized education more generally. Measures of performance only make sense if there is a single continuum or dimension along which all can be judged. One cannot judge competence in musical performance, for example, if students play different instruments. Competence in one instrument differs from that in another. In order to measure, all must be playing the same instrument. At the same time, it would be unfair to make judgments if the players had been trained to play different kinds of music: let's say, jazz, rock, or classical.

Thus, if student performance is being assessed, one must assure that all students are familiar with roughly the same curriculum. Similarly, it would scarcely be a fair test if some students benefitted from skilled teachers and others did not. Thus, one must ensure that all teachers are trained in a similar way. Measurement walks hand in hand with standardization, and the results are everywhere in evidence. By and large, students enter a system of preplanned expectations and demands; the curricula contents are predetermined; personal choices are minimal and monitored to guard uniformity. Teacher training ensures that teachers will perform in specified and regulated ways, their pedagogical practices dictated by the predefined objectives and their relationships with students delimited. In addition to standardized curricula and standardized tests, we move toward standardized class sizes, lengths of class periods, and even standardized rates of progress.[3] As one student-teacher related to us, "If the American public education system could be summed up in just one word, the word would be 'standardized.'"

Over the past century, this view of schools as controlled systems of production has been subjected to additional demands. Of major significance, schools have increasingly become instruments for achieving political goals. A major shift in this direction resulted from the Russian launching of *Sputnik* in 1957—the first man-made satellite in space. In the United States, the result was the National Defense Education Act of 1958, which provided large sums of money for programs to promote science education. In effect, education became an instrument for enhancing national security. In later decades, education was seen as a means of preparing students for jobs that boosted the economy.[4] This economic linkage is intimately tied to a later twentieth-century movement in governance. What we commonly recognize as neoliberal policy favors a deregulated or uncontrolled market, privatization, and a shrinking of government and public spending. Also favored is a vision of society in which progress results from competition among its institutions and individuals. "Progress" in this case is primarily equated with increase in economic growth.

As we shall discuss more fully in Chapter 8, neoliberal assumptions have now crept into all corners of our cultural life globally. When coupled with the factory view of education, the results have been both profound and debilitating.[5] At the most general level, critics argue that the neoliberal approach to education carries an inherent tendency to instrumentalize human activity. Human activity comes to be valued primarily in terms of its economic outcomes. Human well-being is a secondary concern, as well-being is assumed to be a byproduct of capital accumulation.[6] Accordingly, for example, locked in economic competition, universities in the United Kingdom and the United States have continued to raise their tuition fees, thus resulting in the common judgment of degrees and diplomas in terms of economic consequences: "What is the return on investment?" Simultaneously, universities have increasingly become invested in selling education as a consumer product, with students subtly redefined as consumers. Both learning and human well-being become secondary as good education is measured with a monetary yardstick.

With economics in the foreground, the challenge of public education is to maximize educational outcomes at minimal cost. It is therefore imperative that one can measure the end products. At the local level this means frequent tests and periodic examinations to determine students' progress and to ensure that they can pass to the next educational level.[7] Teachers, administrators, and school counselors are certified through tests and exams to guarantee that they are correctly functioning parts of the "assembly lines" and are competent to fulfill their roles as cogs in the machine. Nationalized tests, such as SATs, GREs, LSATs, and MCATs in the United States, serve as gate-keeping mechanisms for students eager for higher education. In the United States, both federal and state inspections are used to judge both the effectiveness of schools and the efficacy of their teachers—all based on the test performance of their students. For virtually every component of the system, assessment is continuous.

More broadly put, the *measurement* of the product has come to determine the *value* of the system. As education becomes less about engagement in learning and more about succeeding in tests, it is stripped of any other value or meaning. Whether the educational process enhances creative potential, curiosity, moral sensitivity, aesthetic appreciation, a sense of justice, openness to others who differ, or capacities to collaborate with peers is of minor significance. Or worse, such considerations only matter as they are related to test performance. Counseling is available to help students overcome stress and anxiety, school programs are developed to boost confidence and self-esteem, drugs are prescribed for those who don't pay enough attention in classes. All these efforts are designed to place students *back into the assembly line* with academic performance as their ultimate goal. Whether students vary widely in their talents, aptitudes, values, and aspirations and have life-challenges that are cared for and respected is rather beside the point. In short, the educational process has fallen victim to a tyranny of testing.

Critics have indeed assailed the emergence of the factory model of education.[8] To capture some of these familiar criticisms, the system functions impersonally, treating students, teachers, and administrators as "machine parts" or commodities. Students are viewed as empty vessels to be filled with pieces of knowledge and information for which they have little interest. They are obliged to master the various contents and skills without question and thus enter society as pawns to the status quo. The assembly line mentality fails to recognize or appreciate the enormous variations among students— their subcultures, interests, needs, social class, gender, race, ethnicity, ability, and more. Curricula tend to be one-size-fits-all and largely designed to produce professionals resembling the elite who devised the system. At the same time, despite cumulative reforms, the system itself is slow to respond to developments in knowledge, technology, and global transformations. Therefore, curricula content seldom invites students to explore contemporary issues of significance to their lives. With its claims to value-free knowledge, the system fails to recognize or deliberate on its ideological biases. And this is just a beginning.

Educational Evaluation in a Relational Key: Transforming from the Bottom Up

Our present purpose is not to expand on these long-standing critiques of our public educational model. Nor is it our intention to turn the clock back to nineteenth-century ideals. However, it is our hope that in challenging the metaphor of the factory so pervading our educational practices, we can open a clearing for an alternative vision. Our specific concern is with a conception of education that places meaningful human relationships at the center. For it is within relationships that we determine what is real, true, and worthwhile— and, indeed, what counts as knowledge itself. Relationships are also the source of all language, and thus it is out of relationships that we learn to speak, listen, read, and write—thus to engage in public reasoning, dialogue, and deliberation, both critical and creative. Furthermore, relationships are at the core of who one may become as a person, as part of a family, as a member of a community, society, the world, and the universe. Relationships are thus paramount to human well-being and a flourishing life. In this way, relationships must be at the heart of teaching, learning, administration, counseling, and parenting. It is not an exaggeration to suggest that the entire educational process lives or dies in terms of the health of its relationships.

We shall expand on this relational vision of education in Chapter 2. However, we also hasten to add that it is not our aim to offer an alternative "blueprint" for future schools. One cannot easily abandon an institutional structure so much entrenched in cultural ways of life. Nor can we begin with a blank slate. More importantly, to offer a blueprint would be antithetical to a relational perspective. It was a mistake at the outset to allow an elite to develop a system of their own choosing, to insert this system headlong into the nation's cultural life without listening to the needs, wants, and hopes of those whose futures would be cast within these institutions. Therefore, our aim is more pointed: to transform a single, critical element within the educational process—the practices of evaluation. In the context of schooling, it may be varyingly referred to as assessing, examining, testing, or appraising—each of which has different but overlapping contexts of usage. For us, the common concern is with a dominant structure in which one or more persons or institutions cast judgment on the worth of others—their qualities, attributes, abilities, performance, capacities, skills, and so forth.

This is no small matter. The traditions of evaluation run deep within the community of educators and the culture at large. One can scarcely imagine education without examinations and testing. At the same time, these traditions of evaluation are pivotal in maintaining the factory model of education. To challenge the "obsession" to measure is to raise questions about the current approaches to educational management and control, the pursuit of standardization and efficiency, and education as an economic asset. Furthermore, if we were to pave the way to relational forms of evaluation, we would also be inviting new forms of pedagogy. If teaching is not directed to test performance, then creative capacities are brought into play and learning becomes more engaging and exciting. By the same token, fixed curricula are no longer commanding. Teachers may draw together materials from different disciplines or from current societal concerns. The demand for independent disciplines may give way to developing hybrids of greater relevance to the contemporary and pressing issues of our world.

This is not simply a conceptual challenge. Although the factory model is held together by its state-sponsored practices, the discontent with them has long been a stimulus to creativity. As we shall see, many of the resulting innovations are at one with our present focus on relationships. Everywhere, we find a growing emphasis on dialogue, collaboration, group work, participatory action, trans- and interdisciplinarity, parental involvement, distributed leadership, learning communities, global interconnection, and so on. As we discuss later, these shifts are at one with societal needs for individuals who can work collaboratively in a complex world of diversity. The seeds are planted here for a major transformation in pedagogy, curriculum, and school leadership. Standing in the way of such transformation is a major impediment: *assessment*. By transforming evaluation, we may reconfigure the landscape of education.

In the remainder of this chapter we thus turn critical attention to the commonly accepted presumption that tests, exams, and grading are essential for the efficacy of educational systems. We inquire here into the validity of our assessment tools, their impact on the learning processes, and their effects on students. A final discussion will focus on the harms of high-stakes testing. While this discussion will center on the assessment of students, many of its arguments are equally relevant to the assessment of teachers and schools. When we question the validity of performance measures and the way in which measurement undermines the system it is designed to control, we are also speaking to current practices of evaluating teachers and schools. We return to these issues in later chapters. In general, however, if the assessment tradition fails to achieve its goals, the way is open to consider alternatives. It is to a commanding alternative that the remainder of this book is devoted.

Testing and Grades Under Inspection

We have pointed to the central role of assessment in sustaining the factory model of education. Putting aside issues of systems control, it is commonly argued that assessment devices are essential to the educational process itself. If we are to raise critical questions about assessment and offer a meaningful alternative, then it is important to take into account such claims. On the positive side, exams and tests are said to (1) provide students with feedback on the level of their performance, thus informing them of their strengths and weaknesses and where they should direct their attention; (2) help teachers to understand whether students are learning and to inform themselves of how they can improve their teaching; (3) offer parents information about their children's learning so they may provide support; (4) inform the government (and parents and taxpayers) about the school's performance, along with the performance of teachers and administrators; and (5) supply information to higher education institutions and potential employers to assist their selection processes.

The major question is whether current assessment practices actually achieve these goals. To answer this question it is first important to consider the potentials of our common assessment devices in daily school life and in national testing. In the former case we inquire into the validity of our measuring devices and their effects on learning and student well-being. The focus then turns to national testing and its consequences on learning. As we shall find, the goals of education are ill-served by traditional assessment practices. Alternatives must be considered.

What Can Tests Tell Us?

The headteacher of a primary school in Lancashire in the United Kingdom writes to her sixth-grade students after their taking a battery of national tests:

> The people who create these tests and score them do not know each of you—the way your teachers do, the way I hope to, and certainly not the way your families do. They do not know that many of you speak two languages. They do not know that you can play a musical instrument or that you can dance or paint a picture. They do not know that your friends count on you to be there for them or that your laughter can brighten the dreariest day.[9]

So if these tests do not tell us who these students are, what do they tell us? We typically think of measurement as reflecting the properties or characteristics of an independent object or event. We wish to know, for instance, about the weight of an object, its height, speed, and so on, and thus we develop measures to assess these properties. School tests and exams are devised in the same way because teachers wish to know about the knowledge, competency, or capability of their students. Metaphorically, the measure should function as a mirror, giving us an accurate reflection of the object or event in question. If the reflection is accurate, we say that the measure is *valid*. Yet this view of measurement is deeply flawed. Objects or events *in themselves* have no properties. What we presume to be the properties result from our particular interests. What one takes to be the "properties of water," for example, will depend on whether one is interested in chemistry, fishing, pollution, photography, or swimming. The act of measurement, then, is an outcome of the assumptions and interests of the particular groups to which we belong. For example, how do we measure a loaf of bread? A dietician might measure the calorie count, a biologist could tell us of its grain content. In neither the world of dietitians nor biologists does "taste" figure as a characteristic of bread. For a physicist, calories, grains, and taste are all irrelevant.

The same may be said about the way we attribute properties or characteristics to people. Persons *in themselves* have no properties. People are neither intelligent nor unintelligent, ambitious nor lazy, attentive nor inattentive
in themselves. The properties are not *there*—waiting to be discovered and
quantified—but represent the interests, values, and assumptions of different communities to describe people in the way they do. In this context
we see how the educational system has created exams and tests that define
learning and knowledge in terms that are practical and comparable *for its
purposes*. Regardless of the interests of students, teachers, or parents, and regardless of the rich and complex range of activities in which students may
be involved, the student is reduced to single scores or grades. Testing and
grading thus create a world of the competent and incompetent, the smart
and the stupid, the brilliant and the average. Young people are thrust into
an identity-threatening tradition without a voice, either in its constitution
or its effects on their lives. Tests and grades tell us more about those who
apply them—their assumptions and values—than they do about those who
are being judged.[10]

For the moment, however, let us put aside the question of how assessments
create the world of education. Let us temporarily accept the long-standing
assumptions and values that go into creating measures of students' competency, mastery of subject matter, and the like. In this case, we confront a new
question: Do such exams and tests actually provide us with accurate information? Or, in traditional terms, are tests and grades valid indicators of student knowledge and learning? Drawing here from a wide range of criticism,
there is little support for this assumption.[11] Consider scores on an examination. We presume they reflect the student's proficiency, and the student's
future may be shaped by the result. But what else might test performance
reflect?

Life conditions. If a child is hungry, has little sleep, or walks to school in fear,
will their test performance be affected? If a young person lives in a household
where her parents are continuously quarreling, her brother is taking drugs,
and she is bullied online by her classmates, why should she—as an independent student—receive a failing grade? When a mother of a high school
senior discusses her son's work with him every evening, edits his essays before they are submitted, ensures that he has the latest computer technology,
and doesn't allow him to stay out late with his friends, who should be con-
gratulated on the young man's outstanding performance: the mother or
her son?[12]

Interests and passions. Exams typically focus attention on a single aspect of the student: academic performance. Everything else about the student is obscured, such as beliefs, values, passions, moral convictions, spiritual life, sexuality, loves, and hates—virtually everything essential to their daily life. Yet it is this "everything else" that will vitally affect a student's engagement in a given subject matter. Consider the matter of reading. From the earliest primer to the most noble works of the culture, what students understand, appreciate, and remember will largely depend on their interests. Some readers will fasten on the plot, others will feel empathy for particular characters, others will be intrigued by the style of writing, and still others will labor with the relevance of the text to their personal lives. Is it reasonable, then, to use a single measure—let's say plot details—as an index of the individual's competence?

Personal issues. The same examination will mean different things to students in terms of personal issues. Some students approach exams with confidence, some with disinterest, and others will be fearful. These variations in personal orientation will also make their way into performance. There is a substantial literature, for example, on test anxiety.[13] The stress that many children feel when placed under the microscope of examinations may begin in primary school. With an experience of failure, one's stress is increased on successive occasions. Because anxiety can interfere with performance, subsequent examination scores will suffer. Failure and anxiety are mutually reinforcing. As research suggests, students with high test anxiety will score significantly lower than students who are confident.[14] Could we not read exam scores as indicators of emotional state?

Test training. Like any other complex challenge, experience and training contribute to success. Thus, for example, with increased experience one gains an idea of how multiple-choice tests are constructed, one listens to lectures in terms of the questions that can be asked, one learns rules for writing short answers and budgeting time during a longer exam, and so on. With greater experience in taking tests, performance is enhanced. One might even draw the conclusion that the longer students remain in school, the less valid are tests of their knowledge of subject matter. As one student remarked at the chapter opening, tests measure one's ability to take tests.

Classroom culture. Whether students strive for high performance on exams is largely a matter of their cultural lodgment. As illustrated by Willis's classic ethnography, working-class youth may ridicule the academically successful students. The high-performing students seem like children, unadventurous and knowing little about "real life."[15] More generally such students may be demeaned as "grade grubbers," "rate busters," or "greasy grinds." As Herbert Kohl also proposes, minority youth often feel that their intelligence and integrity are threatened by the educational system and therefore respond with forms of "creative maladjustment."[16] Asian subcultures can offer a dramatic contrast: failing to devote oneself to studies is virtually unthinkable. So, are we assessing individuals or their subcultures?

Teacher style. Teachers vary widely in teaching styles. Some are warm and chummy with their students, while others are formal; some are full of humor and others serious, and so on. Teachers' personal styles also invite varying responses among their students. Some students are drawn to a teacher who can be a father or mother figure; others may thrive on support for their independence. These various affinities and discords will be reflected in the student's learning. Indeed, many students select their subjects or courses based on the personality of the teacher. Furthermore, teachers also vary significantly in their investments in particular students. As Rosenthal and Jacobson's classic studies of the "Pygmalion effect" made clear, if teachers have a positive view of a student, they relate to that student in ways that will boost his or her performance.[17] Research also suggests that teachers may alter their style of teaching in ways that facilitate the failure of lower-class students.[18] In general, teachers and parents typically view failing grades as a reflection of the student alone.[19] One might equally argue that for every failing student there is a failing teacher. However, we may also ask: If it takes a village to raise a child, isn't a child's failure also the failure of the villagers?

Pedagogical practices. What we have said about teaching styles also applies to pedagogical practices. Student performance on exams will depend significantly on the pedagogical practices to which they have been exposed. Students vary widely in their taste for such practices. Some students thrive on the teacher's use of PowerPoint technology because the structured material gives them a comforting sense of clarity; others are bored with what they feel is spoon-feeding. Some students are innervated by distance-based learning, while others are energized in face-to-face discussion; some thrive when working in collaborative groups, while others fare better working alone. It is in this context that critics point to the ways in which traditional pedagogical practices are structured in ways that alienate minority and disadvantaged students.[20] Others experiment with pedagogical practices that propel the interests of otherwise marginal students. The general point is that examination scores for students reflect their many and varied relationships to pedagogical practices.

As we see, a host of factors can affect student performance on exams and tests, including their socioeconomic backgrounds, family circumstances, teachers' personalities and teaching practices, personal needs and capabilities, interests and passions, personalities and aspirations, and the interrelationships of all these factors with each other—among other things! Measures in themselves tell us little or nothing about what is being measured, and it is fallacious to conclude that they are measures of the student alone.

The Subversion of Learning

In an autumn day, Malik, an 8-year-old boy, used his recess to create a leaf design in the school yard. The sweeping swatches of red and yellow were striking to all who passed. The activity was not compulsory nor did Malik expect to be examined on his design. But what if Malik had been assigned the task of using the leaves to create art and told that he would be graded on the result? Would the creative effect be superior? This is difficult to say, but we can presume that the activity would now become suffused with tension, and Malik would become curious about the criteria for grading. In fact, a common complaint among high school students is that course requirements reduce their enjoyment of learning, such as reading, writing, researching, and thinking. Where they had once delighted in reading novels, poems, history, or philosophy, it was now a task. Even with books they wanted to read, their experience went flat when grades were at stake.

By inserting instruments of grading into the process of learning, the potentials of learning are reduced. Intrinsically meaningful activities are instrumentalized. While reading a novel, a student might be drawn into a rich vicarious life, experiencing the dynamics of the unfolding relations; in reading a poem, the student might be swept away by the imagery, the metaphor, the rhythm; in reading history a student might imagine the relevance for current events; and a student might have been challenged in philosophy to ponder the meaning of life. All these life-giving possibilities are snuffed out when one's efforts are bent to alien standards of judgment.

As many see it, grades now serve as the only marker by which to judge that learning has taken place. Because this is the single indicator of worth, grades come to be defined as the sole reason to learn. Tod Wodicka captures the sentiment in his novel *All Shall Be Well; And All Shall Be Well; And All Manner of Things Shall Be Well.* [21]

> "Will this be in the examination, Mr Hecker?" was the limit of my students' interest in any given subject. If it was going to be in the test they took notes, if it was not going to be in the test they did not take notes. Their silent, depth-less stares were unnerving. I told myself that they were not stupid— for how could the final attainment of thousands of years of human progress be stupid?

If the purpose of study is to achieve a high mark on an exam, the learning process is emptied of any other value. If one didn't receive a good grade, the time spent on learning would have been "wasted." If one could obtain the grades without the study, so much the better! Insofar as young people come to regard their education in this way, learning becomes merely instrumental to achieving some external goal. Lost is an appreciation of the learning process itself—the joy of discovery, the intellectual challenge, the flight of imagination, or the creativity and inspiration.

Life and Death in Schools

In a traveling exhibit organized by Active Minds, 1,100 backpacks were spread on the ground to represent the approximate number of American students committing suicide each year.[22] Increasing reports from around the world also suggest that students' anxiety and depression are closely related to exam-induced stress. Like most institutions, schools create their own internal definitions of what is appropriate or inappropriate, what is meritorious or malfeasant. For schools the central standard of the good is academic performance, with test scores and grades serving as the major indicators. Hence students continuously live under threat. It may be a pop quiz, grades on homework, an end-of-the-week test, or a final exam; it could also be the intimidating judgments made by the teacher and classmates on one's class recitation.

The threat of judgment is not simply about academic performance, but also about one's identity. Poor performance defines one's mental capacities. When children enter school they are little concerned about their "level of intelligence" or "academic aptitude"; after 12 or more years of life in the closed culture of schools, these qualities become pivotal to one's sense of self. Abundant research demonstrates a strong relationship between grades and self-esteem.[23] For example, a University of Michigan survey study found that 80 percent of the students felt their self-worth depended on their academic performance.[24] Assessing young people through testing and grading passes judgment on their worth as persons. It should scarcely be surprising that myriad programs have been launched in schools to boost students' self-esteem. However, such programs primarily chase after symptoms without attending to the disease. Why should students' sense of self-worth require a special program in the first place?

The pressure of performance is often amplified by the additional factor of parental ambition. Parents' self-respect is often tied to the school performance of their children. Poor performance may be regarded as a symbol of sub-par parenting or poor-quality genes. Furthermore, to an even greater degree than their children, parents may be caught up in the heat of competition for their offspring to get into "a good school." Thus, parents may incessantly goad their sons and daughters to be more diligent in their studies. With anything less than a strong performance they may revoke privileges and withdraw respect. For poorly performing children, parents are also seduced into defining their children as mentally disordered. Here they join teachers in seeking a diagnosis for attention deficit hyperactivity disorder (ADHD). The child is thus drugged to ensure he or she pays attention and makes better grades. And this is to say nothing of the incentive that such students garner special privileges at exam time.[25] In the United States, the number of children between 11 and 14 diagnosed with ADHD is now more than 6 million, nearly 10 percent of the school population, and the figure increases annually.[26] Pharmaceutical companies supplying medication for ADHD simultaneously take in more than $13 billion, a significant portion of which goes into research to bolster the case that ADHD is actually an illness.

We should scarcely be surprised, then, at reports such as the following: Between 2009 and 2017, the rate of depression in the United States for students between 14 and 17 rose by more than 60 percent; for those between 12 and 13, the increase was almost 50 percent. A recent survey of 11th-grade students at a handful of private high schools found that about half of them were chronically stressed.[27] Nearly half of the students reported feeling heavy stress on a daily basis. Schoolwork, grades, and college and university admissions were identified as the greatest sources of such stress.[28] Pressure by parents and schools to achieve top scores also begins as early as elementary school, and the levels of stress are so high that some educators regard it as a health epidemic.[29]

Few would doubt the relationship between exam-based stresses and students' well-being.[30] We find that student suicides are significantly related to levels of academic stress.[31] A poll by the National Education Union (NEU) found that "more than half (56 percent) of school staff said youngsters had been self-harming or thinking of self-harming" due to exam stress.[32] Furthermore, between 2007 and 2015, the number of children and teenagers arriving in emergency rooms with suicide problems doubled.[33] For children, the rate of suicide attempts during months when they are in school is twice that of when school is not in session.[34]

Why should we create educational institutions in which stress and anxiety are the norm and where the most vulnerable are pressured to such an extreme that they no longer wish to live?

High-Stakes Testing: A Failing Grade

"High-stakes testing" refers to practices in which regional or national governments employ standardized assessment devices to ensure the performance of students, teachers, and school administrators. Although such testing has a long history, its implementation began to soar in the late twentieth century. In the United States, such tests have been advocated by every president of recent decades. The cost to the states for blanket testing in grades 3–9 reaches more than $1.7 billion a year.[35] In the United Kingdom, national testing has yielded a hall of fame or shame. High-scoring schools receive accolades, while the poorly performing may be threatened with closure. Critique of high-stakes testing has become widespread and increasingly caustic.[36] A full review of the agonies is beyond the scope of this chapter. Indeed, if the many writers on this topic were to constitute a team of judges, high-stakes testing would receive a grade of "F." However, to set the context for seeking alternatives, it is important to bring several issues into focus.

At the outset, high-stakes tests suffer the same problems of validity as classroom tests and exams. They do not give us an objective understanding of students' learning; rather, they *construct* reality through the narrow lens chosen by the examiners. The equivalent would be a group of self-proclaimed experts assessing the quality of a book by the number of its adjectives while paying no attention to the strengths of its argument or the aesthetics of its prose. Even with carefully composed tests of verbal or math performance, validity is elusive. As discussed, such tests may appear to tell us about the performance of students, but, with equal validity, they can be interpreted as tests of the teacher, the parents, the school culture, the students' mental health and stress levels, the multicultural makeup of the class, the state of the surrounding community, and more. Each interpretation will also suggest different policies or remedies, from raising salaries, providing more counseling, and adding armed guards to firing teachers or closing schools. With respect to policy-making, test scores in themselves are empty of direction.

An intensive barrage of criticism has also centered on the effects of such testing on the learning process. Perhaps the most common complaint is the way such testing invites "teaching to the test." All other learning interests are set aside to ensure that students are prepared for the tests. Pedagogical practices and curriculum are radically narrowed; student curiosities, innovation, collaboration, and projects are all sacrificed. Such preparations may consume weeks of class time. Teacher morale plummets, not only because teaching autonomy has been usurped, but also because test scores may mean the loss of dignity—or a job! Student engagement falls because the challenge set before them is as difficult as it is meaningless. There is little educational value in such tests. Students simply cram in information, without knowledge of its importance, without interest, and without critical or creative thought. As noted earlier, the chief educational payoff for such preparation is increased skill in taking standardized tests.

Standardized testing is also unresponsive to the multiple ethnic, religious, and racial enclaves in society, along with the local needs of school systems. In the United Kingdom, exclusive and elite private schools are compared along the same continuum as large inner-city academies; in the United States, schools in upper middle-class suburbs are compared with schools in lower-class urban settings, Hispanic communities in the rural Southwest, and so on. Yet, in each of these settings, the educational needs may be quite specific. In one school setting, the goal is to prepare young people to compete successfully for placement in good universities; in another, the concern is with their students merely graduating; in another still, the challenge is one of teacher attrition or surviving a slumping economy. In some communities there may be companies seeking graduates with particular kinds of skills, while other communities might need farmers, builders, or school teachers. To assume that there is single test relevant for all is not only insensitive to local needs, but also robs schools of providing functional education.

A final shortcoming must be addressed: the uncontrolled, *upward spiraling of effort*. When school systems can be compared on national or regional tests, a hierarchy of worth is created. The same may be said in comparisons of student performance among nations, such as the Programme for International Student Assessment (PISA) listings published by the Organisation for Economic Cooperation and Development (OECD). Given such a hierarchy, every school and every nation that is not at the top is urged into trying harder: increasing rigor, giving more homework, establishing incentives for more diligence, and so on. When schools successfully raise their performance, they advance in the hierarchy while others are displaced. Those with lowered standings strive even harder to compete: more homework, more incentives, and more pressure to succeed. Again competition is set in motion, with a steady increase in effort after worth. (And, of course, the top-scoring systems or nations try to protect their high standing with increasingly greater effort as competitors gain ground.) There is no deliberation on educational values, learning ideals, or students' work ethics; instead, there is only the continuously increasing standard of excellence, with intensifying demands for effort. Students and teachers pay a dear price.

Defenders of high-stakes testing point to evidence that such tests can sometimes succeed in elevating student performance. What appears to be successful in raising learning, however, cannot easily be disentangled from efforts to drill students to perform well on these tests. The important question is whether test performance is the aim of education. If the ends of education are other than test performance, then what kind of evaluation can contribute to these ends?

Educational Evaluation: Why Do We Bother?

Earlier we sketched out some of the major purposes of testing and grading in education. We now return to these hopes in light of the present analysis. Evaluation is a necessary aspect of the learning process, but to what extent are its purposes achieved by current assessment devices? If little is gained through these devices, the stage is set to consider alternatives. It is to a promising alternative that the remainder of the book is dedicated. Consider again the following major aims of evaluation:

Feedback for students. Feedback on students' learning is integral to the learning process itself. However, examinations seldom furnish students with the kind of feedback necessary for improvement. At the outset, tests and grades primarily focus on the student's "failures." They presume that the attentive and well-prepared student will succeed, and thus the student is primarily informed of shortcomings: "Where was I less than perfect?" More importantly, tests and grades chiefly function as summaries of the past. They grade students on their mastery of subject materials already covered. What students take away from a less than perfect performance is a thin resource for the challenges ahead. Grades seldom illuminate what matters to the student: their personal trajectories of learning, their interests and curiosities, their relationship with classmates, or their sense of well-being in school. This point is closely related to a second.

Guidance for teachers. To facilitate and support students' learning, it is important that teachers receive feedback and guidance about their practices of teaching. However, student test performance is minimally useful for this purpose. As argued, tests are ambiguously related to what has been taught. Exam performance may result from a wide range of factors including the student's subculture, home life, emotional state, and so on. What then, does a teacher learn about from student performance? Teachers may indeed find areas of study in which a class as a whole has scored poorly, but such findings are also open to multiple interpretations. Is the failing the result of the day or time the materials were covered, the intrusion of a major school event, the season of the year, the pedagogical tools, or possibly the students' disinterest in the subject? With multiple interpretations in hand, nothing clearly follows.

Information for parents and carers about students' learning. Ideally, information on their children's learning should help parents and carers to provide guidance and support. Under current conditions, test scores and grades have become markers of competitive success, but they say little about what children have learned, what they care about, how they see their future. Similarly, because one doesn't know how to interpret such performance markers, tests scores, or grades, parents typically fall prey to the same fallacy as many teachers: they treat these markers as judgments of the children. This is to disregard all the circumstances that may affect student performance: poverty, subculture, their teacher's personality, and so on. And this may include the parents' relationship with each other and the student. Interestingly, if a student fails, the parents will typically hold him or her blameworthy, but they may well take credit for their child's success.

Information for institutions of higher education and potential employers. Accurate indicators of competence are essential to efficient selection among

pools of applicants. Yet test performance tells little about students' suita-
bility for college or employment. More sensitive and probing inquiries into
the relevant capacities and interests are sacrificed for the convenience of a
single and summary number or letter grade. Colleges and universities are
thus caught in a difficult dilemma. There is indeed a broad understanding
of the fallacies of grades and test scores as reflections of an applicant's ability.
Admissions boards search continuously and creatively for other means of
drawing judgments, but simultaneously struggle with overwhelming numbers of applications. We return to the challenge of alternative selection processes in Chapter 8.

As we find, tests and exams are not only deficient in fulfilling the functions
for which they were developed, but they actively undermine the learning
process. They radically reduce the aims of education to exam performance,
thus robbing the learning process of its enormous potential. They undermine
the curiosity, creativity, and critical thinking of both students and teachers
while steadily increasing levels of stress for high performance. Teaching and
learning are drained of joy.

Beyond the Shadows

Let us not conclude from this analysis that evaluation is dispensable—that
the desires of students, teachers, parents, administrators, gatekeepers, and
policy-makers for useful information about the learning process are mis-
guided. This is not our proposal. The significant question is whether the
continuing needs for such information might be served in a less harmful
and more illuminating way. What if the evaluative processes deepened an
understanding of what counts as learning, progress, development, and a
worthwhile becoming? What if such practices could enhance appreciation
of the learning journey and foster collaboration with teachers, students, and
communities in building futures of significance? And what if the results
of such evaluation provided nuanced insights into the learning of each
individual?

To these ends, we replace the traditional relationship between subject and
object—the evaluator or assessor on the one side and the target of evaluation
on the other—with a relational orientation. Here we recognize the pivotal
place of relationships in teaching and learning and in fostering the well-
being for all concerned. Evaluation in education should not only draw from

the wellsprings of relationships but also nurture them. As we hope to demonstrate, when relational well-being is primary, educational evaluation can enrich the meaningfulness of learning and the flourishing of the student, the teacher, the school, and the surrounding community.

Notes

1. Gill, S., and Thomson, G. (2012) *Rethinking Secondary Education*. London: Pearson Education.
2. Key thinkers who promoted such visions include Jean Jacque Rousseau, Johann Pestalozzi, Francis Parker, Johan Herbart, Maria Montessori, Rudolf Steiner, and many others. In the twentieth century, thinkers such as John Dewey, Alfred North Whitehead, and Nel Noddings continue to be proponents of progressive, human-centered, and relation-centered education.
3. Stokes, K. (2013) "The impact of the factory model of education in Central Texas." Unpublished Honors Thesis, Waco, TX: Baylor University.
4. In 1967, the US government established the Education Commission of the States, an office that would systematically assess progress in American education.
5. See, for example, Shumar, W. (2013) *College for Sale: A Critique of the Commodification of Higher Education*. New York: Routledge; Schwartzman, R. (2013) "Consequences of commodifying education," *Academic Exchange Quarterly*, 17(3): 1–7.
6. Thomson, G., and Gill, S. (Forthcoming) *Happiness, Flourishing and the Good Life: A Transformative Vision of Human Well-Being*. London: Routledge.
7. As an illustration of the expanding emphasis on standardized testing of students, the ProEd Inc. catalogue of student assessment devices features more than 300 tests of student abilities, including tests for "language processing disorder," "expressive language disorder," "loudness of voice," "emotional control," and "phonetics." See https://www.proedinc.com/Request-Catalog.aspx
8. See, for example, Coffield, F., and Williamson, B. (2011) *From Exam Factories to Communities of Discovery: The Democratic Route*. London: Institute of Education; Jacobs, J. (2014) "Beyond the factory model," *Education Next*, 14(4): 34–41; Serafini, Frank. (2002). Dismantling the factory model of assessment. Reading & Writing Quarterly. 18. 67-85Gottesman, I. (2016) *The Critical Turn in Education*. London: Routledge.
9. Belam, M. (2018) "'These tests only measure a little bit of you'—the teachers' letters that go viral," *The Guardian*, May 15, 2018.
10. For more on the social construction of reality, see Gergen, K. J. (2009) *An Invitation to Social Construction* (3rd ed.). London: Sage.
11. For example, Ravitch, D. (2000) *The Death and Life of the Great American School System: How Testing and Choice Are Undermining Education*. New York: Basic Books; Popham, W. J. (1999) "Why standardized tests don't measure educational quality,"

Using Standards and Assessment, 56(6): 8–15; Ryan, R. M., and Netta, W. (1999) "Undermining quality teaching and learning: A self-determination theory perspective on high-stakes testing," *Theory and Research in Education*, 7(2): 224–233; Jones, M. G., Jones, B. D., and Hargrove, T. Y. (2003) *The Unintended Consequences of High-Stakes Testing*. Lanham, MD: Rowman and Littlefield; Kohn, A. (2000) *The Case Against Standardized Testing: Raising the Scores, Ruining the Schools*. Portsmouth, NH: Heinemann; Sacks, P. (1999) *Standardized Minds: The High Price of America's Testing Culture and What We Can Do About It*. New York: Perseus; Guskey, T. R. (2015) *On Your Mark: Challenging the Conventions of Grading and Reporting*. Bloomington, IN: Solution Tree; Koretz, D. (2017) *The Testing Charade: Pretending to Make Schools Better*. Chicago: University of Chicago Press.

12. Herein lies one of the significant critiques of meritocracy's claim that it rewards those with high performance. See, for instance, Dixon-Roman, E. J. (2017) *Inheriting Possibility: Social Reproduction and Quantification in Education*. Minneapolis: University of Minnesota Press.

13. McDonald, A. (2001) "The prevalence and effects of test anxiety in school children," *Educational Psychology*, 21: 89–101; Devine, A., Fawcett, K., Szucs, D., and Dowker, A. (2012) "Gender differences in mathematics anxiety and the relationship to mathematics performance while controlling for test anxiety," *Behavioral and Brain Functions*, 10: 8–33.

14. Kahan, L. M. (2008) *The Correlation of Test Anxiety and Academic Performance of Community College Students*. Cambridge: ProQuest.

15. Willis, P. (1977) *Learning to Labour*. Farnborough: Saxon House

16. Kohl, H. R. (1995) *I Won't Learn From You: And Other Thoughts on Creative Maladjustment* (2nd ed.). New York: The New Press

17. Rosenthal, R., and Jacobson, L. (1968) *Pygmalion in the Classroom: Teacher Expectations and Pupils' Intellectual Development*. New York: Holt, Rinehart and Winston. For long-term effects, see Hinnant, J. B., O'Brien, M., and Ghazarian, S. R. (2009) "The longitudinal relations of teacher expectations to achievement in the early school years," *Journal of Educational Psychology*, 101: 662–670.

18. For example, Cohen, D., and Hill, H. (2000) "Instructional policy and classroom performance: The mathematics reform in California," *Teachers College Record*, 102(2): 294–343.

19. Conversely, in the context of high-stakes testing, poor student performance will stand as a failure of the teacher.

20. See, for example, Emdin, C. (2016) *For White Folks Who Teach in the Hood . . . and the Rest of Y'all Too: Reality Pedagogy and Urban Education*. Boston, MA: Beacon.

21. Wodicka, T. (2009) *All Shall Be Well; and All Shall Be Well; and All Manners of Things Shall Be Well*. New York: Penguin Random House, p. 116.

22. See https://www.activeminds.org/programs/send-silence-packing/about-the-exhibit/

23. Thomsen, M. (2013) "The case against grades," *Slate*, May 1, 2013.

24. Crocker, J. (2002) "The costs of seeking self-esteem," *Journal of Social Issues*, 58(3): 597–615.

25. Here we refer primarily in the United States to the National Assessment of Educational Progress (NAEP), along with specifically designed tests in each state, and in the United Kingdom to the Standardized Attainment Tests (SATs) which are designed to measure students' achievement in answering questions that check their knowledge, skills, and academic progress. There are also international tests, such as the PISA, aimed to assess sample students in different countries, compare their attainment levels, and seek international trends.

26. The 2016 National Survey of Children's Health (NSCH) interviewed parents and reports the following ADHD prevalence data among children aged 2–17 Danielson M.L., Bitsko, R.H., Ghandour, R.M., Holbrook, J.R., Kogan, M.D. and Blumberg, S.J. (2018). "Prevalence of Parent-Reported ADHD Diagnosis and Associated Treatment Among U.S. Children and Adolescents, 2016", *Journal of Clinical Child and Adolescent Psychology*, 47(2):199-212: 6.1 million children (9.4 percent) have ever been diagnosed with ADHD. This includes about 388,000 young children aged 2–5 (or 2.4 percent in this age group), 2.4 million school-age children aged 6–11 (or 9.6 percent in this age group), and 3.3 million adolescents aged 12–17 (or 13.6 percent in this age group).

27. *The Atlantic*, October 9, 2015.

28. Leonard, N. R., Gwadz, M. V., Ritchie, A., Linick, J. L., Cleland, C. M., Elliott, L., and Grethel, M. (2015) "A multi-method exploratory study of stress, coping, and substance use among high school youth in private schools," *Frontiers in Psychology*, 6(1028): 1–6.

29. Palmer, B. (2005) "Pressure for good grades often leads to high stress, cheating, professor says," *Stanford News*, February 23.

30. For example, Koyama, A., Matushita, M., Ushijima, H., and Jono, T. (2014). "Association between depression, examination-related stressors, and sense of coherence: The Ronin-Sei study," *Psychiatry and Clinical Neurosciences*, 68: 441–447;

31. Harley, N. (2016) "Exam stress among causes of teen suicide," *The Telegraph*, May 26. The increasing needs of students for therapeutic help has led many to speak of a "silent epidemic"; in Europe, mental health in schools has become a significant policy focus.

32. Busby, E. (2018) "Pupils self-harm and express suicidal feelings due to exam stress and school pressure, warn teachers," *Independent*, April 10,

33. Twenge, J. M. et al. (2019) "Age, period, and cohort trends in mood disorders indicators and suicide related outcomes in a nationally representative data set, 2005–2017," *Journal of Abnormal Psychology*, 128: 185–199.

34. Brooks, K. (2019) "We have ruined childhood," *New York Times*, August 18.

35. Ujifusa, A. (2017) "Standardized tests costs states 1.7 billion a year, study says," *Education Week*, December 2017.

36. Ravitch. *The Death and Life of the Great American School System*; Kamenetz, A. (2015) *The Test: Why Our Schools Are Obsessed With Standardized Testing—But You Don't Have To Be*. New York: PublicAffairs; Delpit, L. (2012) *"Multiplication Is For White People": Raising Expectations for Other People's Children*. New York: The New Press; Kohn. *The Case Against Standardized Testing*; Leman, N. (1999) *The*

Big Test: The Secret History of the American Meritocracy. New York: Farrar, Straus and Giroux; Hoffman, B. (2003) *The Tyranny of Testing*. Mineola, NY: Dover; Hanson, F. A. (1993) *Testing Testing: Social Consequences of the Examined Life*. Berkeley: University of California Press; Nichols, S., and Berliner, D. (2007) *Collateral Damage: How High-Stakes Testing Corrupts America's Schools*. Cambridge, MA: Harvard Education Press.

2

Education as Relational Process

In the beginning is the relationship

—Martin Buber, *I and Thou*

We may shudder at the vision of schools as factories, but its underlying rationale remains very much alive: If we want our schools to *produce* well-educated students and effective teachers, assessment is essential. After all, exams and tests provide students with information about their performance, reward the dedicated, and motivate the laggards. They also ensure the accountability of teachers, administrators, and entire school systems. The successful are inspired and the ineffective eliminated. And such indicators allow us to assess the economic costs and benefits, thus ensuring that we get the most performance for our money. As concluded in Chapter 1, these same "good" reasons are strangulating the educational processes. Given the caustic effects on all concerned and the continuous critique of the factory metaphor, why must it be sustained?[1] In fact, our entire educational system has become part and parcel of a greater ideological project,[2] a paradigm shift that has shaped values toward a focus on cost-effect and the individual as the unit of measurement.

To be sure there are innovations and refinements, but most remain comfortably within the paradigm of manufacturing. The major question thus becomes: Are there promising alternatives available? Interestingly, there are clear and cascading intimations from both past and present, all pointing in one way or another to human relationships. There is, for example, Dewey's pronouncement that "Education is a social process,"[3] and Vygotsky's emphasis on relationships for enhancing the learner's cognitive growth.[4] Jerome Bruner's 1990 book, *The Culture of Education*, also makes a strong case for viewing educational systems as forms of cultural life. As Bruner proposes, the participants are tied together through shared understandings. The culture "provides us with the toolkit by which we construct not only our worlds

Beyond the Tyranny of Testing. Kenneth J. Gergen and Scherto R. Gill, Oxford University Press (2020). © Oxford University Press. DOI: 10.1093/oso/9780190872762.001.0001.

but our very conception of our selves and our powers."[5] This social emphasis is widely shared among educators,[6] and embodied in a vast array of collaborative, dialogic, and relations-based pedagogies. Slowly we turn from individual learners to education as a social process.

In this chapter, we deepen the exploration into a social alternative to the factory metaphor of education. Here we make a radical shift in understanding the idea of relationships. Rather than viewing a relationship as the meeting of two or more independent persons, we propose that relational process precedes the very idea of individuals. This proposal invites an exploration of the *conversation* as an alternative to the *production* metaphor for schooling. We also begin to appreciate the way in which the co-creative process of relating gives birth to knowledge, rationality, and value. With this theoretical background in place, we briefly address the question of the aims of education. Moving beyond the tradition of school as a place for imparting subject matter for student mastery, education now invites students into generative relationships. From these relationships come engagement in learning for life. We complete the chapter by considering the impact of traditional assessment practices on relational process. Reinforcing the critiques of Chapter 1, we see how measurement-based approaches to assessment destroy the relational processes on which meaningful education is founded. The way is thus prepared for relationally sensitive evaluation.

From Manufacturing to Co-Creating

If relationships are central to the educational process, then what is a relationship? This may seem an odd question as we commonly define a relationship as a connection between two or more persons or entities. Thus we understand that individual persons come together to form couples, families, groups, teams, organizations, and even society as a whole. However, if we embrace this particular concept of relationship, we may never move beyond the factory model of education and its dependence on assessment. The factory metaphor is founded in the assumption of *individual* performance. If each individual performs as required, the factory will be productive. Assessment is used to ensure individual accountability. Roughly speaking, if the teacher does a *good job*, and each student does *good work*, the result will be *good education*. Concern for the performance of the individual units is primary; relationships are secondary.

On this view, failure is thus an individual responsibility. If a student fails, it may be attributed to laziness, innate dullness, or poor study habits. Or, we may hold the teacher responsible for the student's failure because of his or her poor teaching. By the same token, the poor teaching might be traced to the lax attention of the principal, and so forth. In each case, it is the individual who is accountable. In this world of independent individuals, relationships slip into the shadows. Thus, while we may champion collaborative learning and dialogic classrooms, these initiatives will ultimately be subverted by the traditional idea of individuals as the building blocks of relationship.

How else could we view relationships? There is little help in this case from either of the classic fields of psychology or sociology. Psychologists typically presume a world made up of individuals whose behavior is dictated by mental process. On this account relationships are of secondary concern, merely the sum of two or more individuals interacting. Sociologists, in turn, typically focus on the larger units of society—structures of class, religion, ethnicity, and so on. They presume that relationships occur within these various groups, but relationships themselves fall between the cracks of concern. Yet there is a more recent movement in the scholarly world in which we can locate the seeds for a vision of relationships as central to all that we say and do.[7] Without tracing these intellectual roots, the effect can be grasped in the image of the *conversation within a community*—people conversing and acting together. This seems simple enough, but the implications are far-reaching.

The most salient feature of a conversation is that *one cannot act alone*. The act of speaking is not in itself conversation. In the same way, one cannot dance the tango, play a game of basketball, or sing a duet by oneself. Two or more people must participate, but what they do together is not the sum of their individual actions. In the same way, what takes place in a classroom cannot be reduced to the individual acts of each student and the teacher. Remove an individual's acts from the dance of classroom activity and it may become nonsense.[8]

Consider a second feature of a conversation, less obvious but more profound: its dependency on *co-creation*. To clarify, consider the relationship between a question and an answer. If you ask a colleague, "Do you have the time?" and she continues to stare at her computer screen, you have not effectively asked a question. It is when she looks up, glances at her watch and says "It's 2:30" that your utterance becomes a question. If she looks up and says with a glare, "You are interrupting me!" what you considered a question is now defined as an irritant. In her reply, your utterance is granted meaning, and, until she has replied, your words mean nothing. But now consider your colleague's words. If you saw her walking by herself, and she suddenly blurted out, "It's 2:30!" you might wonder about her mental stability. By itself, the phrase is empty of meaning. It only becomes "an answer" in light of your asking for the time. In effect, a question becomes a question when coordinated with an answer, and an answer is only an answer in light of its following a question. Question and answer are co-created. A conversation, then, is an ongoing process of co-creation. Each individual's words become meaningful as they are taken up by the other, and vice versa. Meaning is a joint achievement, the product of neither person alone.

A third feature of conversation is its *dependence on preceding conversations*. When we speak together, virtually all our words are borrowed from preceding conversations. No single individual can create a word because the sound from an individual's lips only becomes a "word" when at least one other person agrees that it is a word. Meaningful language is a co-creation. When we speak together, then, we don't struggle with inventing entirely new ways of making sense. Rather, we draw almost exclusively from a reservoir of words that have already been made meaningful by others.[9] On the one hand this means that we owe an enormous debt to our traditions of making meaning; our conversations are made possible by others before us. At the same time we are not governed or determined by these traditions. We together can create new ways of speaking and acting together. In this sense, the future of education is ours to make.

There is a final important feature of conversations: *they are not governed by cause and effect but by collaboration*. The production metaphor is lodged in a traditional view of cause and effect. In the same way a machine produces standardized sausages, so should schools produce educated students. By contrast, the way we converse together emerges from norms developed in the past, such as responding to a question with an answer. And, too, the conventions are not fixed. A person can offer an opinion, but our conventions offer dozens of ways of replying—agreement, disagreement, critique, delight, and so on. None is required, and indeed one might even reply in a nonsensical way. A rationally planned educational system, replete with trained teachers, standardized curricula, and rigorous testing, does not *cause* learning to take place. It has no *effects* on test scores. Without the collaboration of others—students, their families, and their communities, among others—top-down policy-making means nothing. As we now explore, when we understand our schools in terms of conversations as opposed to factories, we open the way to engaged and inspiring participation in learning.

Co-Creating Realities and Forms of Life

To appreciate the power of the co-creative process in shaping education, there are two important matters to consider: the construction of our realities and the co-creation of our forms of life. In the former case, consider what we commonly call a "student" in a classroom. At home that same individual might be understood as "my son" or "my daughter"; at the doctor's office, he or she would be described in biological terms; some classmates might describe the individual as "really funny," while others might say he or she is "a loner" or "invisible." None of these descriptions are required by the person's existence; each is created within conversations in given settings. Other characterizations are possible and still others could be invented. At the same time, for those who have co-created these understandings, these become the realities they live by. The utterances, "This is my son" or "She is our daughter" are not just "ways of talking"; they become *facts* of the kind that one might defend with one's life.

These co-created realities are central to life in schools. While some students see school as boring, oppressive, or a waste of time, others may value school as a way to be with their friends or to make their parents proud. These co-created realities are closely related to students' engagement in school activities—whether assignments are taken seriously, whether there is commitment to homework and class participation, or whether they remain in school at all. Similarly, teachers may vary in the way they understand and experience their work—challenging, burdensome, frustrating, inspiring, and so on. Parents also participate in this process of reality-making, with schools variously understood as an opportunity for their children to succeed in a new country, a means of social climbing, and so on. These realities emerge from the flow of conversation, drawn from tradition and now reborn and reshaped in the ongoing circumstances. Because conversations are in continuous motion over multiple sites, the experience of school may be constructed in numerous and even competing ways by different participants. There is no uniform reality of school life, but multiple realities emerging and shifting across time. School life is a buzzing beehive of co-created worlds, and the transformation of school life can begin with the next conversation.

Consider as well as the common view of education as a means of acquiring knowledge. With a good education, students should master basic knowledge in history, biology, geography, and so on. But we must also realize that what we take to be knowledge of the world is equally the fruit of co-creative process.[10] All the descriptions, explanations, and logics are formulated within the process of *conversation*. Whether it is an account of osmosis, a description of the Atlas Mountain range, or a complex mathematical formulation, all are the outcomes of conversation within professional communities—biologists, geographers, and mathematicians in this case. These accounts are not universal truths that stand beyond history and culture. Rather, they are ways of speaking and writing useful to these communities for accomplishing their own particular goals. As scientists work together and invent a shared language to help them coordinate their efforts, so do they create their own specific realities. Mathematics, for example, is a co-constructed world, a world of shared language and logics for solving the problems that mathematicians have created together.

To put it boldly. if we removed from our vocabularies of daily life everything that did not issue from relational process, we would be left with nothing to say about the world. There would be no "good" or "bad," "true" or "false," no "reality" or "fiction," no poetry, proper grammar, or algebra. This is not to say that nothing exists, but simply that it is through relational process that the world takes on its particular meaning. In effect, not only is the knowledge that we hope students to acquire forged within relationships, but also the significance of education as a whole.

As we co-create the meanings of our worlds, so do we shape our actions. When students come to agree that a biology class (taught by a particular teacher) is boring (as opposed, let's say, to "the teacher trying hard to be clear and complete"), their actions will also be affected. They may roll their eyes as the teacher speaks, ridicule him after class, and avoid taking biology classes. As students share this idea of "biology is boring," they are creating a way of life together, with words and actions seamlessly woven together.

We also discover here significant origins for our valued ways of life. This is easy enough to see in the public sphere. Throngs of people devote time, energy, and money to see sports events. Indeed the most widely witnessed event in the world today is the football World Cup. Watching young men kick a ball into a net acquires its value only within a process of co-creation. In the same way, people are willing to sacrifice themselves for their country or religion, but only for the country or religion in which they participate in making meaning together.

Closely related is the issue of engagement in education. How much do students care about learning or about each other? Are teachers dedicated to their students, do they enjoy teaching? Do parents support their children or are the disinterested? These are all questions of engagement, and all depend on the process of co-creating value. If a child shows her friend a beautiful leaf she is taking to biology class, and her friend smiles and searches for a similar leaf, they may enjoy learning about biology. If her friend laughs at the leaf and calls it "stupid," interest in biology may wane. If teachers find their students appreciative, their own enthusiasm will be sparked. When parents express interest in their child's school project, asking interesting questions, their child's curiosity may be ignited. Interest, curiosity, and enthusiasm in the classroom will find their primary origin in relational process.

We may extend this account to what we call school culture. Life within our schools is generated through a continuous process of relating. Schools, like communities, are not composed of individual students, teachers, principals, and so on, each following their own independent path. And even though each person is unique, their differences will largely be lodged in different histories of relationship. We may all listen to different drummers, but all drummers have their traditions. Virtually everything that is said and done within schools emerges and is sustained (or not) through a process of co-creation. There is nothing sensible to do or say that falls outside this relational process.

In sum, the success of our educational institutions does not ultimately rely on the factory-like properties of accountability, clarity of assignment, performance assessment, and the like. Their success depends on the meanings people make of their activities, their lives together, and the world beyond. When a school is designed as an assembly line, it reduces human actions and potentials to mere utility. By contrast, when a school is understood as a complex and ever-moving matrix of meaning-making, it prioritizes human relationships and their vast potential for creating ways of life. Herein lie the seeds of a profound shift in understanding both education and evaluation.

Relations in the Balance: How Shall We Go On?

Parents often ask their children, "How was your day at school?" The question may be ordinary but it is not insignificant. School days can be filled with drama—a friendship blossoming, a teacher's scolding, an invitation to a party, a poor recitation. Emotions can rise and plummet. Much the same can be said for teachers, where friendships, cliques, jealousies, and competitions are commonplace. And, of course, there are the overarching antagonisms resulting from class, ethnic, racial, and religious differences. Relational process may hold enormous potential for learning and development, but the reverse is also true. Relationships can also result in bitter arguments, alienation, exploitation, and the like.

It is vitally important, then, to consider the relational process itself. If together we create both anguish and inspiration, how then shall we go on? The issues here are both challenging and vast as we are speaking in a broad sense about all our daily practices of making meaning. Practically speaking, how is it that we succeed or fail to understand each other, to co-create both love and animosity, to become insulated from others or open to new ideas? It is one thing to celebrate kindness, compassion, and understanding, but how do we actually accomplish these in the process of relating? Clearly, they cannot be accomplished alone; we must focus on the "dance" or "coordination" among those involved in the process. The implications for learning and life in schools are enormous. If together we can master the process, pathways to energized learning and human well-being are in our grasp.

In this section, we first lay out a framework for understanding the potentials and problems in relating. We explore what we bring to relationships and how these potentials may limit or liberate. We then turn to the trajectories of relationships in motion. When we come together, in what directions will our relationship take us? If we understand the perils and promises, we also see that we have choices. With these grounding ideas in place, we then return to the question of evaluation and the corrosive influence of exams and tests on relational process.

The Emergence of Multi-Being

Perhaps the most radical idea in this chapter is the reconstruction of the concept of relationship. We replace the traditional idea of a relationship as composed of independent persons with a vision of relational process from which individuals emerge as who they are. Thus, for example, we shift from the idea of *a boy* and *a girl* coming together to form a relationship to a vision of a relational process from which they draw on a tradition of distinguishing be-tween genders. If they rely on the tradition they will become a *boy* and a *girl* and act according to relevant traditions of what boys do as opposed to girls.[11] As we increasingly realize in today's world of gender fluidity, it could be oth-erwise. At the same time, this radical idea may also meet with resistance. At least in Western culture, there is a long tradition of viewing society as made up of individuals.[12] Our democracy is indeed based on this idea: one person, one vote. In education we commonly speak of educating minds, we hold students responsible for their own performance, we give drugs to the indi-viduals with "attention deficits," and, of course, we assess the academic per-formance of individual students and teachers. One might say that all these are expressions of an individualist ideology.

Embodied Relationships

There is an important reason for individualists to resist these relational proposals: the obvious fact of separate bodies! After all, we do observe two embodied beings in conversation, and these embodied beings will move on to other conversations. In each conversation the participants will arrive with their own beliefs, values, and preferences. And in education, there are ob-vious variations in students' abilities and proclivities. Caring about these in-dividual differences is essential to teaching. Should we not gladly join with those who see individual flourishing as a major focus of our education?[13] How can we reconcile the vision of relational process with these observations and ideals? Let us explore.

First, we all agree with the obvious point that human relationships involve the activity of two or more embodied beings. The question is: How do these embodied beings live their lives from day to day? In the case of students, for example, do they talk with each other, attend classes, post updates on social media, play football, and so on? It is precisely this range of activities that we are tracing here to relational process. The words we speak, our ideas about education and how we engage in class, the values we attach to social media, our interests in sports, and so on all arise from relational process. To be sure, when single individuals, as biological entities, meet with each other, they will typically carry with them certain ideas, opinions, logics, and values; they will know how and when to laugh, to argue, and the like. Again, all these potentials are prepared in preceding relationships.

Broadly speaking, we never step out of relational process.[14] Even when there are no other embodied beings present and we describe ourselves as "being alone," we are not truly alone. Consider what do when alone— possibly listen to music, read, watch TV, take a bath. Al these activities have been acquired and become valued through relational processes. We may suffer in private, feel love and longing, dwell in anxiety over what is to come, wrestle with self-doubts, and so on. All these private journeys have their origins in widely shared narratives. As bodies in action, we are always already immersed in relational process.

Meeting as Multi-Beings

When people meet for the first time, they are carriers of past relationships. They are simultaneously co-creators of the future. Consider, for example, the first day of primary school when Mark, a student, meets his teacher. Mark brings echoes and deposits from a history of relating—possibly with his father, mother, a grandmother, a sister, young friends, a neighbor, a priest or pastor, and so on. He also carries residues of vicarious relations—from watching videos, playing computer games, or reading books. He carries the potential to solve puzzles, ride a bicycle, and build fancy Lego structures. We may say that Mark is a *multi-being*: he can play and fight, be generous and self-centered, swear and pray, cooperate and resist, and so on. In other words, young Mark enters this meeting with his teacher as a multi-being, carrying multiple potentials for becoming.

As the conversation with the teacher begins, questions also arise. For example, will the relationship enable Mark's interests, needs, or passions to be ignited in the learning process?[15] Will standardization in curricula, pedagogy, or testing limit the teacher's sensitivity to the particular potentials that Mark brings into the relationship? From what relational resources will he be drawing when participating in class activities? Will the power difference between teachers and students, along with the fear of being judged, inhibit his expressions?

Of course the teacher, too, is a multi-being, carrying a rich array of potentials garnered from the past. But does the teacher have the freedom, either by dint of training or teacher evaluation demands, to open herself to her students? If students vary significantly in their proclivities, needs, and so on, don't teachers need to use a wide range of their potentials? For example, shouldn't expressions of affection, humor, serenity, and delight along with dis-appointment, irritation, sadness, and wonder be ready resources for relating?

And finally, there is the question of "Who and what shall we become?" While entering the relationship as multi-beings, the past does not dictate the future. In his relationships with his teacher, will Mark acquire new potentials? And, if so, what kind and for what purpose? Similarly, will the teacher move beyond the familiar routines to acquire new and enabling potentials? How can educational policies contribute to expanding the dimensions of human potential both for the student and the teacher? What shall be added to the wings of multi-being such that the human flight of relationship is enhanced? It is this latter question of development that deserves special attention.

Relations in Motion: Generative and Degenerative

We began this chapter by proposing the conversation as a replacement for the production metaphor central to the factory model of schooling. The met-aphor of conversation prepared the way to appreciate how education is fun-damentally a process of coordinated action or co-creation. To extend and amplify the significance of this shift, it is useful to scan the relational pro-cess in motion. Consider here the mechanical orientation to relationships invited by the factory metaphor. When the teacher's task is to produce high-performing students, the relationship becomes both impersonal and me-chanical. In contrast, the conversational metaphor places a strong emphasis on the well-being of the relational process and invites exploration into forms of relating. We are sensitized to the ways in which conversations can vary. Some forms of dialogue are life-giving, others yield boredom, and still others lead to anger and alienation. In each case we are co-creating our lives to-gether. How, then, should we think about the forms of relating favorable to learning? Let us explore:

First consider a brief exchange between a teacher and 11-year-old Larry.

TEACHER: Larry, you didn't do your homework.
LARRY: I'm sorry, I just had a lot of things on my mind.

There is nothing especially remarkable about this exchange. The teacher notices Larry was irresponsible for his homework, and Larry apologizes and explains why. But Larry could have drawn from his potentials in another way.

LARRY: Well, what do you expect when you load us down every day with homework!

Here, Larry has turned the tables; what seemed like his own failing is now treated as the teacher's shortcoming. Consider a third alternative.

LARRY: I just didn't understand the assignment. Can you help me?

Here, Larry has turned what could be seen as the teacher's admonition into a reason for inviting help.

These interchanges first underscore the significance of relational process. Neither the utterances of the teacher nor Larry would make sense standing alone. Out of communal tradition the teacher couldn't inform Larry about his failing to do homework any more than Larry could walk up to his teacher one day and apologize because he had a lot on his mind. It is only in their coordinated actions that each becomes a "sensible person." But consider further: each of Larry's replies changes the sense of the teacher's utterance. The first reply defines the teacher's utterance as an admonishment; the second defines the teacher as a tyrant; while the third suggests she is an understanding person. Is the teacher admonishing, tyrannical, or caring? She herself doesn't control the meaning of her words. It is Larry who is in control, at least until the teacher replies to Larry. Her reply may now change the meaning of Larry's words. Identities continuously unfold in the co-creative process.

Let us now use these exchanges to contrast three scenarios or forms of co-creating meaning: first, there are *conventional patterns* or scenario of interchange. These are the well-worn patterns of coordination that constitute most of our daily relations. One asks a question and another answers; one asks for assistance and another helps; someone tells a joke and others laugh. Because they are so embedded in cultural traditions, such patterns largely go unnoticed.[16] The consequences can be positive, negative, or both simultaneously. On the one side, these conventional coordinations provide fundamental stability in everyday life: one knows what to do; when, where, and how to do it; and has confidence in communal support. Establishing these patterns is a major challenge for early education. Children do not necessarily listen when a teacher speaks, remain quiet unless called upon, sit in chairs as opposed to lying on the floor, or carry out assignments when asked. As many believe, mastering these patterns is essential to effective education.

At the same time, every ordering is a necessary closing of doors. If it is ordinary for teachers to design curricula, lecture to classes, and assign homework, then students are denied participation in co-creating their future. Conventions are guileful in this way, as we comfortably cease to explore the possibilities of doing otherwise. Thus, while conventional coordination may be essential to our daily sense of well-being, a critical consciousness should be its companion. It is precisely this kind of consciousness that is represented in the critical education movement.[17] And it is just this kind of critical reflection that set our present writing in motion. What is gained and what is lost, we ask, when exams and grades are just ordinary constituents of school life?

In contrast to these more conventional patterns of everyday life, consider a second pattern of coordination, one that is *degenerative* in its trajectory. The flow of life is frequently disrupted by irritations, blame, criticism, verbal abuse, disrespect, indignation, jealousy—the list goes on. It is important to realize, however, that all such actions are also created and made sensible in relational process. Blaming another person is not a natural act. Rather, we learn how to blame, including for example, the necessary words, facial expressions, tone of voice, body posture, and so on. We also learn when it is appropriate to blame others and when it would be irrelevant. We also learn many ways of responding to another who seems to be blaming us. But now consider: If another's remarks are understood as blame, how do we go on? If you apologize and the apology is accepted, life may go on as normal. However, if you respond to the blame by arguing that it is unwarranted or even malicious, the relationship begins to weaken. And if the other then responds with more pointed remarks about your faults, the relationship is further threatened. Emotions may flair, criticism becomes harsher, voices increase their intensity, until. . . . The result of such escalation is often physical separation and sometimes physical violence.

In a degenerative scenario the participants move toward the termination of relationship altogether. Sharp words and expressions of irritation, inattention, dismissal, teasing—all may invite disconnection. The educational implications are substantial. Partly owing to the divisive impact of grading, schools are rife with potentials for conflict. Differences in race, gender, class, and politics are all small powder kegs. When explosions occur, harassment, hostility, fear, and physical abuse may result. But, as just pointed out, there are choice points. Responding to blame with an apology is only one example; there are others. And these, too, must be learned; they must be added to the resources for multi-being.[18] As we shall explore, if degenerative scenarios obstruct the learning process and undermine well-being, these should be of focal educational concern. More broadly, when we lack the capacities to halt downward trajectories in relationships, society as a whole begins to suffer. Communities become unsafe, organizations are riven with litigation, governance becomes contentious, and so on.

Conventional and degenerative scenarios may be contrasted with a third and more promising pattern of relating; we term this *generative* relating. In a generative interchange, the vitality of the relational process is enhanced. Such scenarios may feature delight, insight, curiosity, and creativity; they could be occasions of illumination, heightened understanding, empathy, or a shared struggle against an oppressive force. Consider, for instance, what is often called "deep dialogue,"[19] where participants listen to each other with care. They offer something of personal importance and learn from each other with appreciation; they may come to a richer understanding of each other and themselves. As a further illustration, there is an increasing range of organizational practices featuring "creativity by design."[20] Here practitioners from differing fields come together, and, through sharing, questioning, prototyping, gathering opinions, and so on, bring new ideas to life. As many commentators agree, such creativity is essential for organizations to remain viable in the global flow of innovation.

Again, the educational implications are important. Unlike conventional patterns of relating, generative coordination can inject excitement and enthusiasm into the learning experience. It is through generative patterns of relating that students come away with new and interesting ideas and are inspired to invent and to develop a sustained curiosity. Perhaps most importantly, students may emerge from these conversations with an appreciation of the relational process itself and increased capacities to contribute to such practices in the future. Until recently little attention has been given to ways in which generative relations are fostered. How do we learn to co-create in these ways? They are not natural actions. Often we treat such interchanges as magical: they were just outcomes of the right time and place. We champion critical thinking skills without question, but relationships would be imperiled if mutual critique and antagonism were to dominate our classrooms. Our hope in this volume is to move significantly toward both an appreciation of generative process and its applications in education.

Educational Aims from a Relational Perspective

In the light of this emphasis on relational process, how are we to understand the aims of education? The question of educational aims is as significant as it is disregarded. As Gert Biesta proposes, because educational success has become increasingly identified with test performance, the deeper questions about aims are thrust aside.[21] Students themselves can scarcely articulate the purpose of their years in school; the most common answer is "so I can get a good job." Given the vast resources devoted to education, we can scarcely afford to let the question of aims escape. And because ideas, cultures, values, and technologies continue to change across time and culture, dialogue on these matters should be unceasing.

As an invitation to such dialogue, and to further understand what is at stake in the present account, let us consider the aims of education from a relational standpoint. As already proposed, the life blood of the educational process lies in relationships. It is out of relationships that meaning emerges, that the world comes to be what it is for us, that we generate what we take to be knowledge, that our potentials are formed, that learning does or does not take place, and that education does or does not become valuable or worthwhile. At the same time, what is said about educational institutions also applies to families, business organizations, religions, government, and more. In short, through a relational lens, society is constituted in and through relational activities and relational practices. Together people co-create friendships, intimacies, families, professions, religious institutions, governments, armies, and so on. Outside of what people have co-created as meaningful activity, life becomes senseless or empty. Relational process, then, should be somewhere toward the heart of our concerns with education.

What does this mean more specifically in terms of educational aims? In an important foreshadowing of the present work, John Dewey wrote, "All education proceeds by the participation of the individual in the social consciousness."[22] In the present offering, however, we might paraphrase Dewey: "All education proceeds through participation in social process." But this conclusion must be expanded in two significant ways. First, while education is a social process, it should also *enable the active participation in the social process.* Second, education should *sustain and enrich the potentials of the social process itself.*

To elaborate, whether we are speaking of business, medicine, government, research, the military, farming, religion, the arts, or any other field of endeavor, the patterns of activity rest on a relational foundation. All depend on the co-creation of meaning and relevant patterns of coordinated action. A primary aim of education, then, should be to enable the young to participate in these processes and practices in skilled and resourceful ways. In terms of the earlier metaphor of multi-being, the aim should be to enrich the potentials for effective collaboration.

Such an aim might appear to echo the widely shared idea that education should equip students with the knowledge necessary to join the workforce. But the echo is only faint. To be sure, exposure to history and geography is important to participating in a culture, just as information about the body and the environment may be useful to live a healthy life. However, factual information in these cases is cut away from the relational processes and the relationships in which it is meaningful. The curriculum content is itself but an entry into conversation; it is akin to knowing a vocabulary but without knowing how to use it in conversation. One may learn that "the world is round" but must abandon this way of putting things when planning a drive across the Great Plains. From a relational standpoint, we are drawn to pedagogies that recognize the importance of learning in context.[23]

Yet preparing to "enter the conversation" is only the first step toward effective participation in social processes. Curricula have largely been built around subject content—biology, physics, literature, geography, and so on. From relational perspective, however, such focus is severely limiting. The *knowing that* something is the case is far less important than *knowing how* to participate generatively in ongoing relational processes from which something becomes meaningful and significant. What one takes to be useful knowledge will change over time and circumstance. In fact, students tend to remember little of the contents they have acquired in the first 12 years of schooling. But the challenge of relating to others, the communities, and the wider world in a possibly enriching way will remain for a lifetime. This is so not only in the demands for continued learning, but also for human well-being more generally.

The emphasis on "knowing how" is especially relevant to the educational aim of enriching the potentials of social process itself. To expand, let us return to the three relational scenarios described earlier. To be sure, schools should enable students to participate in *conventional* forms of cultural life, the first and most common scenario. It is valuable to know how to listen attentively to others, to reply coherently and cogently, and to comply when appropriate. However, the challenge here is far greater. Cultural vitality depends on one's expanding as a multi-being, capable of relating to many different people in different situations. Required here are capacities for suspending rigid beliefs, predetermined rationalities, and fixed values and opening oneself to multiple vocabularies of meaning and living. Here we place a value on such capacities as accepting ambiguity, balancing inconsistencies, and co-creating realities with others.

Unfortunately, when entering school most students are already well-versed in *degenerative* scenarios. Many will know how to be angry, belligerent, jealous, and intolerant; they will be skilled in blaming, criticizing, threatening, and so on. Within competitive classrooms, students will then learn ways of subtly abusing and undermining the weak, the failed, and the different. As outlined earlier, when these forms of relating are carried into adulthood, they are perilous. Consider here scenarios of domestic violence, gang warfare, incessant political battles, the interminable cycles of ethnic and religious violence—for starters. It is imperative that education fosters capacities not only for avoiding degenerative relations but also for *reversing* downward spirals. On the simplest level this means learning to engage in civil exchange, to relate in mutually respectful ways. More demanding is learning how to disagree without offending. Even more challenging are skills in turning escalating enmity into mutual appreciation and harmony. How can students learn, for example, to turn bitter disagreements into creative planning or intergroup conflict into friendship? In the case of bullying and restorative justice, such challenges are slowly making their way into public education.[24] This is a promising beginning.

Cultivating capacities for contributing to a *generative* process in education cannot be overestimated. Without relational resources, conforming conventions can lead to inflexibility, intolerance, and ennui. Maintaining order and avoiding degeneration may simply allow conformity to be sustained. However, as the global flows of information, ideas, values, cultural practices, and ways of life increasingly shape and reshape our world, we must consider anew the challenges of education. Education that is concerned with students mastering "What is the case?" is essentially "downstream" education. We stand on a bridge looking at the waters that have already passed beneath. We live now, however, in a world in which "upstream" capacities are essential, where attention to the approaching turbulence is critical. What is required, then, is preparation for participating in the generative processes of co-creation. How can our pedagogies and curricula enable the young to work together creatively, balancing continuity and interruption, passion and restraint, progress and renewal? How can education enable the collaborative creation of new ideas and new forms of life?

As we shall explore, new forms of evaluative practice in education can play an essential role. To put a practical edge on this proposal, research demonstrates the increasing dependency of organizations—great and small—on the ability of their participants to collaborate. This is especially owing to the fact that in the context of rapid change, fixed structures are stultifying. Organizations must adapt to changing conditions, and this requires capacities for collective innovation and coordination.[25]

Finally, it is important that we not equate schooling with preparation. While preparing students for full participation in social process is vital, we must also consider the life quality of all those participating in the cultures of the school. Young people spend from 12 to 22 years of their lives in institutions of learning, too often experiencing fear, boredom, alienation, frustration, and anger. Some even find schools a form of imprisonment. Schools are social creations; they are not demanded by or required by anything other than our negotiated agreements. We do not view our adult lives as preparation for old age. As adults we would scarcely tolerate years of fear, boredom, oppression, and the like. This should be no less the case for the younger generation. The educational process should in itself be engaging, energizing, and inspiring.

Assessment and Relational Deterioration

It is in this context that it is useful to consider once again the functioning of examinations, grading, and testing in school life. In the preceding chapter, we explored the many ways in which such practices undermine the process of learning that they were designed to serve. Given the present focus on the centrality of relationships in education, a new range of questions emerge: If learning crucially depends on the flourishing of relational process, what kinds of relationships are fostered by examinations, grading, and high-stakes testing? When assessment is set in motion, what happens to the quality of relating?

We begin with the classroom. Exams and tests are not only imperfect vehicles for assessing learning, they also establish *hierarchies of worth*. Out of all the many ways in which students vary, grades declare a narrow spectrum of actions as worthy or unworthy. These declarations are often converted to scale points, suggesting objective support for a student's placement on the continuum. Through their mere participation in the school system, children and youth thus come to learn that they are able or *dis*abled in ways they never imagined.

This hierarchy of worth ripples through relationships among students. A small number of students will learn that they are superior to others. They are justified in looking at themselves as better than their mates in matters that count. They may feel obliged to accept the "average kids" but avoid and privately ridicule those who struggle. The bulk of the students will learn that there is nothing special about them, nothing to celebrate. By all standards they can anticipate lack-luster lives of quiet satisfaction. For these "invisible children,"[26] there is little reason for enthusiastic participation in school life. Then, a small number of students will be informed that they are "failures," "dull witted," or "stupid," and their future is bleak. Some will retaliate by demeaning or attacking the system and what it represents. They may argue that for the life they want to lead—possibly free, close to the earth, out of the "rat race"—book learning is useless. They may also scorn those with high grades—"sissies," "stuck up," "teachers' pets," "slaves."[27] For many others, the repeated assaults on their self-respect will become an invitation to exit. If the classroom is a source of continuous humiliation, dropping out is the route to liberation.[28]

With the imposition of grading, students also become aware that the classroom is essentially a competition of all against all. As they are subtly informed: "You are in a race; your classmates are all trying to beat you; they hope you will fail." Under these conditions, students will avoid sharing notes, ideas, or insights. They may even lie to each other about how little they have studied, hoping their classmates will slacken their efforts. The high-scoring students may also avoid collaborative learning because the poor students will *contaminate* the outcomes and lower their grades. Classroom culture becomes grounded in the assumption of fundamental alienation.

Relations between students and teachers are similarly affected. Realize first that there is nothing about relationships between the young and their elders that is necessarily alienating. Depending on time and circumstance, the young may eagerly seek council from their experienced elders, take them as role models, listen enchantedly to their stories, rely on their mentoring, or collaborate with them in their endeavors. In all cases, the young are learning, often with pleasure and satisfaction. Importantly, in none of these situations are they assessed. When tests and grades are thrown into the relationship, all this changes. As critics note, the relationship between teacher and student is best characterized as a relationship of power.[29] The teacher structures the activities of the class and sustains order. The primary means of ensuring attention to the lesson is the threat of assessment. In effect, evaluation serves as an instrument of coercion. Alienation becomes a "natural state."

High-stakes testing typically increases the distance between teachers and students. Student performance on these tests is often used to assess their teachers. Poor student performance may affect their teachers' salary and career. Thus, the teacher begins to take an instrumental orientation to students. They cease to be interesting young people whose development contributes to one's fulfillment as a teacher. Instead, they become something akin to machine parts that must be shaped to specification.[30] Spending time exploring students' personal hopes and fears is time wasted. The pressure on students to perform well on tests is also an invitation for them to cheat. For teachers, this simultaneously invites an attitude of suspicion.

Consider as well relationships beyond the classrooms. The instrumentalist orientation favored by the use of testing also carries over to family relations. Parents often come to define their children in terms of the school's hierarchy of worth. They become "good" or "bad" depending largely on their grades. Empathy and understanding are replaced by the same alienated attitude as the teacher's. If a son or daughter fails to succeed, scorn, humiliation, and punishment are invited. Even an average grade may mean the loss of privileges, along with the loss of parental regard. Otherwise sparkling children fall into silent resentment.

Ironically, many parents and carers have also come to embrace the possibility that their children are mentally ill. If a child's poor test performance can be attributed to an "attention deficit" disorder (ADHD), the child may be "treated." With daily chemical dosages and special privileges at exam time, these students' performance might just improve. Teachers are also advantaged by such diagnoses because chemically treated children will contribute to ordered classrooms. And higher achievement scores on national or regional tests will also contribute to their own "report card." It should not be surprising that the classification of ADHD was invented at roughly the same time that high-stakes testing took root. Nor should we be shocked that, in the United States, roughly 1 in 10 children are considered to be "disordered" and are medicated for it.[31] Chemical "cures" for the "disease" of "not performing well on tests" now support billion-dollar industries.

There is finally the relationship between governmental policy-makers and administrators of local school systems. Here we have an additional tier in the structure of power, with government presiding over school administrators, administrators over teachers, and teachers over students. In each case systematic testing sustains the distribution of power and control. Those in the lower echelons will thus tend to fear those above, while those above will tend to distrust those below. Ironically, while tests are used to generate confidence and reassurance that the system is working properly, the result is more often the reverse. As school systems are placed in jeopardy by high-stakes testing, the possibility for cheating at the level of school administration becomes attractive. At the same time, the discovery of cheating further feeds the fires of suspicion. The result is increased surveillance. As a case in point, an audit of Pennsylvania state exams recently flagged 38 school districts and 10 charter schools for possible cheating.[32] Following such findings, the governor proposed a 43 percent increase in funding for educational assessment. School funding in general remained at its existing level! We thus have a degenerative spiral in which tests generate the rationale for cheating, which then provides the grounds for more formidable means of testing. Similar stories are found in elsewhere in the United States[33] and the United Kingdom.[34] Where our educational system could be guided by collective understanding and collaboration, we find division, alienation, and distrust.

In brief, traditional practices of assessment contribute to a culture of schooling marked by conflict, fear, alienation, arrogance, jealousy, self-denigration, misunderstanding, and suspicion. This is so for relationships among students and between teachers and students, administrators and teachers, parents and their children, and policy-makers and educators. Why should we sustain such conditions?

The Challenge of Relational Evaluation

As we propose, meaningful education depends on the flourishing of relational process—within the classroom, the school at large, the family life of students, the community, and the culture of education more generally. The dependency of education on traditional practices of assessment undermines this life-giving process. When added to the critical problems of testing and grading outlined in the preceding chapter, it is essential to explore alternatives. It is our belief that practices of evaluation can contribute significantly to the aims of education. In the following chapter, we thus open discussion on evaluative processes that draw from and contribute to flourishing relationships. As we propose, practices of relational evaluation are not set apart from learning, but are integral to its thriving.

Notes

1. Critics are indeed concerned that the entire educational system has become part and parcel of a greater ideological project, one that has shaped values toward a focus on cost-effectiveness, individualism, and competitiveness. See, for example, Lipman, P. (2013) *The New Political Economy of Urban Education Neoliberalism, Race, and the Right to the City*. Florence: Taylor and Francis.

2. Ibid.

3. Dewey, J. (1907) "Chapter 1: The School and Social Progress," *The School and Society*. Chicago: University of Chicago Press, 19–44.

4. Vygotsky, L. (1978/1995). *Mind in Society: The Development of Higher Psychological Processes* (M. Cole, V. John-Steiner, S. Scribner, & E. Souberman, Eds., and Trans.). Cambridge, MA: Harvard University Press.

5. Bruner, J. (1990) *Acts of Meaning*. Cambridge, MA: Harvard University Press, 10.

6. Major educational proponents of relationships in education include Paulo Freire, in Freire, P. (1970) *Pedagogy of the Oppressed*. London: Continuum; Carl Rogers, in Rogers, C. (1961) *On Becoming a Person*. Boston: Houghton Mifflin; Basil Bernstein, in Bernstein, B. (1996) *Pedagogy, Symbolic Control and Identity. Theory, Research, Critique*. London and New York: Taylor and Francis); and Parker Palmer, in Palmer, P. (1998) *The Courage to Teach. Exploring the Inner Landscape of a Teacher's Life*. San Francisco: Jossey-Bass

7. For a more extended account, see Gergen, K. J. (2009) *Relational Being: Beyond Self and Community*. New York: Oxford University Press. This account places relational process in the center of concern and may thus be contrasted with contributions to relational theory that emphasize either the self in relation to the other or communities as a whole. The former would be exemplified by care-centered approaches in education, such as those of Carol Gilligan, in Gilligan, C. (1982) *In a Different Voice: Psychological Theory and Women's Development*. Cambridge, MA: Harvard University Press.; and Nel Noddings, in Noddings, N. (1984) *Caring: A Feminine Approach to Ethics and Moral Education*. Berkeley: University of California Press. The community view is represented by educational thinkers such as Lave and Wenger, in Lave, J., and Wenger, E. (1991) *Situated Learning. Legitimate Peripheral Participation*. Cambridge: Cambridge University Press; Wenger, E. (1999) *Communities of Practice. Learning, Meaning and Identity*. Cambridge: Cambridge University Press; and Day, C. (2004) *A Passion for Teaching*. London and New York: Routledge Falmer.

8. As the philosopher Wittgenstein would put it, our words acquire their meaning within our "games of language." Thus, if we remove the phrase "strike one" from a conversation about baseball, it may cease to make sense. Wittgenstein, L. (1953) *Philosophical Investigations*. Trans. G. Anscombe. New York: Macmillan.

9. See Bakhtin, M. M. (1981) *The Dialogic Imagination: Four Essays*. Austin: University of Texas Press.

10. See, for example, Poovey, M. (1998) *A History of the Modern Fact: Problems of Knowledge in the Sciences of Wealth and Society*. Chicago: University of Chicago Press; Latour, B., and Woolgar, S. (1979) *Laboratory Life: The Construction of Scientific Facts*.

London: Sage; Knorr-Cetina, K. (1999) *Epistemic Cultures: How the Sciences Make Knowledge*. Cambridge, MA: Harvard University Press.

11. Butler, J. (1990) *Gender Trouble: Feminism and the Subversion of Identity*. New York: Routledge.

12. For instance, in the idea of social contract supported by Thomas Hobbes, in Hobbes, T. (1651/2017) *Leviathan*. London: Penguin Classics; Jean Jacque Rousseau, in Rousseau, J-J. (1987) *The Basic Political Writings* (Trans. Donald A. Cress) Cambridge, MA: Hackett Publishing Company); and John Locke, in Locke, J. (2003) *Two Treatises of Government and a Letter Concerning Toleration*. New Haven, CT: Yale University Press.

13. Gill, S., and Thomson, G. (2012) *Rethinking Secondary Education: A Human-Centred Approach*. London: Pearson Education.

14. If we add the material world to the relational process—the air we breathe, the objects about us, and so on—the case for continuous immersion in relational process becomes indelibly clear.

15. For a compelling account of the need for sensitivity to the interests and needs of students from minority cultures, see Delpit, L. (2012) *"Multiplication Is for White People": Raising Exceptions for Other People's Children*. New York: The New Press.

16. See also Macbeth, D. (2010) "Ethnomethodology in education research," *International Encyclopedia of Education*, 6: 392–400.

17. See, for example, Freire, *Pedagogy of the Oppressed*; Gottesman, I. (2016) *The Critical Turn in Education*. New York; Rutledge; and Wink, J. (2010) *Critical Pedagogy: Notes from the Real World* (4th ed.). London: Pearson.

18. Promising movement in the direction of such learning is represented in school programs for restorative justice. See, for example, Winslade, J. M., and Williams, M. (2012) *Safe and Peaceful Schools: Addressing Conflict and Eliminating Violence*. Thousand Oaks, CA: Corwin; Lund, G. E., and Winslade, J. M. (2018) "Responding to interactive troubles: Implications for school culture," *Wisdom in Education*, 8: 1; www.rjoyoakland.org.

19. See chapter 4 in Gill, S., and Thomson, G. (2019) *Understanding Peace Holistically*. New York: Peter Lang.

20. Senge, P. (1990) *The Fifth Discipline: The Art and Practice of the Learning Organization*. New York: Doubleday.

21. Biesta, G. (2010) *Good Education in an Age of Measurement: Ethics, Policy, Democracy*. Boulder, CO: Paradigm Publishers.

22. Dewey, J. (1897) "My pedagogic creed," *School Journal*, 54: 77–80.

23. For a more extended rationale for learning within context, see Rose, D. (2009) "Weaving philosophy into the fabric of cultural life," *Discourse*, 9(1): 165–182.

24. Good examples are found in, for instance, Montessori, M. (1949) *Education and Peace*. Chicago: Henry Regerny; Beckerman, Z., and Zembylas, M. (2012) *Teaching Contested Narratives: Identity, Memory and Reconciliation in Peace Education and Beyond*. Cambridge: Cambridge University Press; and Harris, I. (2013) *Peace Education from the Grassroots*. Charlotte, NC: Information Age Publishing

25. See for example, Hansen, M. R., (2009). *Collaboration: How leaders avoid the traps, create unity, and reap big results.* Boston: Harvard Business Review, and Rosen, E. (2009). *The culture of collaboration: Maximizing time, talent and tools to create value in the global economy.* San Francisco: Red Age Publishing. Wagner, T. (2012) *Creating innovators: The making of young people who will change the world.* New York: Scribner.

26. Pye, J. (1988) *Invisible Children: Who Are the Real Losers at School?* Oxford: Oxford University Press.

27. Willis, P. (1977). *Learning to Labour: How Working Class Kids Get Working Class Jobs.* Farnborough: Saxon House.

28. A *Guardian* article suggested that some British secondary schools use student exclusion as a strategy to seek better overall SAT results; see https://www.theguardian.com/education/2018/aug/31/dozens-of-secondary-schools-exclude-at-least-20-of-pupils.

29. See, for example, Bernstein, B. (1975) *Class and Pedagogies: Visible and Invisible.* Washington, DC: OECD; Freire, *Pedagogy of the Oppressed*; and bell hooks (1994) *Teaching to Transgress: Education as the Practice of Freedom*, New York: Routledge.

30. Noddings, *Caring.*

31. Danielson, M. L., Bitsko, R. H., Ghandour, R. M., Holbrook, J. R., Kogan, M. D., and Blumberg, S. J. (2018) "Prevalence of parent-reported ADHD diagnosis and associated treatment among US children and adolescents 2016," *Journal of Clinical Child & Adolescent Psychology*, 47(2): 199–212.

32. Paslay, C. (2012) "The mighty testing juggernaut," *The Inquirer*, February 21, 2012, https://www.philly.com/philly/opinion/inquirer/20120221_The_mighty_testing_juggernaut.html, accessed April 29, 2019.

33. Strauss, V. (2015) "How and why convicted Atlanta teachers cheated on standardized tests," *The Washington Post*, April 1, 2015, https://www.washingtonpost.com/news/answer-sheet/wp/2015/04/01/how-and-why-convicted-atlanta-teachers-cheated-on-standardized-tests/?noredirect=on&utm_term=.9ea0f3ee9f20, accessed April 2019.

34. Perraudin, F. (2018) "Thousands of teachers caught cheating to improve exam results," *The Guardian*, February 11, 2018, https://www.theguardian.com/education/2018/feb/11/thousands-of-teachers-caught-cheating-to-boost-exam-results, accessed April 2019.

3

Toward Relation-Centered Evaluation

Everything begins with dialogue. Dialogue is the initial step in the creation of value. Dialogue is the starting point and unifying force in all human relationships.

—Daisaku Ikeda

Our tradition of educational assessment damages relationships, undermines well-being, and radically constrains the potentials for learning. These were among the prominent messages of the preceding chapters. For many readers these critiques were unnecessary. Most of us have suffered both directly and indirectly from this tradition. We are well aware of the sense of dread, fear of failure, deflating comparisons, family tensions, threats of a gloomy future, and the enormous numbers who have dropped out from our schools. Few need to be reminded of these experiences and their emotional stress. In fact, many of us in the teaching professions have tried in various ways to develop means of resisting the regimens of assessment. We have challenged administrative demands for grading on the curve, allowed students to retake tests, and used achievement targets in the place of summative grading. Piecemeal, in quiet corners and in countless creative ways, we have sought to resist the tyranny of testing. We watch with hope the innovative schools and isolated movements from which new and promising developments are emerging.

What would be required, however, to bring about more sweeping and significant change to education? How can we go beyond these scattered attempts to chip away at the numbing oppressiveness of our traditions? In our view, there are three major challenges for transformation. First, it is crucial to provide a conceptual framework for deliberating on the process of education along with its aims and aspirations. This was the task of the preceding chapter, in which we shifted from the factory view of education to an understanding of education as a relational process in which dialogue and collaboration are pivotal.

Beyond the Tyranny of Testing. Kenneth J. Gergen and Scherto R. Gill, Oxford University Press (2020). © Oxford University Press. DOI: 10.1093/oso/9780190872762.001.0001.

The second challenge is to draw from this relational perspective a conception of educational evaluation. If we see education as a relational process, how are we to understand the practice of evaluation? How would evaluative practices fit within the goals of fostering learning and enriching the relational process at its core? Traditionally, there has been a significant distinction between learning and assessment: assessment is used to judge how well and how much one has already learned. In our view, the separation is artificial and misleading. By thus separating the two, we are blinded to the corrosive impact of assessment on learning. Required is a way of approaching evaluation not as measurement *of* learning, but as constituted within and *contributing to* the process of learning. We take up this challenge in the present chapter.

In later chapters, we take up the final challenge: fusing relational theory with practices of evaluation. We accomplish this by introducing multiple examples of relationally rich alternatives to assessment—not only in primary and secondary school, but also in the evaluation of teachers and schools This further allows us to connect the many relevant educational innovations currently in motion. In effect, relational theory enables us to build conceptual bridges among myriad islands of sparkling potential. By illuminating the coherence among these endeavors, we glimpse the contours of a broader movement among educators. Readers may find inspiration for innovating in their own special locales, but most importantly, they can see the way forward to broader change in practice and policy. We explore this broader movement in the final chapters of the book.

We open our discussion by outlining what we take to be key features of evaluation from a relational perspective. How can it be characterized, and how would it differ from traditional assessment? As we propose, relationally informed evaluation should contribute simultaneously to processes of learning and to relational flourishing. In effect, evaluation, learning, and relational process should be mutually supportive. We then turn to the chief goals of relational evaluation. What do we hope to accomplish with evaluation in a relational key? Finally, we turn attention to major sites of relational evaluation. If examinations, grades, and testing are abandoned as the locales of evaluation, where and how would evaluation take place? We focus on evaluation in two different registers: within the ongoing learning process and as periodic reflection on learning over time. These discussions set the stage for our later exploration of specific practices.

Educational Evaluation in a Relational Key

As proposed, it is within the process of relating that the world comes to be what it is for us. We draw from this process our understandings of the world, the meanings and values that motivate our actions and shape our moral and ethical horizons. It is within this process of relating that all kinds of knowing take place and learning processes come alive. However, as we have seen, traditional assessment practices, including high-stakes testing and grading, tend to subvert the very process of relating on which learning depends. How are we to envision the alternative? How might it be realized in practice?

Our focal interest is with illuminating forms of educational evaluation that draw strength from relational process in stimulating and sustaining learning while enriching the relational process itself. We refer to this orientation as *relational evaluation*, or educational evaluation from a relational perspective. We have intentionally chosen the term *evaluation* as opposed to such terms as assessment, examination, measurement, or appraisal, all of which carry strong connotations of independent and objective judgment. Here we return to the Latin root of the word "evaluation," which means "to strengthen" or "to empower." We emphasize evaluation as a process of valuing, or appreciating the value of something.[1] This enables us to replace the traditional focus of assessment on student deficiency—pointing to where students have fallen short of perfection—with an emphasis on opportunities, possibilities, and potentialities for growth and well-being. The attempt is to build from strength, thus fostering hope and engagement. Equally, a relational orientation to evaluation pays special attention to the relationships among those who are involved in the evaluative processes—for example, teachers, students, parents, and administrators—within the cultural contexts in which evaluation takes place. Evaluation should draw from the resources inherent in all these relationships.[2]

There are two primary features in our conception of relational evaluation: first, it is a *process of co-inquiry*. This emphasizes both the *process* of inquiry and the importance of *inquiring together*. In the former case, the process of evaluation might include questioning and listening, attending and caring for the many lived realities of the participants. Inquiry is not a process intent on locating a single answer and thus terminating the conversation. With multiple values and realities ever in motion, there is no final point of "knowing." Precluded here is the logic of affixing grades and making summary judgments of students' work. At the same time, such an inquiry should be dialogic and collaborative. In contrast to impersonal measurement practices, evaluation should be lodged in mutually appreciative interchange. We have in mind here the kinds of generative dialogues discussed in the preceding chapter, in which trust, transparency, and creativity are central.[3] Ideally there should be a sharing of the views and values of all relevant stakeholders. Invited is an understanding and appreciation of the different values and realities that enter into the educational process. There is the cultivation of a collective consciousness, a sense of "we are all in this together." That is, we are learning together, and together we are responsible for the educational process and its outcomes.

Indeed, educators will readily recognize here the limitations on what is called *summative assessment,* that is evaluation at the end of an instructional unit that establishes what has been learned. Such assessment typically compares and grades students against some standard or benchmark. It naturally follows from the preceding emphasis on dialogue and resource development that, in contrast to summative assessment, relational evaluation is radically *formative* in its emphasis. It places less emphasis on marks of achievement and more on the continuous enrichment of learning. At the same time, a relational approach adds further dimension to this understanding of the formative process. It stresses dialogue among multiple voices, the sharing of diverse perspectives, and the inclusion of different lived social realities, all directed at the enrichment of learning. It also gives special importance to the ongoing relationships among the various stakeholders. The idea of formative evaluation is now moving across the educational spectrum. However, there is an abiding temptation to fold such evaluation back into the testing tradition, where the scope of evaluative criteria is narrowed and deliberations are constrained.[4] In a relational frame, learning and evaluation remain continuously flowing and enduringly formative.

The second major feature of relational evaluation is its *focus on valuing.* As outlined in the preceding chapter, it is within the relational process that various activities, persons, ideas, or objects acquire value.[5] Unlike assessments that place an individual's identity in jeopardy, relational evaluation should unswervingly affirm the value of the learner and his or her hopes, aspirations, and general well-being. Rather than the way in which performance measures drain subject matters of interest, evaluation should also give life to the subject in focus. Indeed, evaluation should give life to the process of learning and infuse with value the very process of evaluation. Evaluation need not be experienced as a threat, a weight to be endured. It should ultimately be understood as constitutive of the process of growth, illuminating the path to a flourishing future. And, finally, relational evaluation should bring to light the significance of the relational process and its vast potentials.

To be sure, evaluating students in the process of their learning is a focal point. However, taking our conception of evaluation as a whole, it can be applicable to evaluative practices throughout the educational system. A relational orientation extends equally to the evaluation of teachers, schools, and administrators. All have fallen victim to the logic of measurement and control. Ideally, within the evaluative process all relevant stakeholders—parents, community members, policy-makers—should be engaged. We are speaking, then, of an approach to evaluation that contributes to the flourishing of the full learning community.

Aims of Relational Evaluation

Given this general conception of relational evaluation, how would it be applied in action? What would be its specific objectives in various school settings? What specific practices are invited, and how would these objectives be reached? Here, we address these questions. This discussion will prepare us for subsequent chapters in which we focus on a range of innovative practices that illustrate the achievement of these objectives. We propose three central goals of relational evaluation. The first is to *enhance the process of learning*, the second to *inspire sustained engagement in learning*, and the third to *enrich the process of relating*. While overlapping and interdependent, it is helpful to consider them separately.

Enhancing the Learning Process

If learning is the primary focus of education, then practices of evaluation should principally serve to enhance the learning process. Under the domination of assessment, this fundamental requirement has all but disappeared from view. Assessment devices are primarily used for checking and boosting academic performance, with scores and grades serving as prods to the low performers and rewards for the high achievers. Putting aside its many damaging effects (as described in Chapters 1 and 2), the extent to which this carrot-and-stick approach actually facilitates learning remains controversial.

In our view, the chief goal of relational approaches to evaluation is the enhancement of the learning process.

At the outset this means that evaluation should draw from and inspire the motivation of the learner. As argued, students' interest and enthusiasm in learning depend importantly on relationships. From biology to baseball, from grammar to government, whether one values such activities as exploring biology, drawing, singing, doing math, or writing a poem will significantly depend on the relationships in which one is embedded.[6] With the co-creation of value, one will welcome evaluation. One wants to know "how it goes," which also means knowing "how it doesn't go." Valuing and evaluation walk hand in hand. Consider, for example, the hours spent by youth to improve their skills in video games: they talk to each other as they play, they watch experts, they tirelessly practice a particular move, they observe each other's maneuvers and offer each other feedback and tutorials. In all these ways, they voyage toward the next level of the game. Evaluation in schools should be no less motivating.

Here the preceding emphasis on collaboration and dialogue in evaluation is reinforced. It is in just such contexts that teachers and students can together inject learning activities with value or significance. Evaluative inquiry and dialogue can cultivate students' curiosity. This may mean a teacher's asking questions that prompt students to consider the value of their experiences, concerns, and dreams of the future. It may also mean encouraging students to set directions for themselves, considering the steps they would have to take and helping them reflect on their progress. If students feel that others care about their interests, they may welcome evaluative comments to help them with their learning. "How well have I understood this?" "What else do I need to do to understand this better?" "Would you suggest a book that might help me?" Such are the questions of engaged students.

The emphasis on co-creation of value may also be extended to the classroom as a whole. Students and teachers can explore together the ends they wish to accomplish with one another and how they may collectively reach these objectives. Such discussion may ideally include a focus on what is worthwhile to learn, who might contribute to their learning, and how. For students, this would not only make clear how valuable the teacher's offering can be to their undertaking, but also sensitize them to the meaningful ways that students can support to each other. Together the class and teacher may also expand their vision to include individuals outside the boundary of the school who could assist them in learning. Indeed, these deliberations might also center on how and what kind of evaluation process would assist them in their pursuits.

Inspiring Sustained Engagement in Learning

Learning should be ongoing throughout life. Yet, when test performance serves as the major goal of learning, the examination functions as a termination. The goal has been reached, and there is little motivation to continue. So often we hear, "Thank god that's over!" or "I was up all night for that one, I'm so glad that's behind me." Interests in further engagement are minimal. When the next module or semester starts, the teacher is confronted with the same challenge of prodding students to enter another demanding race, neither to their liking nor their choosing. By contrast, we see the second major aim of relational evaluation as inspiring and encouraging students' continued participation in the learning process. Rather than regarding learning as a chore to complete or a threat to overcome, evaluation should function to renew and sustain engagement. The challenge here is to lay down tracks for life-long curiosity. Evaluative reflection should become a valuable ally for life.

By the same token, relational evaluation can encourage students to embrace responsibility for their learning. The factory model of education places the sole responsibility for educating students in the hands of the teachers and the school. As assumed, if teachers "deliver" and "do their job," and if the school leaders are "accountable," the students will receive an education. On this view, students themselves have little or no responsibility for learning. They are simply objects to be fashioned by the teachers and the institution. Relational evaluation attempts to reverse the effects: to inspire students to care about and become responsible for their own learning in both the present and the future.

There are several key ingredients to achieving these ends. At the outset is the focus on *building confidence* for further engagement in learning. For the majority of students, assigning grades has the opposite effect: their inadequacy is virtually assumed by the practice of grading. Relational evaluation invites us to abandon the single standard against which all are judged. It should foster appreciation of the complex patterns of a student's life circumstances and differing paces of development. In its emphasis on valuing, relational practices can accentuate the various ways in which students do achieve, such as meeting their personal aspirations or independently developing a special interest.

Also required in sustaining learning engagement is *developing an appreciation of learning*, and especially its role in reaching valued goals. In its emphasis on dialogue, relational practices may enable students to identify meaningful preparation for the next chapter in their life adventures. Given their current interests and curiosities, what steps would follow? Whether it is learning a topic within sciences, an idea for an art project, writing a story, or doing a piece of social research, what are the next moves? How would the student like to see these steps taken? Why are these particular moves so important? Such questions may be posed, for example, in the ongoing reflection on one's learning experiences or during an overall evaluation at the end of a course of study. The exploration can then be extended to ways that learning can fulfill hopes for the future.

A third key to sustaining learning engagement is by *cultivating consciousness of resources*. When exam performance is the goal of learning, from what resources do students draw? Typically their interest will be limited to resources yielding maximal outcome with minimal effort—for example, assigned readings, underlined notes, past exam papers, or cues from the teacher about what might be included in the test. All else would be superfluous. In comparison, relational evaluation emphasizes valuing each student's learning journey and stresses multiple routes to personal development. In collaborative reflection, an expanded domain of resources may come to life. Given a topic of interest and an abiding enthusiasm, the student may scan the riches of the Internet, spot a relevant book in the library, see the potentials of a random post on social media, or realize the knowledge that can be supplied by family or neighbors. The potentials are unlimited.

Enriching Relational Process

As discussed, traditional assessment practices undermine trust, friendship, and authenticity and lend themselves to anxiety, alienation, and antagonism Yet, if the learning process is inherently a process of relating, and relations suffer, so too, does learning. Enriching the relational processes is the third major aim of relational evaluation. This is no small matter. Consider that, in the structure of testing, we have the assessing agent on the one hand and the objects of assessment on the other. Pains are taken to ensure a minimal (or neutral) relationship between them. Exams and tests are standardized artifacts, ideally administered independently of any relationships (machine administration preferred). As commonly reasoned, feelings of attraction or antipathy would only interfere with the process and bias the outcomes. Feelings of stress and anxiety are irrelevant.[7] From a relational perspective, we turn the assessment tradition on its head: we propose that the evaluation process can and should significantly enhance the quality of relating.

There are several possible ways to approach this. Primary among them is to build *mutual care and appreciation* into the process of evaluation. Lest this seem utopian, consider the father teaching his son to ride a bicycle. He runs alongside the peddling child, affirming and encouraging the right maneuver, propping the boy as he lurches one way and the other, pointing out the direction, guiding the next move, finally letting the child peddle on his own, and then chasing after him to prevent his falling. There is no standardized examination of the child's skills nor comparison of his mastery against other children's. Yet there is corrective feedback and helpful comments at every turn. The act of teaching is an expression of care, and, through the child's appreciation, a lifetime bond may take shape.

When evaluation is a process of co-inquiry, as opposed to machine-like measurement, there is maximal opportunity for expressions of care. The very act of a teacher's expression of interest in the student's welfare is already a sign of respect. When discussions emphasize the student's learning progress, strengths, and personal development, they are expressions of abiding support. With innovative effort, mutual care and appreciation can also be nurtured within classrooms as a whole. As a class is invited into dialogic reflection, they share their hopes and plans with one another, and, as they offer their appreciation of each other's efforts, they, too, are invited into a posture of mutual care.[8]

A second significant key to enriching relations through evaluation is a focus on *building trust*. As discussed, the assessment tradition breeds distrust and even fear. When one sits in judgment of another, the stage is set for mutual suspicion. Teachers cannot be certain their students will not cheat; students become cognizant of surveillance. Each party becomes an instrument to the other's calculations. Virtually all that we have said about linking evaluation with caring also applies to building trust. In these caring forms of co-inquiry and dialogue, students become more confident that the teacher has their best interests at heart and will protect and support them in pursuing what matters to them. When students engage in activities of mutually caring evaluation, they will come to feel they can depend on each other's support.

Importantly, this focus on enriching relationships also paves the way to solving one of the chief problems of the factory orientation to public education: its *ethical sterility*. Partly owing to the view that education should be about objective facts and not subjective feelings, issues of ethics or human values are seldom addressed.[9] With the waning of organized religion, there is virtually no remaining site within the culture for exploring issues in ethics, morality, or values. And in a world in which the plural cultures and religions of the world are increasingly thrust together, an education focused singly on test performance is potentially lethal.

With an emphasis on enriching relationships and the foregrounding of dialogue and collaboration, we open a space in which matters of "ought" can be safely explored. On the one hand, in fostering mutual understanding, an appreciation of multiple perspectives, and a sensitivity to the riches and complexities of the participants' experiences, schools can provide an education in pluralism. Furthermore, by recognizing the validity of valuing, students are invited to become robust citizens in society and the world. In this case, students' passionate concerns with such issues as gun control, gender diffusion, and climate degradation would not be extracurricular. The educational value of such activity cannot be overestimated.

Sites of Practice in Relational Evaluation

Our discussion of the aims of relational evaluation is surely idealistic. The vision is attractive, but is it too remote from reality? We don't think so. As we shall explore in later chapters, there are many teachers and educators who are already pioneering such relational alternatives to testing and many schools in which some of these possibilities are being realized. Without them, we would not have begun this book. Before exploring this landscape, however, one further step in this conceptual grounding of relational evaluation is required. Specifically, we must distinguish between significant sites of evaluation and the kinds of evaluative processes relevant to each.

Measurement-based assessment is viewed as a periodic appraisal of a student's performance. Tests may be interspersed across a term or semester to ensure that students are "keeping up," and exams are administered at the end of a term or semester to assess comparative competences. As noted earlier, these assessments are considered ancillary to learning: they may judge and rank, but they do not contribute to the learning process itself. As we propose, evaluation and learning should not be separated but intertwined and integral. To be sure, periodic moments of focused relational evaluation can make a valuable contribution to learning, sustaining interest, and building relationships. At the same time, it is important to realize the potential for relational evaluation in the ongoing everyday learning process. Let us distinguish, then, between evaluation within the learning process, or *evaluation-in-process*, and evaluation at interspersed intervals, or *reflective evaluation*. Each draws out particular features of relational evaluation.

Evaluation Within the Learning Process

To appreciate relational evaluation within the learning process, consider the way a small child learns language. The process is informal and there are no exams. However, within the ongoing give-and-take between parent and child there are subtle signals, feedback, affirmations, demonstrations, corrections, verifications, directions, and encouragements. Facial expressions, tones of voice, posture, gaze, and so on, all carry evaluative potential. This subtle but significant evaluation practice is integral to the process of learning. At the same time, we must realize that the child is not the only "student." In bringing the child into language, the parent is no less a learner than the child. In order to "teach," the parent must also attend to the signals, feedback, and affirmations offered by the child. The parent must learn what kinds of utterance make a difference to the child, what kinds of movement draw the child's attention, and what challenges the child is confronted with, as well as how to correct without disrespecting. In this interchange, the child informs the parent how to be a better "teacher." That is to say, mutual evaluation is at the core of learning.

Across the lifespan this informal dance of coordination is the major source of learning. Whether it is learning with a parent to catch a ball, with friends to play outdoor games, or to flourish in relationships—as friends, intimate partners, neighbors, parents, community members, or professional colleagues—we learn in and through our relationships with others. The mutual adjustments of the participating parties are dependent on these subtle signs of evaluation. An action "works" within the dance of coordination or not, a sentence proves felicitous within the conversation or not, and so on.

In the present context we draw attention to three features especially related to evaluation. First, if evaluation-in-process of learning is akin to dance, it should be *invitational*. Traditional assessment practices are based on forced compliance. The student has no choice. Both teacher and student must be attuned to each other, adapting and changing their behavior according to each other's actions. In the relational case, the challenge is how to effectively invite students into the dance and to do so in a way they are willing—if not enthusiastic—to join in. Drawing from our earlier discussions, one can again appreciate the significance of a teacher's listening for the interests of students. These may contain meaningful cues for crafting invitations. Likewise, when there is good classroom rapport, the teacher's own expressions of value may be beckoning. If a teacher unfolds her personal passion for a given subject— from poetry to geometry—there may be an empathic resonance.

A second significant feature of evaluation-in-process is its reliance on *interdependence*. Traditional assessment practices are based on a conception of autonomous individuals with independent minds. Hence, each student should be held accountable for his or her own performance; each is graded in comparison to others as independent units. One cannot dance the tango, waltz, or salsa alone: collaboration is required. It is thus useful to understand in-process evaluation not as a relationship between two fundamentally independent units—for example, the teacher and student—but as a single unit: teacher-*with*-student. This *with-ness* adds an extremely important dimension to evaluation, directing attention specifically to how the relationships itself is faring.[10] For example, for a teacher to suspend the flow of classroom activity and invite comments on how "we" (as a class) are doing, is a powerful evaluative option. "Is this activity going well; are we getting the most out of it we could; are we helping each other; could we do this better?" Such questions shift attention to the interdependent character of learning and to the potentials of the relationships themselves. Similarly, a focus on the interdependent unit may be more helpful in understanding parental involvement in the child's education. The question is not who has done well or ill, but how is their relational process faring?

Finally, the emphasis on evaluation-in-process invites us to attend to its *improvisational* character. Consider a classroom of students, all multi-beings with a host of potentials that may be realized or not at any point in the ongoing flow of learning. Like our everyday conversations, the ongoing changes in a classroom are never repeated and seldom predictable. For some students, a teacher's simple request to read aloud will be welcomed as an opportunity to shine; for others, it may result in shivers of fear. What one says acquires its meaning from others' responses, and the possibilities for responding are innumerable. Furthermore, as classroom exchanges continue across time, so do they create histories. These histories also enter into the relations of the moment. At any moment, a smile of the past may be recalled; so may a harsh or an encouraging word, laughter, enthusiasm, and so on. As the school term progresses, the dance gains complexity.

Thus, with evaluation-in-process, there are no standardized practices. In spite of the years of preparation, teachers are always learning. Their education may furnish them meaningful residues; teaching experiences will add further to their potentials. However, to remain effective, evaluation within learning process is a challenge of continuous improvisation. So long as teachers and students are attuned to the ever-emerging dance in which they are engaged, learning will be enriched.

Evaluation Through Periodic Reflection

We turn here from evaluation within the learning process to evaluation during periods of reflection. One might look at exam and test scores in this way. They represent intervals in which the student might look back at their learning experience as a whole, assess strengths and weaknesses, and plan for future study. However, traditional assessment practices provide very little of either kind of information. Students may see where they succeeded or failed in an exam, but scores themselves do not explain why. As discussed, there are no clear answers to questions of why. Was more study required, was the test fair, did the teacher adequately explain, was there too little sleep, were they unmotivated, was there anxiety over the exam? All of the above, none of the above, or some combination? And to whom does one discuss such questions? Classmates are usually loath to talk about such matters because they are in competition with each other. Few students want to confess a low score or brag about a high one. Both family and teachers will typically view low scores as the student's fault: something "*you* failed to do."

In contrast, our attempt is to bring these intervals of reflection into alignment with the major purposes of relational evaluation outlined earlier: enhancing learning processes, sustaining engagement, and enriching relational well-being. There are several emphases that should ideally figure in reflective evaluation. The first is the importance of *multivocal* or *multiparty dialogue.* Traditional exams and tests are monologic. That is, the judgment of the student represents only a singular perspective, and this perspective is reduced to a single point on a continuum. Little or no attempt is made to engage students or other stakeholders in reflection on students' experiences in learning.

In replacing monologue with dialogue, reflection should minimally include conversation between students and their teachers, and this conversation should not be centered on rating the student's academic performance in comparison to others. Instead, dialogue should involve a mutual exploration of the learning process, conditions that support or obstruct, where improvements could be made, and future goals to be served. A teacher's questions might include: "What have you found most interesting in your school work?," "What progress do you think you were able to make over this period of time?," "What has contributed to such progress?," "What resources would be useful to help you now?," "How can I support you in your learning?"

Ideally such conversations should extend beyond teachers and students. Parents and caregivers should also play an important part in such reflection. Creative attention should be directed as well to ways in which classroom peers can be drawn into such dialogue about learning. Ultimately, the span of periodic reflection should be extended to administrators, government representatives, and future employers. Here we find a radical expansion in *evaluative criteria.* In traditional assessment, what cannot easily be measured about learning is all dis-*counted.* In multiparty dialogue, diverse perspectives are brought into play. Concerns with the student's attitudes toward learning, experiences of well-being, development in personal qualities, relationships with peers, parental support, family relations, hopes for the future, and so on may all enter the conversation. The range of "what is to be valued" and the criteria for evaluating are vastly expanded. This is again an education in pluralism. When skillfully facilitated, such dialogues should also contribute to enriching students' capacities for *reflective articulation.* A distinction is often made between first- and second-order learning, where first-order learning is a process of acquiring knowledge or skill, and second-order learning is learning about that process. This step represents a capacity to reflect on what has taken place, where it might be improved, and how one might proceed to the next steps. Exams and grades fail to enrich this capacity. In the process of dialogue, however, second-order articulation is a staple. As children listen to others speak about their experiences, they acquire the capacity to speak about these topics.[11]

From Classroom to Community and Beyond

Our discussion has centered so far on evaluation in the learning lives of students. Yet, as pointed out in the opening chapter, a relational approach to evaluation has far greater implications. Teachers are also subject to systematic assessment, as are administrators and schools. The factory model requires surveillance of all participants. In effect, the potentials of a relational approach to evaluation should be realized throughout the educational sphere.

To illustrate, we had much to say about the contribution of relational evaluation to sustaining students' interest in learning. However, a thirst for continued learning should scarcely be limited to students. Evaluative practices should equally sustain teachers and their engagement in teaching and learning. Teachers should find themselves curious, motivated, and inspired in their profession; willing to take risks in their teaching; and looking forward to relationships with their students. When they are limited to a standardized curriculum and evaluated in terms of their students' performance on tests, their horizons dwindle and excitement wanes. When evaluation becomes a process of co-inquiry, however, the door is open to mutual learning. For example, consider teachers who give students the freedom to write on topics that expand on their interests. Such teachers often find themselves fascinated by what they read, realizing new wellsprings of opportunity and possibility in their students, eager to converse with them, and to take part in fostering their further growth. In Chapter 6, we explore the practices of relationally sensitive evaluation of teachers, and, in Chapter 7, practices relevant to whole-school evaluation.

Yet there is more at stake than evaluation alone. There is no principled end to who or what is included in the process of relating. Generative relationships thus have the potential for indefinite outreach. The positive potentials can be realized within the network of all immediate stakeholders and beyond. Locally this should include school administrators, supporting staff, parents or caregivers, and kinfolk. As we shall explore, many of these may be drawn directly into the process of evaluation—of students, teachers, and schools. For example, reflective dialogues on students' work may include parents, administrators, and community members. When drawn into discussions of students' work, they will be invited into relations of caring and trust. And they, too, may also find themselves curious and energized to expand their horizons.

More indirectly, we may also cast the relational net outward to include processes of co-inquiry within wider communities, the region, the nation, and the globe. Such potentials are realized when secondary or high school students are offered opportunities to participate in work-study programs and apprenticeships, The European Vocational Education and Training initiative is but one case in which young people contribute to wider transformation. We are also impressed with the School2Home initiative in California, where learning communities are formed across the state. Schools within a district or in several districts share learning resources, experiences, technology, and ways of collaboration and mutual learning.[12] Internationally, we are drawn to the way in which students—young and old—increasingly interact with peers from the far corners of the world in collaborative educational projects. In all cases, evaluation is inherent in the process of learning.

Notes

1. A similar interpretation of the word "evaluation" is also found in Gitlin, A., and Smyth, J. (1989) *Teacher Evaluation: Educative Alternatives*. London: Falmer Press.
2. For insight into how such an orientation applies to evaluation at the university level, see McNamee, S. (2015) "Evaluation in a Relational Key," in T. Dragonas, K. Gergen, S. McNamee, and E. Tseliou (eds.), *Education as Social Construction: Contributions to Theory, Research and Practice*. Chagrin Falls, OH: Taos Institute Publications, 336–349.
3. See chapter 4 "Deep Dialogue," in Gill, S., and Thomson, G. (2018) *Understanding Peace Holistically*. New York: Peter Lang.
4. For example, the widespread practice of *Assessment for Learning* (AfL) embraces a formative orientation and employs dialogue to enrich learning. However, the AfL dialogues can easily be aimed at "seeking and interpreting evidence" related to the curriculum tasks and predefined content mastery. The chief goal remains that of *assessing* goal-oriented tasks and activities. When applied too rigidly, it can provide support to a factory-like vision of education structured around mastery of a fixed curriculum.
5. Cooperrider, D., Sorenson, P., Whitney, D., and Yeager, T. (2001) *Appreciative Inquiry: An Emerging Direction for Organization Development*. Champaign, IL: Stipes.
6. See Gill, S. (2019) "Caring in Public Education," Special Issue on Public Education, *Forum*, 62(3).
7. According to American Test Anxiety Association, "The majority of students report being more stressed by tests and by schoolwork than by anything else in their lives. About 16–20% of students have high test anxiety, making this the most prevalent scholastic impairment in our schools today. Another 18% are troubled by moderately-high test anxiety." http://amtaa.org/

8. Mao, Y. (2020) "Cultivating Inner Qualities Through Ethical Relations," in S. Gill and G. Thomson (eds.), *Ethical Education: Towards an Ecology of Human Development*, Cambridge: Cambridge University Press, 127–147.

9. For a more extended account of the ethical cleansing of education, see Gergen, K. J. (2020) "Ethics in Education: A Relational Perspective, in S. Gill and G. Thomson (eds.), *Ethical Education: Towards an Ecology of Human Development*, Cambridge: Cambridge University Press, 15–26. See also hooks, b. (2000) *Teaching to Transgress: Education as the Practice of Freedom*. New York: Routledge; Noddings, N. (1984) *Caring: A Feminine Approach to Ethics & Moral Education*. Berkeley: University of California Press.

10. See Shotter, J. (2011) *Getting It: Withness Thinking and the Dialogical in Practice*. London: Sage.

11. There are many examples in student voices movement where students can learn to become researchers and reflect on the classroom processes and where students join adults in making key decisions affecting the whole school community. See, for instance, Fielding, M. (2010) "The radical potential of student voice: Creating spaces for restless encounters," *International Journal of Emotional Education*, 2(1): 61–73

12. www.school2home.org/learning_communities

4

Relational Evaluation
in Primary Education

They are children . . . not robots, not machines.
—Bradbury and Roberts-Holmes[1]

It has often been said that education is the basic means of preparing children and young people to join the nation's workforce and strengthen the country's competitiveness in the global economic race. It is only natural, then, that measurement, performance outcomes, efficiency, and comparative scores carry significant weight in fashioning educational policy. Yet for many educators these instrumental terms are calloused intrusions into the learning process and the ethos of the school. In the pursuit of maximal performance, today's students are becoming the most measured in history—and possibly the least engaged. To measure means to test, and to test means sorting students into categories: the intelligent, the average, and the inadequate. As we have detailed in preceding chapters, this sorting is not only detrimental to learning, it also undermines the very basis of flourishing in schools and society.

In recent years we find that even in primary education, there are strong demands for consistent measures of academic performance. In part, this represents a desire for a *baseline* that can be used to assure that all students are making progress toward specified educational goals.[2] However, as critics point out, a standardized testing approach to achieving equality is fraught with methodological problems, disrupts children's education, is burdensome to teachers, and squanders time and money that could otherwise be used to support education.[3] As described in earlier chapters, nonstop testing has already placed children under undue stress.[4] And those who are at the margins and whom baseline measures are supposed to serve end up even more deprived by the system.

Beyond the Tyranny of Testing. Kenneth J. Gergen and Scherto R. Gill, Oxford University Press (2020). © Oxford University Press. DOI: 10.1093/oso/9780190872762.001.0001.

At the same time, we also recognize that primary education finds itself consistently confronted with competing interests from different groups surrounding the child—the state, teachers, parents, religions, and ethnic traditions, as well as the children themselves. The result is endless debate with regard to educational values, ethics, what counts as useful knowledge, and even conceptions of the child and childhood. Many have succumbed to the instrumentalist focus on test performance and grades. Others have struggled to find a compelling alternative to treating school as a production site.[5] Surely our children's well-being is important in itself. Isn't their enjoyment of life in schools, freedom from fear, engagement in meaningful activities, and participation in nourishing relationships with each other, adults, and with learning all part of their flourishing?

In this book, we propose a relational vision of education as an alternative to the prevailing production orientation. In the context of primary education, this vision draws from an abundant literature emphasizing the importance of joyful unstructured time and play; a safe, supportive, and stimulating environment; open-ended exploration and inquiry; an intimate and warm connection with adults; friendship with peers; and collaborative relationships in and between families, schools, and the community.[6] This vision does not disregard the learning outcomes of primary school, but rather explores the ways that a nourishing present is at one with a future in which children emerge as curious, confident, creative, imaginative, trusting, sociable, and open to differences. This is not an idle dream, but has served as the driving force in many locales and movements.[7]

Thus, despite the global prevalence of testing-oriented models and sausage-factory schooling, inspiring innovations abound. In this chapter, we move beyond critique to illuminate the potentials of relational evaluation in primary education. Here we explore specific practices contributing both to learning and to the relational process that gives life to learning.

Relational Evaluation and the Flourishing Child

While it is a common practice to assign grades to primary school children, there is also broad resistance. More intense is the resistance among parents and teachers to the insertion of national tests into the lives of their children and students. At the same time, there is a continuing hunger for evidence that students are progressing in their learning, that teachers are effective, and that standards are maintained, and measures for comparison are in place. Thus, in much of the world, primary school children are still being assessed and graded in various ways, and they remain subjected to standardization and national testing.

How can a relational praxis alter the landscape?[8] To begin, we shift the focus from evaluation as a means of judging or assessing to its contribution to learning and to processes of relating. As we propose, evaluation should not stand as a method or practice outside of learning but should be integral to the process of learning itself. The remainder of this chapter is thus structured around the three key aspirations of relational evaluation developed in the preceding chapter: (1) enhancing the learning processes, (2) inspiring further learning engagement, and (3) enriching the quality of relating. In each of these areas we explore relevant ideas and practices that point the way to educational transformation.

As proposed in Chapter 3, relational evaluation takes place both during the ongoing learning process and at periodic intervals of reflection. *In-process evaluation* could include evaluative comments from peers and teachers, feedback from the teacher, and self-evaluation. *Periodic reflection* might feature such evaluative practices as portfolio work, individual and group review, end-of-year student-led report meetings, and project exhibitions. As we shall explore, in-process evaluation should improve the quality of a child's experience, enhance the learning processes, and facilitate ongoing engagement. Periodic reflection is more systematic, focusing on such topics as the child's interests, learning priorities, and future planning. Both work synergistically to support children's development as whole persons, inspiring them to learn and linking their education to personal interests. They also draw from and contribute to meaningful relationships between teachers and students, friendships among students, relationships between school and home, and more.

Enhancing Learning Through Evaluation

There are many ways relational practices of evaluation can enhance the ongoing learning processes. In focusing here on in-process evaluation, it is useful to contrast two classroom stories:

In a public elementary school in Washington state, 6-year-old Lucy is enjoying the first grade. Last week, her class listened to the story of "Jack and the Beanstalk," and, in activity time, each child planted a bean in a small pot. This week, Lucy was happy to see that hers has already geminated—a thin feeble stalk supporting two tiny leaves. Now it is time to complete a lined worksheet where the children are asked to report on those elements required for the growth of a beanstalk and to illustrate each element.

Lucy fills the lines with confidence: bean—soil—water—light, writing down these well-rehearsed words, one on each line, with a drawing next to it. She is really pleased with herself as she scarcely needs to look up at the spellings on the board—she knows her letters! With concentration, Lucy completes all four lines of the words and drawings and is about to raise her hand in triumph. Suddenly, however, she notices a fifth line on the worksheet! She holds her breath, stares at the line and freezes: she has no idea of what to write or draw on that line. Looking around, she sees other children are still bowing their heads over their worksheets. Lucy feels lost.

The teacher notices Lucy's frown and comes over. "How are you doing, Lucy?" Lucy casts her eyes on the worksheet, and answers: "I think I got these all right!" The teacher continues: "Yes, I see you have, and the writing is neat." But Lucy is not yet relaxed and points her finger to the fifth line. "I don't know what to write here." Now the teacher understands why Lucy looks so worried and apologizes. "You must have missed what I said earlier: that line was just a mistake." Lucy sighs with relief.

Traditional school culture favors obedience to authority. Just like Lucy, many children never question why they must do as they are asked; they simply follow instructions. Lucy is beginning to realize that what counts in education is filling in the lines with correct answers. A possible fascination with how beans grow will be replaced with the pressure to perform. Unless children are actively engaged in the learning process—participating in the rationale for what they are doing, finding meaning in the activities—they may soon find schooling an alien chore. They will simply do as they are told, and education will rapidly approach coercion.

As we have advanced, evaluation can be accomplished without such deadening effects. As a form of inquiry, relational evaluation can serve as an integral part of ongoing teaching. For teachers, evaluation can return what is meaningful to themselves, that which has been taken away from them by a system of testing. Let's return to Lucy's classroom and see how a relational approach to in-process evaluation could stimulate her learning and prevent her from feeling defeated or waiting for the voice of authority.

Lucy's teacher asks the class to take a few minutes to think about how they will care for their plants in the future. What steps will they take to help their plant have a healthy life? And if the plant does produce some beans, what will they do with them? Giving the class a few minutes to reflect in silence, the teacher invites the children to imagine and share stories about raising their plants.

Lucy was one of the first to raise her hand. She talked about how she would remember to water the plant and make sure that the sun could reach it each day. Lucy confessed she didn't know what to do if there were too many cloudy days. She smiled once to say that she thought her plant needed a lot of love. And she laughed when she finally said that she didn't like beans, so she would feed them to her little brother.

Lucy's teacher joined Lucy and the class in laughter, and then commented on how she liked the way Lucy was so attentive to the plant and understood its needs. She thought "love" was a great way to talk about caring for the plant. She then asked the class, "How can we help out with this question about cloudy days? Does anyone have an idea about what we could do if there wasn't much sun?" An active discussion ensued.

Drawing from this vignette, let's pay particular attention to the use of affirmative feedback, collaborative inquiry, and reflective questioning in enhancing learning.

Affirmative Feedback

The most common way of combining relational evaluation with ongoing classroom learning is through *affirmative feedback*. Feedback in itself is in total contrast to the alienating effect of testing and grades.[9] Much has been written, in particular, about shifting from a deficit orientation to assessment—pointing to a student's errors—in contrast to feedback focusing on strengths. As commonly agreed, strength-based feedback builds confidence and enhances participation in learning while simultaneously alerting students to areas needing improvement.[10] It sets the stage for generative relating between teacher and student.

In this last vignette, the teacher's affirmative feedback is prominent. It begins in the subtle but important act of attentive listening. In this small act, Lucy is already positioned as someone "worth listening to." In commenting on how Lucy understood the plant's needs, the teacher equally affirms Lucy's learning. Then, a relational touch is added to the teacher's feedback by inviting the class to join in reflecting on the question about how plants survive long periods of cloudiness. Here the teacher not only grants significance to Lucy's questioning, but also creates a classroom atmosphere in which the students feel they are working together.

Affirmative feedback may also draw attention to the child's learning process. When children recognize the care and attentiveness in affirmative feedback, they are invited to take an interest in their own learning. When the class laughed at Lucy's conclusions (e.g. feeding her little brother with the beans), they were in effect complimenting her on adding an unexpected twist to the end of the story. And when the teacher expressed particular enthusiasm for Lucy's introducing the metaphor of "love" in her care for the plant, she was also congratulating Lucy for taking a creative leap in her story.

Yet the idea of building individual confidence through affirmative feedback doesn't take us far enough. The common focus on building self-esteem through affirmative feedback comes at the cost of supporting an individualistic vision of education. From the standpoint of our book, individuals cannot be separated from the relational processes of which they are a part. We return to this challenge shortly.

Reflective Questioning

When teachers address their students, questions and answers are common stock. Questions are sometimes addressed to individuals and sometimes to the class as a whole. The practice typically distinguishes right from wrong answers and identifies who knows what and who doesn't. This often comes at a cost to relationships. The eager children who answer quickly and correctly soon learn they are "superior"; others hesitate in fear they may make a mistake. And, through it all, the teacher sits in judgment.

Yet relationally sensitive inquiry can stimulate curiosity and inspire learning. In particular, *reflective questioning* is not intended to elicit correct answers or judge a student's mastery of knowledge. Rather, it attempts to stimulate children's curiosities and expand their horizons of learning. Such questioning doesn't anticipate cookie-cutter answers, but instead invites opportunities to enliven and deepen the learning experience. Here we can distinguish between questions directed to *subject matter* and those directed to *processes of learning*. In the former case, for example, a teacher might encourage children's imagination and kindle their curiosity by asking the class: "Do you think your plants would grow well in the Sahara Desert or the North Pole?" Bringing the biology lesson closer to home, the teacher could ask, "Do you think you would like to be a farmer and plant beans or corn?" "Why?" and "Why not?" Turning to the learning process, thoughtful questions can develop students' interest in why and how to learn. For example, to inject importance into the topic at hand, a teacher might ask, "Why is it important to know about what plants need?" And to give the lesson global importance, one might ask, "If people know what you know about how plants can grow, why do you think so many people in the world are starving?" "Do you think this could be helpful for you to know some day?" In terms of learning how to learn, the teacher might ask, for instance, "If we wanted to know more about how plants grow, where would we go? Who could we ask?"

Furthermore, reflective questions may be used to expand the teacher's professional horizons. For instance, Lucy's teacher might ask herself: "How well will the children understand and appreciate the meaning of this activity?" Or, "How can I expand this activity in ways that will appeal to the children?" Teachers might also share with their students such self-questioning. A teacher might ask the children, for instance, "I wasn't sure if you would be interested in this topic, and I thought we might take it in this direction. What do you think?" Or, "This didn't make much sense to me when I was your age. I wonder if you can see why we should learn this?" In sharing such questions, the teacher not only models the kind of questioning that can enhance the children's learning experience but also contributes to a culture of learning.

Collaborative Inquiry

A third significant contribution to in-process evaluation can be achieved through *collaborative inquiry*. Collaborative learning has long been recognized as an important part of primary education.[11] Value is placed on children's development within their relationships with peers, teachers, and other adults. Collaborative work can invite active participation, expand the children's knowledge, and simultaneously act as a multifaceted process of evaluation. It can bring into view diverse perspectives, values, and ways of understanding. When different ideas and perspectives arise, with possible tensions between them, children can be prompted to reexamine and question their own ideas and beliefs. Learning and evaluation are simultaneous.

A collaborative approach to evaluation is well-suited to pairs or small groups of three or four students. In Lucy's class, there are tables at which three to four children share ideas and work on tasks together. Following the children's stories about how they helped to make their plants grow, the teacher asked if they could work together on how much or how little sunlight and water a plant would need to be healthy. The question challenges the children to think about how they can gain knowledge from different sources, appreciate multiple possibilities, and learn from each other. Inquiries are open-ended and they help demonstrate to the students that learning is unrestricted and unlimited.

Of course, when children are working collaboratively it is an ideal time for feedback and reflective questions that would enhance the value and understanding of the relational process itself. The teacher might, for instance, comment on the strengths displayed by various collaborating workgroups or congratulate the class on "how well we all have worked together on this task." Each group might be asked to reflect on how they managed to work together. What did it require to collaborate well? Congratulating the class as a whole would also make visible the process of relational interdependence.

Affirmative feedback, reflective questioning, and collaborative inquiry are only three of many ways in which relationally oriented evaluation may inspire learning in everyday classroom activities. Much more can be said, and the potentials for innovation are unending. For instance, we are drawn to the Reggio-inspired approach to making learning visible and reflecting on learning in process.[12] Here, teachers talk with students about photographs or video samples of their work and invite student conversations about projects. Within such discussions, the evaluative process is everywhere at work.

Sustaining Engagement in Learning

We now shift the focus from inspiring learning to ways in which relational evaluation can lay the groundwork for sustained interest in learning. We illustrate this with three well-documented approaches to periodic reflection drawn from both mainstream and alternative schooling: the *learning review, formative feedback,* and *portfolio work.* Together they provide powerful illustrations of the ways in which relational evaluation can inspire and facilitate students' further engagement in learning.

Learning Review: Students Lead the Way

A learning review meeting is increasingly common in mainstream schools in the United Kingdom.[13] It is a shift from judging the effects of learning to fostering continued commitment to learning. Let's take a closer look at a learning review meeting through an illustration.

On a sunny day in July, in a quiet room of a primary school in Midland, England, a learning review meeting is about to start. Ten-year-old Paul stands with ease in front of his teacher, his parents, and the school's headteacher. The boy smiles broadly: "I am not doing a powerpoint, but I will show you what I have been learning this year with this!" The audience looks on with anticipation at the tastefully decorated cover of Paul's learning review folder. In the next 10 minutes, Paul gives a carefully prepared account of his learning journey over the course of the year. Using drawings, photographs, clippings, and other artifacts, Paul provides a visually rich narrative of his learning experience. He speaks of his enthusiasms—languages, arts, drama, church performances, and sports; he also points to areas of challenge—math, science, and punctuality. The review emphasizes how he has negotiated tough patches during the year with the help and support received from his friends, teachers, parents, and others.

At the end of Paul's review, his teacher offers her congratulations on his achievements. She comments on the progress he has made during this fourth year in the United Kingdom since arriving as a refugee from Africa. In particular, she expresses her admiration of how well he has collaborated with others on math, at which point, Paul briefly tells the interested audience about the math group work. After that, Paul's father expresses his delight in finding out about his son's enthusiasm and dedication to learning in spite of earlier hardships; his mother praises his helpfulness at home and in the church. The headteacher asks Paul how else his teachers might support him in the coming year. The conversation ends with encouragement for Paul to continue drawing on his strengths and on help from others as he goes on.

Such evaluative practices tend to offer an overview of a student's learning journey over time. They can encourage students to understand and appreciate the value of their activities and experiences in school. Equally, they can also inspire students' curiosity in the learning processes while supporting them in taking risks. When sensitively developed, such practices contribute to the student's overall well-being and development as a person.

Learning review is usually scheduled once a school year, as in Paul's school, but can also be held at shorter intervals, such as once a term. Review meetings tend to last 15 minutes and are always led by the child. Children as young as 9 years of age are encouraged to take responsibility for preparing a presentation about their learning journey. The presentation outlines the student's experience over time and can help teachers and parents understand the child's interests and aspirations, how the child engages with challenges, along with what and how learning has taken place. The review is usually attended by the class teacher, the parents or caregivers, and, ideally, the school's principal.

We are drawn to learning review not only because of its relational sensitivity, but because it can also be a powerful way of inviting students to take part in the evaluation of their learning. The review process prioritizes the student's voice while incorporating the parents' perspectives. It stands in stark contrast to the more typical parent–teacher meeting where the teacher simply discusses the child's levels of attainment in various subjects. Unlike the way in which Paul was the main speaker in the review meeting, parent–teacher meetings are often short and dominated by the teacher, sometimes even without the student's attendance. Furthermore, the purpose of a conventional parent–teacher meeting is primarily to instruct parents on where the child needs to improve, which implicitly places responsibility with the parents rather than the student. When assessing students using target levels, age-related expectations, ability-sets, progress scores in grids, boxes, graphs, performance indicators, audits, and other forms of performance tracking,[14] the child becomes an object to be shaped by others. In comparison, the learning review places the child as the subject or agent who is encouraged and supported to take the initiatives to shape his or her learning pathways.

We are also interested in the ways that learning review can encourage students to understand and appreciate the value of their engagement in learning. As we have seen, Paul reflects on both his strengths and his capacities to embrace challenges. Such reflection holds potential for further stimulating his curiosity in the learning processes and provides an opportunity for him to be more creative about learning. Thus students may link the learning process to their lives at home and in communities.[15]

How did the learning review accomplish these ends? Here we focus on two relevant components: the discourse of evaluation and the relational process. As proposed in Chapter 2, through language, we give meaning to the worlds we inhabit. Here we distinguish between the discourse of *assessment* and the discourse of *evaluation*. The former now dominating our school systems centers on scores, grades, outcomes, proficiency, and so on. Such terms come to inhabit our ways of life, thus fashioning the way teachers relate to their students. Alice is an "A" student; Jimmy is failing—regardless of their other many talents, ambitions, and needs. This narrowing of definition also narrows the sphere of relating to actions specifically bearing on performance. Slowly the discourse of assessment also becomes prevalent in the way teachers' own activities as teachers are judged. It may cease to matter whether one is generous, kind, or compassionate as a teacher—unless such ways of being can improve student performance.

By contrast, in preparation for the learning review, students are introduced to the discourse of evaluation, by which we mean a multiplicity of voices giving expression to relevant values. Multiple perspectives are invited into the conversation about learning. In the present case, Paul could use his own terms to describe his experiences of learning, his interests, and objectives along with what he has learned and how. Moreover, Paul was also invited to integrate stories, workbooks, arts, PowerPoint, and other means of helping the teacher and parents understand and appreciate his learning journey. The teacher will also add to the review the discourse of educational concern and possibly the languages of communities outside the school. The more diverse the values entering into the review, the more promising the preparation for life in the social worlds to come.

The power of the learning review in sustaining engagement also lies in its reconfiguration of relationships. Traditional education is based on a hierarchy in which the knowers are on top and learners at the bottom. This structure has several effects. It favors monologue over dialogue, with the teacher presenting and leading a class of the monitored silent. It thus fosters obedience among learners and a reliance on authority for direction. When coupled with testing, it also creates a condition of fear and alienation for students and fosters an attitude of surveillance and suspicion among teachers. Within this hierarchical model, parents are typically allied with the teacher to ensure the academic success of their children.[16] The learning review wholly restructures this configuration. Here the playing field becomes more level: students are now credited with being the "knowers." They can deliberate on their activities, formulate their perspectives, and share what they value in learning. As their voices are honored by both teachers and parents, they become full-fledged participants in discussion about education. Paul's learning review involves major partners in learning, and the respect he receives in these discussions plays a significant role in building his confidence in having something valuable to offer.

With this shift toward participatory dialogue a new consciousness is also invited. As noted in Chapter 2, with its long-standing emphasis on the performance of the individual—at one with the practice of testing and grading—traditional schooling lends itself to an individualist ideology. As monologue is replaced by dialogue, however, one may begin to appreciate the significance of the relational process in which he or she is embedded. The *you* and *I* give way to an appreciation of *we*. This is especially noteworthy in Paul's experience with math, and the headteacher's final remark asking how the other teachers could support Paul's work in the coming year. Paul now finds that he is not alone; he is a member of a community of support.

To be sure, the power of the learning review for sustained learning engagement depends on more than a new language of evaluation and a restructuring of relationships. The evaluation process cannot be separated from classroom pedagogy and school ethos. A culture in which students' voices are honored and collaboration is invited can make a significant difference to the potency of the learning review.

Formative Feedback: Vocabulary for Growth

Earlier we described *affirmative feedback* as a form of relational evaluation built into the process of everyday learning. However, there is another form of feedback that can also contribute to a continued interest in learning. We call this *formative feedback* because it is specifically directed to developing a more holistic orientation to students' learning and development. In contrast to affirmative feedback, formative feedback may focus on the student's personal engagement in learning, including his or her interests, motivation, confidence, determination, and direction. It is an exercise in learning to learn, and linking the learning process to a flourishing life with others. The feedback typically takes place at specific intervals and is nurtured by a language of evaluation aimed at holistic growth and generative relationships.

To appreciate the potentials, we draw from an end-of-term formative feedback session hosted by Paul's teacher Miss Levy. To set the context of this particular formative feedback session: Paul's family lost a child when escaping from their war-torn native country, and Paul's parents have consistently encouraged him to treasure the life he was given and to work hard: Miss Levy starts by telling Paul that his motivation for learning is appreciated by both his teachers and peers. They discuss a few examples of Paul's work where he points out how he has persisted and succeeded in story-writing and arts work, and where he is with regard to math as the subject that he finds most challenging. Miss Levy also mentions that Paul's friendly demeanor and eagerness for friendship is truly infectious. Here she talks about Paul's reaching out to and translating for a newly arrived refugee student, what a talented linguist Paul is, and how admirable that he is using his talent in helping others. Paul beams throughout at these positive comments. He knows that he is a hard-working student and he is a good friend.

Miss Levy then cautiously shares an observation that sometimes Paul's enthusiasm for learning could be so overwhelming that he might to be stressed. Paul keeps quiet for a while and whispers with his eyes casting downward: "I do not know how to stop. . . . Just want to try my best in everything." Miss Levy nods reassuringly and comments that his desire to do well is a great asset. However, she points out, "sometimes this pressure to do well can get in the way of having a good time." She then asks whether Paul might like to have special times for another kind of learning. For instance, he could join several classmates in listening to music from various parts of the world and talking about what they like. "Just having fun." Paul smiles and nods at the prospect.

In this example, we see that formative feedback focuses on the learning process and the student's learning engagement in a holistic way. The feedback is rooted in who and where the child is, and it supports his aspirations from there. Rather than distracting the student from his learning trajectory by imposing external targets, it enables him to deliberate on his learning experiences. Its gentle and caring quality provides support for Paul's learning journey. Throughout the conversation, Paul's views are respected, and trust is established between him and his teacher.

Formative feedback can also be used on a peer-to-peer basis. Consider an example drawn from Paul's classroom. At the end of each half term, the teacher encourages her class to have a group feedback session. On these occasions, students talk about their work, what they like, how they are doing, and where they could use some help from their classmates. In one such group session, Paul told his group that he was afraid of math as he made so many errors. "I can never get anything right!" he exclaimed in an exasperated way. Alice responded: "But when you write stories or do drawings, you don't seem afraid of trying, and you always try different ideas." Other children joined in, also pointing out Paul's fearless and creative qualities in other activities.

These conversations provided an opportunity for Paul to consider how he might take a similar approach to learning math. Such comments from peers can help students to shape their ways of learning as well as sustain their engagement.

Portfolios: Linking Worlds, Linking Lives

In the learning review meeting, Paul presented a collection of his work to his teachers and parents. This kind of collection is often called a *portfolio*. Portfolio work is a well-researched alternative to examinations and is most helpful in evaluating and documenting students' progress over a period of time. There are two major considerations in establishing a portfolio: its particular *purpose*, which determines who collects what, when, where, how, and for whom; and the *range of sources* to be included.[17]

Portfolios can serve different purposes. Some are intended to show growth over time,[18] some can be used to support teachers' decisions in terms of how to plan the next phase of teaching and learning,[19] others can provide rich illustrations of students' learning journeys and progress.[20] Despite the varying purposes, in general, portfolios can offer major opportunities for demonstrating and reflecting on students' activities and their learning experiences. Portfolios are also intended to improve the quality of teaching as they contribute (indirectly) to teachers' self-reflection.[21]

For these reasons, it is necessary that portfolios comprise a wide variety of artifacts.[22] A generic portfolio might include evidence of completed tasks, notebooks, drawings, diaries, reports, charts, posters, software, certificates, student self-evaluation, and so forth.[23] There can be pieces of the students' best work,[24] or any work in which the child takes pride or effectively represents his or her knowledge and skills.[25] Likewise, the audience of a student's portfolio can include multiple stakeholders, such as the teachers, school administrators, parents, others in the community, and above all, the child him- or herself.

The widespread use of portfolios represents a major step toward relational evaluation, and a viable and meaningful alternative to measurement-based assessment. For instance, because portfolios can be extensive, when collected over a period of time, they may help illustrate, from multiple perspectives, the student's learning process, progress, and growth over the same period of time. The evaluative potential of portfolio lies in the processes of compiling the portfolio contents which serve as conversation starters to co-inquire into the student's experiences of learning. Hence portfolios can enable more sustained engagement in learning and continuous effort in inquiry.

While some educators have attempted to standardize portfolio work for purposes of traditional grading,[26] our particular focus is on dialogic approaches to evaluation. For example, in choosing the items for the portfolio, both the teacher and the student collaborate in dialogue which helps deepen their understandings about the student's progress in learning. Dialogue and conversations about each piece of "evidence" to be included in the portfolio will necessarily return to the learning journey itself, the delights experienced, the challenges overcome, and the myriad forms of help the child had received.

Let's return to consider the process Paul had gone through to put together his portfolio. The contents of Paul's portfolio are the result of dialogue between him and his teacher. Because the portfolio is intended to document Paul's learning journey and his progress overtime, they discussed what might be included, and Paul was encouraged to think about what has been important to him during the term. The teacher encouraged him to reflect on questions such as: "What have you enjoyed about learning during this term?," "What has been particularly interesting for you?," "Where do you feel that you have excelled?," "How might you demonstrate these?"

These questions invited Paul first into dialogue with his teacher and then into personal expressions. As the teacher listened and joined in Paul's reflection on what would help him illustrate his learning, her world of understanding also expanded. Similarly, as the teacher might ask, "Why is this a good illustration of your work?" or "Which piece of work would show that you have really learned something?," Paul could be sensitized to the values that would be placed on his work, effort, and experiences.

In fact, in Paul's school, when the children began to select pieces of their work for their portfolios, they also included each other in the discussions, and sometimes their parents and other relevant parties. Such portfolio practices enlarge the circle of dialogue about what counts as learning, progress, development, and growth. The relational nature of dialogic evaluation through portfolio has encouraged Paul and his peers to press further in their learning, thus nourishing their continued growth and engagement.

The three selected practices in this section variously demonstrate how relational approaches to evaluation can help sustain students' engagement in learning. Further practices continue to emerge from around the world. We are drawn, for example, to *family reading diaries* and *records of development* in primary schools in China[27] along with the potentials of performance-based evaluation practices.[28] A common thread among these is a dialogic and collaborative orientation to the way children and adults understand and appreciate learning and being together.

Enriching the Quality of Relating

The third aim of relational evaluation is to enrich relationships among participants in the learning process. As we have argued, when the aim of education is improving test performance, relationships are impoverished. In contrast, we ask, how can evaluation help enrich the qualities of relating, including trust, care, mutual interest, and understanding? The evaluative practices just described do contribute to positive relations. Here, we consider three practices that bring these potentials into sharper focus.

Circle Time Learning

Circle time activities are not uncommon in schools, but how do they contribute to educational evaluation? We begin with a story.

In a small community school in Quebec, 15 children are having a very busy morning. One group is creating all kinds of artwork from variously shaped and colored pieces of paper, while a second group is making designs with small colored blocks, and a third is drawing shapes on white paper. Elsie, the class teacher, moves from table to table, observes the children's work, makes notes of their progress, listens to their discussions, and talks to anyone who seeks her feedback or advice.

Before snack time, Elsie invites the children to sit in a circle. "Going around the room just now, I am really excited by all the new ideas and designs you have made." She surveys the children's beaming faces. "I think it would be great if you would share some of the highlights from this morning." The children nod eagerly. "Which group would like to start?" Jason raises his hand and talks excitedly about how his group has made a large diamond using multiple smaller diamonds. As Jason talks, Una holds out a photo of their effort on the class iPad, and Luca uses his fingers to show how the diamonds have been stacked up. Other children listen with interest. Elsie comments gently: "What a fascinating piece of work. Well done to all four of you!"

Joe, the smallest in this group, raises his hand: "But wait, I think we have a surprise for you." He giggles and in a dramatic gesture touches the iPad to reveal a beautiful cascade of blue-red triangles. The class is fascinated. "Can you tell us how you did this?," asks Elsie. The group proudly attributes this magnificent piece to each other—Jason's noticing that two triangles make a diamond, Luca and Una choosing their favorite colors, Joe's interest in repeated patterns. "Such excellent group work; thank you!" All children clap together in celebration.

This vignette illustrates what is often called *circle time learning*, a long-standing practice in primary education in many parts of the world. Circle time can be particularly helpful in providing an appreciative context where children learn to listen to each other with care and respect, and thus build stronger and more generative relationships.[29] Circle time is often a dedicated time for children and their teacher to reflect on their learning. In the case of the preschool class, circle time is integral to the daily flow of classroom activities. The day is punctuated with circle time sessions—first thing in the morning, before snacks, after lunch, and at the end of the day. Circle time provides a breathing space for the children to arrive and settle in the class, an opportunity to inquire about and appreciate each other's learning, an occasion for storytelling and sharing experiences, and a moment of relaxation. Our discussion here focuses on the way circle time provides an opportunity to evaluate learning and, in doing so, also enrich relationships.

Several aspects are noteworthy. First, circle time is inclusive: it invites the participation of every child in the class. That the teacher sits in the circle at the same level with the children shifts the traditional power structure from hierarchy to one of mutual respect. From within the circle, the teacher can also act as a facilitator of dialogue. Second, the reflections on learning do not stress mastery of content. Simply put, during circle time, students do not make the kind of "I can" statements invited by competition and performance assessment. In circle time, a typical "I can" statement would be "I have made a diamond shape with two triangles." The evaluative reflection is focused on what students have appreciated most in learning together and how they have collaborated to enable these experiences.

Third, the teacher's ways of commenting and questioning are key to enriching relational process. As we have seen, Elsie's way of moving with the flow of conversation is not only appreciative, but also directed at drawing out the collaborative nature of the learning processes. As previously discussed, the teacher's choice of language in this process is an important element in the way children co-create the meaning of learning, evaluation, and each other. Finally, circle time reflection can link the individual student's learning to the shared class experience. Here one child's idea or one group's creativity becomes a resource for the whole class. The class is able to contribute to each other's learning. The care for learning converges with care for each other.

Dialogic Inquiry in a Writing Workshop

Earlier we discussed ways in which evaluation can function within classroom dialogue to support learning. Here we draw attention to ways in which dialogue can enrich the relational process.

In a community school, students aged 11–12 learn to evaluate each other's writing through a dialogic process called *writing workshop*. When a student feels it would be useful for others to help review a draft of writing-in-progress, he or she can nominate three classmates as reviewers. Each writing workshop follows a process of dialogic inquiry, often facilitated by the teacher and lasting 30–45 minutes. The inquiry begins with the *author* stating the reason for the writing workshop: for example, needing help in developing the plot or seeking ways to make the writing more interesting. The author then reads aloud from an existing draft while the reviewers listen with the stated need in mind. They first discuss the draft appreciatively by offering comments on its strengths and then respond by offering constructive suggestions. Once all the suggestions are offered, the group discusses them together and explores possible ways the author might improve the draft. The workshop ends with the author reflecting on ideas to move his or her writing forward and thanking the reviewers and the teacher.

Here we see that evaluating the student's work is synchronous with building positive bonds among students. Each step of the dialogic inquiry builds on the previous and cumulatively shows care, scaffolds learning, and strengthens friendship. Good relationships also feed back into the learning process. The stronger the relationships, the more open the author is to the reviewers' suggestions, and the more he or she will trust and appreciate the process of evaluation.

Project Exhibition: Celebrating a Hundred Languages of the Child

Loris Malaguzzi, founder of the Reggio Emilia schools, maintains that children bring with them multiple "languages," or diverse ways to engage, listen, and explore.[30] But how do our schools allow students to learn in such rich and myriad ways? For many years, Reggio Emilia schools have provided a space where children can *speak* in these different languages. Most importantly, there is always someone listening and documenting, and there is always ongoing inquiry and dialogue about learning. Each language is also an invitation for relating. This is in contrast to the way in which standardized assessment leaves many children mute.

How then might we configure the evaluative process so that there is listening, appreciation, and dialogue? As pointed out, there is a close affinity between the pedagogy of project-based learning and relational evaluation. In project-based learning, dialogue can play a pivotal role from beginning to end. In the framing of the project ideas can be initiated by either teachers or students and shaped in further discussion. If the project is undertaken by a single student, he or she may be encouraged to seek the advice and support of numerous others. If the project is collaborative, active dialogue may ensue within the group. As children work on these projects, they will also begin to consider the responses of others—teachers and peers most centrally. When projects are subsequently presented to a class, a new round of conversation will be triggered. If properly crafted these dialogues will incite enthusiasm for learning, inspire innovation, and favor a deep learning experience. Most important for the present discussion, they will provide a rich palette of evaluative feedback and contribute to generative relationships.

Interestingly, a Reggio-inspired school in the San Francisco Bay area has extended its potentials in a dramatic way. The school puts on a public exhibition for the local community of all the projects children have worked on during the year. Students stand proudly in front of their projects. Each project is accompanied by a written *project journey* that describes the various challenges, successes, and failures along the way and what students have learned from them. The exhibit is attended by friends, family members, the school staff, and interested community members. Active dialogue between students and visitors is typical. The visitors examine the projects, often reading the accounts of the learning journeys and asking the students to tell them about their work. The fruits of these lively conversations are many. As they are drawn into conversation, the children learn through their attempts to explain their projects; new ideas often emerge as they grapple with the questions of differing visitors. Likewise, visitors acquire understanding and appreciation as they enter the many worlds of the children. As these adventures in learning are taking place, so are positive relations developed across generations, genders, ethnicities, and so on. The school now contributes to an expanded *community* of learning.

Liberation for Learning Together

As we propose, practices of relational evaluation have the potential to transform the learning process while establishing life-long resources for living together. We move away from the corrosive effects of testing and grading—pressures to outperform others and to avoid shame and scorn—to a context of growth, guidance, and support. With dialogically and collaboratively oriented practices of evaluation interest can center on the potentials that children bring to the class. Spaces are created for developing generative relationships within the classroom, with learning, and with the surrounding world. Both teachers and children can be open to listening, sharing, and reflecting. They can build on each other's enthusiasm and insights. There is mutual care for the child's learning and ongoing engagement in the process of learning. There is an invited awareness of the potentials and value of the "we." These possibilities in secondary education are the focus of the following chapter.

Notes

1. Bradbury, A., and Roberts-Holmes, G. (2016) "They are children . . . not robots, not machines," *The Introduction of Reception Baseline Assessment*, a Report Commissioned by Association of Teachers and Lecturers and the National Union of Teachers. https://www.teachers.org.uk/sites/default/files2014/baseline-assessment--final-10404.pdf, accessed April 2019.

2. *Baseline assessment* was introduced in 2015 in England, aimed at scoring the literacy and numeracy performance of children within the first few weeks of entering Reception year, aged 4–5. It was intended to create a "baseline" against which to consistently measure these children's progress for the purposes of school and teacher accountability. However, the baseline assessment has been resisted by teachers and parents and rejected by the National Union of Teachers.

3. Bradbury and Roberts-Holmes, "They are children."

4. Hutchings, M. (2015) "'Exam Factories'? The impact of accountability measures on children and young people," National Union of Teachers, http://www.teachers.org.uk/node/24299, accessed April 2019.

5. Gill, S. and Thomson, G. (2012). *Rethinking Secondary Education: A Human-Centred Approach*. London: Routledge.

6. For example, Alexander, R. J. (2004) "Excellence, enjoyment and personalised learning: a true foundation for choice?" *Education Review*, 18(1): 15–33; Marples, R. (ed.) (1999) *The Aims of Education*. London: Routledge; and Wood, E. (2007) "Reconceptualising child-centred education: contemporary directions in policy, theory and practice in early childhood," *Forum* 49(1 and 2): 119–135.

7. Here we draw especially from views and practices of primary education in Germany and Nordic countries, as well as from the child-centered education movement in the United Kingdom, progressive educational traditions found in Waldorf education, Montessori education, the worldwide Reggio Emilia movement, democratic education, community-based schools, and human-centered education. See also Shuayb, M., and O'Donnell, S. (2008) *Aims and Values in Primary Education: England and Other Countries (Primary Review Research Survey 1/2)*, Cambridge: Cambridge University Press, University of Cambridge Faculty of Education; Gribble, D. (1998) *Real Education. Varieties of Freedom*. Bristol: Libertarian Education; and Gill, S., and Thomson, G. (2014) *Human-Centred Education*. London: Routledge.

8. We chose the word *praxis* based on its meanings proposed by Paulo Freire, who suggests that the praxis is both a vision and practice aimed at structural transformation. See Freire, P. (1970) *Pedagogy of the Oppressed*. London: Continuum.

9. Some scholars, especially those of the UK Assessment Reform Group, would argue that feedback is the essence of assessment for learning, which has become a key focus on policy on assessment. See The Assessment Reform Group (ARG) (1999) *Assessment for Learning: Beyond the Black Box*. Cambridge: Cambridge University Press, University of Cambridge School of Education; Black, P., and Wiliam, D. (1998) "Inside the black box: raising standards through classroom assessment," *Phi Delta Kappan*, 89(2): 139–148.

10. Closely related is the emerging emphasis on strengths-based learning and its emphasis on student strengths as opposed to shortcomings. However, where the strengths-based approach tends to focus on how the student can be affected, a relational orientation is more focused on appreciative feedback in the process of enriching relationships.

11. Alexander, R. (ed.) (2009) *Children, Their World, Their Education. Final Report and Recommendations of the Cambridge Primary Review*. Abingdon: Routledge.

12. Rinaldi, C. (2006). *In Dialogue with Reggio Emilia: Listening, Researching and Learning*. London/New York: Routledge.
13. Swann, M., Peacock, A., Hart, S., and Drummond, M. (2012) *Creating Learning Without Limits*. London: Open University Press.
14. Mansell, W. (2007) *Education by Numbers: The Tyranny of Testing*. London: Routledge.
15. Although learning reviews may accomplish these ends, there has been a tendency in some schools to reformulate them in ways that are more congenial to the testing tradition. For example, when learning reviews become dependent on students' reliance on PowerPoint representations of their accomplishments, they lose most of their value in inspiring and sustaining learning.
16. Pérez-Álvarez, M. (2017) "The four causes of ADHD: Aristotle in the classroom," *Frontiers in Psychology*, 8(928): 1–13.
17. Gillespie, C., Ford, K., Gillespie, R., and Leavell, A. (1996) "Portfolio assessment: Some questions, some answers, some recommendations," *Journal of Adolescent & Adult Literacy*, 39: 480–491.
18. Mullin, J. (1998) "Portfolios: Purposeful collections of student work," *New Directions for Teaching and Learning*, 74: 74–87.
19. Gillespie et al., "Portfolio assessment."
20. Ibid.
21. Brady, L. (2001) "Portfolios for assessment and reporting in New South Wales primary schools," *Journal of Educational Enquiry*, 2(2): 24–43.
22. Cole, D., Ryan, C., Kick, F., and Mathies, B. (2000) *Portfolios Across the Curriculum and Beyond* (2nd ed.). Thousand Oaks, CA: Corwin Press.
23. Freeman, R., and Lewis, R. (1998) *Planning and Implementing Assessment*. London: Kogan Page.
24. Richter, S. (1997) "Using portfolios as an additional means of assessing written language in a special education classroom," *Teaching and Change*, 5(1): 58–70.
25. Jones, J. (2012) "Portfolios as 'learning companions' for children and a means to support and assess language learning in the primary school," *Education 3-13*, 40(4): 401–416.
26. Benoit, J., and H. Yang (1996) "A redefinition of portfolio assessment based upon purpose: Findings and implications from a large-scale program," *Journal of Research and Development in Education*, 29(3): 181–191.
27. Mao, Y-Q. (2019). "Cultivating Inner Qualities through Ethical Relations," in S. Gill and G. Thomson (eds.), *Ethical Education in Schools: Towards Ecology of Human Development*. Cambridge: Cambridge University Press, 127–147.
28. Palm, T. (2008) "Performance assessment and authentic assessment: A conceptual analysis of the literature," *Practical Assessment Research and Evaluation*, 13(4): 1–10.
29. Cefai, C., Ferrario, E., Cavioni, V., Carter, A., and Grech, T. (2014) "Circle time for social and emotional learning in primary school," *Pastoral Care in Education*, 32(2): 116–130; Mosley, J. (2009) "Circle Time and Socio-Emotional Competence in

Children and Young People," in C. Cefai and P. Cooper (eds.), *Promoting Emotional Education: Engaging Children and Young People with Social, Emotional and Behavioural Difficulties*. London: Jessica Kingsley, 119–130.

30. Malaguzzi, L. (1996) *The Hundred Languages of Children: The Reggio Emilia Approach to Early Childhood Education*. Norwood, NJ: Ablex Publishing.

5

Relational Evaluation
in Secondary Education

> I remember at secondary school, everything was about
> GCSEs . . . and then in college, it was all about A-levels. So our ed-
> ucation is not just driven by exams, and also sort of run by exams,
> dominated by exams. Now, all we ended up with are grades, but have
> no idea what we'd learned.
>
> —Molly, an 18-year-old UK student

For most young people, the greatest misery of their education is the pressure of exams. This is particularly pronounced during secondary education for students between 12 and 18 years of age.[1] It is not only they must confront high-stakes testing and college entrance exams but also that grade point averages can affect the direction of their entire future life. For secondary school students, the future is now! Not only is this common condition needlessly noxious, it also undermines a major aim of education: to foster meaningful learning. When exams and tests define one's identity, and these definitions affect the course of one's entire life, the point of education is reduced to performance on the battlefield of testing. If we really care about whether young people are engaged in learning, eager to explore, and capable of working together with others, we must abandon the obsession with assessment.

Our aim in this chapter is to explore a range of relationally inspired alternatives to assessment in secondary schools. These practices demonstrate the potential for evaluation to enhance students' everyday learning while simultaneously deepening the relational process from which their well-being derives. To be sure, there is common desire to know if schools are providing high-quality education to their students, but, as discussed in previous chapters, we learn little from exams, grades, and standardized tests. Our hope is to demonstrate that relational practices of evaluation can furnish

Beyond the Tyranny of Testing. Kenneth J. Gergen and Scherto R. Gill, Oxford University Press (2020). © Oxford University Press. DOI: 10.1093/oso/9780190872762.001.0001.

the kind of comprehensive and detailed information needed for enriching the educational process. In preparation, it is useful to consider more fully the toxic relationship between measurement-based assessment and the specific life conditions of adolescent students.

Adolescence Under Siege

Echoing John Dewey's famous dictum, education is not a mere preparation for adult life; it is life itself. Students' well-being matters as much in their present as in their future. Adolescence marks a special time of personal development. As widely acknowledged, teenagers tend to live in a unique space between the worlds of childhood and adulthood. Accompanying rapid biological growth are myriad unanswerable questions about one's identity. "Am I strong . . . beautiful . . . smart . . . well-liked . . . weird . . . ?," "Am I worth anything . . . ?," "Where am I going with my life?," and "What is my significance in the world?"[2] Adolescence is also a time when one begins to identify one's talents and strengths and cultivate interests. "What am I good at?" "What really interests me?" "Which are the things that I can do well?" Relationships with others also begin to take on a new and vital dimension. Emotions can be intense.[3] Whether one feels "liked," "valued," "talented," or "attractive" may rapidly shift as interpersonal relationships wax and wane. Rapturous excitement may hold hands with emotional explosions.

It is imperative that schools provide opportunities, facilities, resources, support, and, above all, care for adolescents' well-being. Ironically, it is precisely at this tenuous time of life that students are assailed by major testing and exams, with stakes of life-long significance. Indeed, in secondary school, grades begin to "really count," and students are under increasingly intense pressure to perform from their teachers, families, the school, and from themselves. There are also graduation exams, university placement exams, and country-wide high-stakes testing. Almost abruptly, the focus of secondary education is narrowed to exam preparation. Even in the most progressive pedagogical environment, such as classrooms that promote project-based learning, students can become anxious about grades. We were told by a ninth-grade Finnish student that she didn't like working in groups on class projects. "What is the point?" she asked, because, "in the end, we all get the same grade. . . . A group grade is almost always lower. So my grades are pulled down. How will I get into a good university without a top grade average?" As the obsession with assessment increases, life quality deteriorates and well-being plummets. Recall from our earlier discussions (Chapters 1 and 2) how adolescent mental health problems such as depression, anxiety, and suicide, are closely connected to exam stress. In short, the gap between assessment demands and student needs is never greater than in secondary education.

Nor is there broad agreement that the conditions should be otherwise. For instance, when New Zealand abolished National Standards in 2017, a national debate broke out on how to judge students' learning. Instead of seeing the decision as a liberation, many were panicked by the absence of systematic evidence. The arguments are familiar: teachers must judge the progress of their students, parents want to know if their children are applying themselves, employers need to be sure of adequate preparation, universities want to know about the potentials of their applicants, and policy-makers must ensure that schools are generating quality "products." Exams, tests, and grades thus continue to serve as a mainstay of school life.

It is just here that a turn to relational practices of evaluation can be welcomed. Sensitively applied, such practices can radically reduce the pressure of assessment and provide a supportive context for adolescents' personal growth and well-being. Simultaneously, relational evaluation can return the focus of secondary education to engaged learning. From a relational perspective, the adolescent's learning and development must be linked to the school context as a whole. Curricula activities, pedagogy, teacher and student relations, peer friendships, classroom environments, institutional ethos, and wider relations with the community should *all* play a part. Favored are practices of listening, dialogue, caring, co-inquiring, co-imagining, and collaborating. When there is synergy among all, evaluative practices will contribute to students' holistic well-being, learning, and the quality of relational process.[4]

Relational Evaluation in Practice

Given the special challenges of secondary education, how can relational evaluation practices successfully replace traditional forms of assessment? Let us return to the three major objectives of relational evaluation. First, evaluation should contribute to the nourishment of the learning processes. This includes providing feedback on diverse activities, enhancing students' understanding of subject matters, and developing their capacities for learning. Second, relational evaluation should inspire continued engagement in the learning process. It is within a relational environment and through relationships that curiosities and enthusiasms are kindled, and a caring attitude (for oneself, for others, for the world, and for learning itself) is encouraged. The third objective is the cultivation of generative relationships. Replacing the divisive effects of traditional forms of assessment, evaluative practices should enrich the process of relating, including relationships with teachers, peers, parents, and others.

Given these aims, let us explore a range of innovative practices contributing to these ends. Similar to practices in primary or elementary education illustrated in the previous chapter, many of our examples are currently used by forward-thinking schools as alternatives to testing-based assessment. Some of these practices are well-established and well-researched, while others are in the experimental stage. Some are used in classrooms along side national testing, others are applied outside traditional assessment systems. Although we discuss separately how a particular practice contributes to one of the three major purposes, we again call attention to the fact that any given practice may simultaneously contribute to more than one objective. We should not lose sight of these multiple potentials.

Enhancing the Learning Process

In 1917 one of the most influential writers of the century, George Orwell (born Eric Blair), was a scholarship boy at Eton College, an elite secondary school in England. Many years later, his English tutor at Eton recalled that his former pupil had done "absolutely no work for five years" and was judged as a young man with neither a work ethic nor ability. This was because Eric Blair had come out near the bottom in his final Eton examination (138th out of 167). However, unknown to most Eton tutors, Eric Blair had been diligently reading the masters of English literature, experimenting with writing, and quietly setting foot on his journey to become an author. This story begs many questions: How do we know where our students are in their learning journeys? What do we do to support their learning and development? How can we nurture their talents and interests?

Here we may draw insight from John Hattie's monumental synthesis of 50,000 studies exploring factors that enhance students' learning and achievement.[5] According to Hattie's research, the most important factors include *cooperative learning, effective feedback,* and *positive student–teacher relationships.* Clearly these echo the major emphases of our proposals in this book. Relational process is at the heart of cooperative learning and providing effective feedback on learning experiences, and a positive connection between students and teachers enhances both. What kind of evaluation practices are thus invited? How do we integrate these practices into pedagogy, and curriculum design? How do we help students to reflect on and appreciate their schooling journeys over time in ways that can improve their learning? Such questions invite ingenuity and imagination, and hence meaningful educational innovation.

Following the pattern of previous chapter, we share some of the practices to which we have been drawn. We look first at the evaluative practices taking place within the classroom learning process itself and then at the reflective practices carried out periodically, such as at the end of a learning unit or when completing a course.

Evaluation in Process: The Pivotal Place of Dialogue

Dialogic learning has its roots in Platonic dialogue, but its potentials have been enriched and expanded by generations of educators, such as Dewey,[6] Vygotsky,[7] Freire,[8] Bakhtin,[9] and Gadamer.[10] As we see it, when properly facilitated, dialogue can be an optimal way to enhance the learning process while simultaneously providing useful evaluation. Consider that, through energizing engagement with others, students may learn through immediate feedback whether they properly *understand a given subject matter,* including their ability to offer critical and creative commentary. Their understandings may be further expanded as they observe the interchange among their classmates. They see what counts in the ongoing conversation as "needing more explanation," "off target," or "an interesting observation." As dialogue unfolds students may also be exposed to a wide range of views and values, thus opening the door to multicultural understanding and appreciation.

Yet, understanding content is only one of the advantages of dialogic learning. In the process students may also *acquire capacities to communicate,* that is, to articulate their opinions, values, and visions in ways that others may comprehend. In this context, evaluation from one's peers may be as subtle as a furrowed brow, a smile, or a delighted laugh. As students watch others, they may also begin to see the potentials and limits of various forms of expression—of humor, metaphor, sarcasm, personal stories, and so on.

Such observations offer students useful comparisons, and an invitation to expand their own repertoires of expression.

Finally, through dialogue, students can *cultivate the art of relating*. Moving beyond the common ritual of relating through question and answer, dialogue makes continuous demands on improvisation. Students may thus learn what kind of actions carry the conversation forward or invite antagonism. By experimenting and observing, they may learn how and when to support each other, or how to criticize without hurting. Ideally they acquire the art of generative dialogue, participating together in co-creating new ideas. Here lie the wellsprings for appreciating the relational process itself.

Of course, not all conversations or discussions are so generous in their results. Exchanges can be superficial, incoherent, suppressive, and contentious. There is always much to learn about participating in meaningful or generative dialogue. The following practice may help illuminate the path:

I/You/We: The Dialogic Linking of Evaluation and Learning

In a math classroom, Herman the teacher and his students sit in a large circle. In the middle, Tristan, 14, is challenging the class with a math puzzle that he created after the previous week's topic on factoring. Barely containing his excitement, he presents the puzzle to the class. "There are different ways of solving it. So be creative!," he encourages his peers. The class's enthusiasm is instantaneous. First, students launch into a discussion on how to understand the challenge. They discuss the wording of the puzzle until the entire class agrees that the task is clear and everyone knows the goal of the activity. Next, each student works on the puzzle alone. Herman, the teacher, reminds everyone to write down the steps taken to solve it. He moves among the students, answering their questions, offering guidance, or simply reassuring their effort. Upon completing the individual work, the students join in smaller groups of four to share with each other their solutions to the puzzle. When one student presents a solution, the other three in the group listen and then give feedback. Because there is no "right way" of solving the puzzle as Tristan pointed out, smiles of appreciation are seen all around. Herman visits each group—joining in the feedback and commending the imagination, and creativity. After the group conversation, the whole class comes together in a circle for more reflection on the different ways to identify factors and check their answers.

The classroom activity depicted here nicely illustrates the way dialogue enables evaluation to be coupled with learning. This model, developed by

Peter Gallin and adopted by schools around the world,[11] stands in bold contrast to the traditional math teaching, which tends to lose students' interest or worse. For Gallin, the starting point of students' interest in learning and understanding is that something appeals to them.[12] The fact that Tristan was already enthusiastic about the puzzle he developed is important, as it immediately invites the students' listening with interest.

Then begins a process in which dialogue and evaluative feedback are folded into the ongoing process of learning. As illustrated, learning starts with a question or provocation that prompts students to enter into dialogue to both understand the question and clarify the learning activity. In this unfolding inquiry, the teacher and the students are also equal partners or co-inquirers. Learning is a collaborative achievement in which students participate in a shared process to determine the shape, direction, and significance of the journey.[13] This dialogic model of inquiry is called "I/You/We."

Once the core challenge is understood, it serves as a guideline for the student's individual or "I"-process of working alone. The "I's" in the class are many, and their ways of completing the tasks and the diversity of their interests, talents, and capabilities form a rich tapestry of possibilities. The "I"-process, although seemingly individualistic, is in fact dialogic—an extension of the earlier discussion of the problem. The "I"-process invites students to record on paper the step-by-step account of their thinking or working out the solutions to the math challenge. Knowing that one's classmates may bring forward something fascinating and different from one's own idea is also motivating. Curiosity runs high.

In the "You"-process the aim is to enhance the process of learning through direct dialogue.[14] Here students offer and receive evaluative feedback from each other. Free from judgment and measurement, these discussions offer a space for building trust and care and appreciating each other's creativity and imagination. This is partly achieved by focusing on the students' accounts of their learning process and not the outcome. This makes it less threatening for both the student being evaluated and the student who is evaluating. For instance, in the evaluative dialogue, Tristan asked Ulrike to talk him through her thinking behind each step she has taken. As she spoke, she realized that she could also find the factor in a different way. Similarly, from Ulrike's explanation, Tristan recognized the ingenuity in Ulrike's use of number tree, a convenient way to identify prime numbers. Thus dialogic evaluation and feedback led to fresh learning. As the feedback exercise is completed, each "I" may come to feel valued and appreciated by a "You."

The final dialogue on these ideas moves the entire class into the *"We"-process*. Here, students reflect on the core idea together and arrive at a shared understanding of the topic they have explored. Because what they have learned was not directly fed to them by the teacher, the "We"-process invites appreciation of the collaborative process in learning. In their reflection on the process, students realize that they are essentially learning to learn. According to Gallin, in this process the teacher is no longer the authority, nor plays the strenuous role of "knower" traditionally performed by the teacher. In this case, for example, Herman doesn't give instructions on factorization and then generate exercises for the students to do, nor does he then spend long hours marking and grading students' papers. He is liberated from his authoritarian perch from which to survey his "workers" and can more freely develop positive relationships with his class. Cultivated is a sense of trust and being "cared for," along with an appreciation of *we together*. The dialogic practice generates learning while simultaneously enhancing its potentials to do so.

There are many other practices that incorporate evaluation into dialogic learning. For instance, since the 1930s, the Phillips Exeter School in New Hampshire has been perfecting what is now called the *Harkness Method*.[15] In a Harkness class, learning takes place through dialogue and discussions held around a circular table, where all members of the class are invited to question, contribute, and reflect together. From English literature to algebra, from African history to chemistry, all learning is facilitated through engaged interaction. Also notable in the Harkness Method is the teacher's support and encouragement. Teachers provide students with additional resources to facilitate their learning journeys. This means that students are involved in a process in which they develop their potentials through interdependence. Dialogue empowers the students to seek their paths to learning in both congenial and creative ways. There is still much to learn about staging, managing, and participating in dialogues that are generative. We are at one, however, with the efforts of myriad educators currently employing dialogic pedagogy,[16] along with related practices of collaborative learning[17] and project based learning.[18] The ongoing process of evaluation is embedded in each.

Evaluation in Reflection: From Branding to Understanding
Traditional assessments are often used as summary markers of a student's performance. They are to answer the question, "How much do they know?" In the same way that ranchers mark their cattle, test scores and grades are like

brands, informing the world that a student is or is not worthy. To be told that one is above, below, or average for the class is also a minimal learning experience. Yet periodic reflection—in which students reflect on their progress, learning habits, strengths and weaknesses, and their interests and learning paths—can be enormously valuable. Instead of summing up a student's achievements, in this case, reflective evaluation serves the purpose of education, including the quality of learning, and relational well-being.

If evaluation is to enhance students' learning processes, it should be closely tied to their learning journeys. In reflecting on the learning trajectory over a period of time—ranging from a few weeks to a year—two issues are prominent. First, evaluative inquiry should enhance the student's learning abilities and thus include a review of the contents of a student's learning. This could include knowledge, skills and understanding, as well as strategies, and craft in learning to learn. Second, reflection should enhance a student's development as a person, including motivation, interests, and aspirations. All are intimately tied to the learning processes. To illustrate, we consider two practices that move significantly in these directions.

The Personal Record of School Experience: A Collaborative Journey

In Chapter 4, we had much to say about the evaluative potentials of the learning review and portfolio work at the primary level. Variations on the learning review are also implemented in secondary education. One highly creative example is the *personal record of school experience*, pioneered by the Sutton Centre in Nottingham.[19] The practice replaces conventional assessment and vitally expands the range of reflection on one's learning.

In this practice, each student at the age of 14 creates a folder containing self-selected highlights of his or her learning experience over time. Similar to portfolio work in primary education, the personal record of school experience might include wide-ranging examples of work in which students took pride or found important in their learning journey. The highlights are not limited to traditional course work but could include documentation and illustrations of experience in activities such as sports, music, and community engagement. Typically, the record contains personalized items, such as written reports, examples of hands-on projects, book reviews, skills they have mastered both within and outside of school, web-based personal profiles, and a personal statement of interest, values, world-view, and aspirations.[20]

The evaluation process is in motion even when students make choices about what to include in their personal records. Here they must reflect on what is valuable in their learning activity and consider the efforts they have put in to make their experience meaningful. In preparing the materials they also reflect on the educational aims of the term/semester and on their personal growth and development. Such reflection invites students to see themselves not as passive recipients of others' judgments, but as active participants in the process of evaluating and appreciating their own learning.

Evaluation is further enriched when students have the opportunity to verbalize their learning experience. For instance, a student may choose to reflect on her experience of a particular project. Here she might recall and reconsider why this project was important for her, what she had set out to do, the steps taken, along with the challenges encountered and how she managed them. Most importantly, she would summarize what she had learned from this experience and in what way the experience had been significant for her growth and development as a person. The reflective process would continue as comments are added to the learning record by teachers, parents, and relevant others. By the time students have completed their secondary education, they will have a complete, personalized record of their learning.

The approach for creating and maintaining learning records is collaborative. That is, the record is regarded as a collective effort to enhance the learning journey. Most importantly in this case, the teacher is not seen as a judge so much as a learning partner. Similarly, both peers and parents are invited as contributors to the process. Students do not find this kind of reflection onerous and disconnected from their learning. Each reflection on achievements, large or small, is always in the light of relationships with others in the class. In this way, what is being documented by the record is not simply a collection of accomplishments; it is also a chart of the student's relational history. In other words, the multi-being we described in Chapter 2 is being detailed in the record.

Materials in the students' folders are reviewed periodically by a teacher in preparation for an evaluative dialogue with the student at the end of term. The dialogue normally takes place between the student and the teacher and sometimes includes the student's peers. The record is also available for ongoing dialogue between the teacher, parents, and the student. It is noteworthy that teachers can also use these learning records and accompanying dialogues as *indicators* of the learning process in the class as a whole. Likewise, learning records can offer feedback for teachers on the qualities of their teaching, and their relationship with students. These records can become an integral part of teachers' professional reflections. The record can further be used to invite dialogue with other stakeholders within the learning community, visitors to the school, and with school inspectors. We expand on this last point in Chapter 7.

In addition to the personal record of school experience, there are other variations of periodic reflection and learning review. For instance, end-of-year portfolios have replaced exams in many parts of the world. In the states of California and Utah, such portfolios often consist of a collection of a student's chosen pieces of work, such as a report on an in-depth research project. The report may reflect a student's learning through months of efforts and activities, including investigating, critical thinking, analyzing, challenging, defending, drafting, and reporting. All these are intense experiences and can demonstrate students' readiness for moving forward in the educational system. This readiness is revealed not only in the content of the projects, but also in the personal qualities of the students—such as their engagement in learning, caring for the form of presentation, patience in improving on drafts, and their resilience when confronted with difficulties. Importantly, such portfolios can illustrate how students can collaborate with others in their learning. In some US high schools, a portfolio is a graduation requirement.[21]

The Personal Road Map

In contrast to viewing secondary education as a process of jumping through pre-designed hoops, schools around the world are exploring relationally sensitive alternatives to evaluating and documenting students' learning journeys. Here a thriving progressive educational movement in Norway provides an example.

The Youth Invest school was established in 2015 in Norway to help young people aged 14–16 return to education after they dropped out of school. Many of these youths are from troubled or broken homes, some have problems with substance abuse, and others have been diagnosed with mental disorders. Most are simply characterized as having little sense of direction or ambition, as having made the "wrong" educational choices, or as feeling themselves misfits in "normal" school.[22] Already disillusioned with education, when these teenagers arrive at Youth Invest, they are often sullen and unmotivated.

To encourage a return to education, at Youth Invest the young people are given time and space to explore who and where they are, and how they can move forward in life through education. Each young person works with an advisor or mentor with whom he or she discusses these topics in-depth. During these conversations, students reflect on their personal qualities, strengths, talents, and interests, as well as on their hopes and dreams for the future. They such questions as: "What would I like to be doing in five or ten years' time?" "What would my life look like then?" "With whom I would be sharing my life?" Such questions direct attention to the students' life beyond schooling, and to what might constitute a good life for them. With such visions in mind, and with heightened self-awareness, the dialogue takes the student to the present: What would they need to move toward this vision, how could education help them to achieve their goals, and whose help and support would they need along the way? These latter questions also invite students to become agents in their learning and personal development.

In collaboration with the advisor, each student develops a *personal roadmap*. If Karsten would like to become an auto mechanic or Sara dreams of setting up her own hair salon, what knowledge, personal qualities, and capacities would they need develop in their education? With the advisor's help, the student then determines which subjects to study and what projects to embark on. Importantly, to emphasize the crucial place of relationships in their learning journey, students are asked to identify significant persons who would accompany them. Are there teachers, peers, family members, or others who are needed and readily available to help them achieve their dreams? Additionally, students' roadmaps are not limited to the resources within the bounds of the school. Indeed, if the school itself does not offer the needed opportunities, they seek out alternative routes to help students achieve their goals.

The roadmaps are also visual references for enhancing evaluation. They are displayed in a public space in the classrooms and shared with peers and teachers. Of course, a student's map may change over time, with learning and development regarded as an unfolding process of map-making. Both students and teachers find this single addition to the educational program especially meaningful in igniting motivational fires. These roadmaps are conversation starters and reference points for discussions between individual students and their mentors: "What progress has Karsten made in math in this term? Whose help has he sought and how has it supported his learning?" or "How is Sara doing in business studies? Has she overcome the fear of numbers when learning how to use a spreadsheet?" These reflective deliberations help students to review progress and improvement over time. They are drawn into discussion about learning objectives and how they are achieving them. Students are thus encouraged to take responsibilities for learning. At the same time, they develop mutually supportive friendships and congenial relationships with their advisors and mentors. For adolescents struggling to develop self-identities, form meaningful relationships, and recognize their place in the world, these are significant supports.

The personal roadmaps at Youth Invest are only one of a number of their practices for reviving the educational journey for these young people. These practices of evaluation have enabled teachers to better understand where their students are along the learning journeys, where challenges and obstacles lie, and how to support their students in overcoming fears and negativity. Teachers become increasingly sensitive to and respectful of students' needs, and can nurture educational experiences that are meaningful for each student. Alongside the students, teachers are also learning and reflecting on how their pedagogical strategies and curriculum structure could be adjusted in the service of supporting students' objectives. We should not be surprised that Youth Invest has won national recognition for its contribution to educational welfare in Norway.

Inspiring Continued Learning Engagement

Classroom apathy hits its zenith in secondary school. With increased pressures to perform in exams, curriculum content disconnected from interests, and the absorbing dramas of adolescent life, one simply suffers along. How, then, can the second objective of relational evaluation be achieved: inspiring students' further engagement in learning? The challenge is to kindle both delight and curiosity in learning while simultaneously incorporating valuable feedback and reflection on one's efforts and progress. In many ways, practices that enhance the learning process can also inspire students' continued fascination in learning. Here we focus on the way two evaluative practices of evaluation contributing to a constructive and meaningful relationship with learning itself.

The Learning Agreement
The *Learning Agreement* is an idea inspired by the work of the Self-Managed Learning College and now used in many countries of the world.[23] Learning agreements are normally formed at the beginning of a semester/term within a small group of six students, facilitated by a teacher or a learning mentor.

Following initial meetings of the group, each student develops an individual learning agreement reflecting personal interests along with objectives and plans for achieving them. The agreement is then presented to the group for comments and questions. Although called an "agreement," it is an informal "pact" with the group. Because it is rooted in the students' relationships, the agreement invites members of the group to respect each other's intentions and honor the "pact" in following an identified pathway to learning.

There are many variations of the learning agreement, but often students answer five questions focused on significant learning objectives and processes.[24] An initial question might be: "Where have I been in my learning journey?" Here, attention is drawn to past experiences relevant to students' current interests and motivations. It is often followed by: "Where am I now?" To reflect on this question, students need to reflect on their current engagement in learning and the directions in which they are heading. Next, students are asked to consider: "Where do I want to go?" Here they begin exploring their personal learning objectives. Having identified the destination, the students are further asked to imagine the journey and voyage: "How will I get there?" Here the challenge is to deliberate on the future learning processes, the relevant resources on which they might draw, and the responsibilities they must take. The final question is more explicitly evaluative: "How will I know if I have arrived?" This invites thoughtful reflection on the criteria for what counts as good learning and how it is demonstrated.[25]

Formulating a learning agreement is not a self-contained event, but instead serves as a starting point for subsequent reviews of students' learning processes and progresses. Each learning agreement provides a basis from which students can think about the aims of learning and evaluate their own hopes and plans. It also provides a framework within which the group can collaborate and support each other's learning. In typical meetings during the semester, each student shares an account of what they had accomplished in terms of what they set out to do. Using the learning agreement as a framework, other students could then respond. This might include offering support, insights, and resources.

The increasing use of learning agreements throughout the world stems in part from the realization that, in secondary education, young people can have extensive experiences from which to draw, and are increasingly capable of planning their ongoing and future activities. Equally, they can more readily identify personal interests and talents and are more resourceful in collaborating with others in learning. The key to the process of developing the learning agreement is that it creates a positive relationship with learning within a group setting. Students share the act of signing the agreement in the presence of each other and a witness. Through this ritual, students are entrusted with a set of responsibilities. As the learning objectives are personalized, the student's commitment and dedication are intensified.

The Learning Journal

Closely related to the learning agreement is the practice of keeping a *learning journal*.[26] Here we use a creative writing class in a US school to illustrate the evaluative potentials:

> The teacher in a high school English literature class has encouraged her students to use learning journals to help develop their writing strategies. The class understands that the journal itself can take any form according to their individual needs and preferences. Each student's learning journey may thus take a different shape.
>
> Although Maya enjoys creative writing she is often unsatisfied with her texts. Her learning journal is like a collage, containing class notes, sketches of ideas, and thoughts that she wants to try out, along with clippings of admired examples. She uses the journal to reflect on how she creates the drafts of her writing. Her classmate Tom had struggled with creative writing, partly because he didn't trust his abilities. His learning journal takes the form of a personal log that documents his fears, anxieties, and doubts about his ideas and how these hesitations seem to block him from writing freely and creatively.
>
> After 6 weeks, the class gathered to evaluate progress in writing strategies. Students formed pairs to review each other's learning journals—focusing on what they had enjoyed, what has yet to be developed, and what steps might assist their further development. Maya and Tom read through their respective journal entries and asked each other questions. In dialogue, Tom was able to show Maya how much she had used the ideas collected in her journal and how these ideas had strengthened her writing; likewise, Maya referred to Tom's logs and observed that, by exploring his feelings about writing, he was able to overcome his fears and was even becoming daring in his prose. This dialogue helped make learning more visible, and encouraged both Maya and Tom to return to their creative writing projects with renewed excitement and engagement.

The learning journal is a dialogic and evaluative approach to strengthening learning engagement. Although individual reflection is important, the participants gain not only through each other's feedback, but also in the task of evaluating each other's work. There are many variations on how the teacher directs the students in creating their journals and in discussing the contents. For instance, the teacher could request that the journals include reflections on particular aspects of the student's writing or comments by peers on their writing. Challenges for discussion could also be varied: for example, asking the pairs to consider their work in comparison to more general standards of excellence in the field. They could also be asked to consider more personal questions, such as "How have I become more confident?" or "Who has helped me most?"

If students do require a comparative review of their work, discussion can also move in this direction.[27] For example, suppose that two students want to find out how meaningful their learning trajectories are in achieving the same objectives. Here they could actually "travel" together, and, during the weekly learning review, their dialogue would be focused on appreciating their respective journeys and how differing directions might be useful in different ways. Likewise, imagine that both Maya and Tom wrote a fictional story and received detailed comments from the teacher on the strengths and merits in the writing. Together the pair might then review their texts along with the teacher's comments. In this case, the dialogue would concentrate on the strengths in one's work, not in comparison to each other or their classmates, but in comparison to more general traditions in writing fiction.

This also suggests that when teachers provide "comparative" comments in the light of *standards*, they should do so in a manner that is less judgmental and more informative than a single grade. For instance, the teacher might provide anonymous high-quality fiction samples written by other students or even a checklist of what might count as the strengths or positive qualities of a work of fiction. The teacher might also offer a spectrum of qualities that are sought in a piece of writing so that students can evaluate the direction in which they are heading. In this way, students learn about the qualities in their writing needing development and about what counts as improvement in this particular context and why.

In sum, relational approaches to evaluation, such as the learning agreement and journaling, can contribute significantly to students' engagement in learning. Such practices help students to develop the criteria of what counts as good and better approaches and standards of learning and why. Students can consider a range of criteria and choose those most helpful to them. In doing so, they can also take into account their own particular needs, skills, and aspirations. Issues of emotional, ethical, political, or spiritual significance can be featured in the mix. Here students begin to take responsibility for their learning through relationally enriching support; abandoned is the kind of divisive competition that invites the deflation of all but a few. Such practices are marked by a mutuality of care and support. In nurturing relational processes, they can ultimately be the foundation of an entire community of learning.

Enriching the Quality of Relating

Testing-based assessment tends to prize competition, prioritize individual success, and undermine students' relationships with teachers, peers, and learning itself. In contrast, relational approaches to evaluation work in the service of enriching such relationships. Here we focus discussion on the use of *learning groups* in classrooms. Consider the following :

> In a secondary school classroom, 16-year-old Asif walks in, beaming. This is the last week before the end of the semester, and the group will be reviewing students' progress. Asif seems eager to begin the discussion. The teacher, Mrs. Jarvis, is facilitating the meeting. She first asks everyone to share their activities and achievements. The class know the process well and have been encouraged to appreciate and evaluate each other's achievements against their stated objectives.
>
> When it comes Asif's turn, he refers to his notes, points to one of his "ambitions," and says proudly: "I had it down as one of my goals here to learn to assemble a motor bike.'" He looks up at his friends, trying to be cool while suppressing the urge to speak fast. "Well, after three months working on it," he pauses for effect, "I can announce that I have just put together a motorbike!" He looks up at his friends wide-eyed, almost as if saying: "And it is working well." A round of loud cheers and applause ensues. In the conversation that follows, the group discusses how Asif has been able to achieve this goal, the steps he has taken, the resources used, and how he would meet the challenges of his next "ambition."

Asif's story took place in a typical mainstream school in the UK, where a small group of young people took part in an action research project exploring innovative approaches to learning.[28] One of the chief outcomes of this facilitated *learning group* was the way in which evaluative feedback contributed to positive relationships—the third goal of relational evaluation. The students' mutual excitement, delight, and support were remarkable.

How were these results achieved? Both *structure* and *process* were significant. The learning group benefited significantly from a number of structural features. First was its dependence on the use of student learning agreements. With this learning agreement as a framework, a shared focus was created on each student's learning journey. A strong sense of interdependency was facilitated. Group trust was also created through dependable group meetings. Knowing they would be meeting on a regular basis, even weekly, reinforced the connective tissue uniting them. The meetings didn't have a pre-planned agenda, other than a space for students to come together and talk about themselves and about learning. Asif's group consisted of six students. They met once a week for 45 minutes. The discussions often became focused around a specific topic, such as substance abuse, politics, or personal finance. However, depending on the students' needs and experiences, the meeting could also be a time of personal sharing—feelings, friendship, romance, practical issues in life, specific learning challenges, and more. When the groups were composed of students from diverse backgrounds, learning blossomed. The more diverse the group—in gender, learning abilities, socioeconomic backgrounds, and the like—the richer the learning experiences and the relationships.

Group process in these meetings was also significant to their success. How students relate to each other in the group is critical. Superficial chatter offers little to learning; conflict in groups is common. The challenge is to foster generative dialogue, the kind that tends to animate interchange from which students collectively move into new spaces of understanding and appreciation. As discussed in Chapter 2, generative dialogue of this kind is infrequent in society more generally and little practiced for most students. This places a strong burden of responsibility on the teacher to provide a model. For example, the teacher must demonstrate that words matter as much in their emotional tone as in their content. It also means crafting questions that invite appreciation and mutual valuing, that enable critical deliberation without disrespect, and that invite open and imaginative offerings without fear of derision. There are clear implications here for curricula in teacher education.

The learning group is only one way of conjoining evaluation with relational enrichment. With care, most collaborative practices can move schools toward becoming learning cultures. When education ceases to be about test performance and grades, school culture can move in directions that favor relational well-being. Here we focused on a practice for strengthening relations among students. However, with minor changes in the practice, the network of affected relations may be extended to teachers, parents, and the broader community. Consider the following possibilities:

- A daily check-in session where students meet briefly with the teacher to update on their work
- A weekly learning reflection with a teacher to discuss progress over time, to readjust personal goals and ways to meet the challenges ahead
- A mid-term/semester learning review in which parents are also invited into the discussion about the student's work progress, special needs, and possibilities for collaborative support
- An end-of-term/semester learning fair organized by students to showcase their work and to which parents, teachers, school administrators, and staff are invited. During the learning fair, students present their projects, discuss learning experiences, and share their challenges with the community. Presentations might take the form of performance, drama, a fashion show, an art display, and so on.
- An annual learning conference organized by students (in collaboration with the staff) where adults from the community are invited to come together and explore a theme of common interest (e.g., guns and school security, climate change). To spark discussion, students might make presentations, show films, and organize focus groups.

With proposals like these, we move not only toward expanding the range of relational enrichment, but also toward building a broad and engaged community of learning.

Toward Well-Being in Education

Adolescence can be the most exciting time in one's life, but it can also be the most challenging. Proust even claimed that adolescence is the only time when we can learn almost anything. Indeed, while life seems to open up new possibilities, adolescence is also riddled with emotional and relational complexities. For young people to thrive during adolescence, education must simultaneously meet their personal development needs and cultivate their appreciation for learning. A one-size-fits-all approach to educational assessment through testing will fail spectacularly to meet these related goals. Alternatively, relational evaluation practices can enhance students' motivation, deepen the learning process, and enrich the myriad relationships central to their well-being.

Notes

1. In this book, we use UNESCO's International Standard Classification of Education categories to describe levels of education. Therefore, the education of 12- to 18-year-olds is termed "secondary education." Because the evaluative concerns addressed in this section are applicable across secondary education, from this point on, we use the term "secondary education" to refer to both lower and upper secondary education.
2. See Peter Blos and his theory of a second individuation. Blos, P. (1967) "The second individuation process of adolescence," *Psychoanalytic Study of the Child*, 22: 162–186.
3. Rosenblum, G., and Lewis, M. (2008) "Emotional Development in Adolescence," in G. Adams and M. Berzonsky (eds.), *Blackwell Handbook of Adolescence*. Oxford: Blackwell Publishing, 269–289.
4. Gill, S., and Thomson, G. (2012) *Rethinking Secondary Education: A Human-Centred Approach*. London: Pearson Education; Gill, S., and Thomson, G. (2016) *Human-Centred Education: A Handbook and Practical Guide*. London: Routledge.
5. Hattie, J. A. C. (2009). *Visible Learning: A Synthesis of over 800 Meta Analyses Relating to Achievement*. London: Routledge.
6. Dewey, J. (1939) "The Modes of Societal Life," in J. Ratner (ed.), *Intelligence in the Modern World: John Dewey's Philosophy*. New York: Random House, 365–404.
7. Vygotsky, L. S. (1978) *Mind in society*. Cambridge, MA: Harvard University Press.
8. Freire, P. (1970) *Pedagogy of the Oppressed*. New York: Continuum Books.
9. Bakhtin, M. (1981) *The Dialogic Imagination: Four Essays*. Austin: University of Texas Press.
10. Gadamer, H-G. (1976). *Philosophical Hermeneutics*, trans. and ed. David E. Linge. Berkeley, CA: University of California Press.
11. See Gallin, P. (2010) "Dialogic learning from an educational concept to daily classroom teaching," translated from "Dialogisches Lernen. Von einem pädagogischen Konzept zum täglichen Unterricht," *Grundschulunterricht Mathematik*, 02-2010 (Mai), Oldenbourg Schulbuchverlag.
12. Gadamer, H-G. (1975). *Truth and Method* (W. Glen-Doepel trans.). New York: Crossroad.
13. Ibid.

14. Carless, D. (2015) *Excellence in University Assessment: Learning from Award-Winning Practice*. London: Routledge, 192.

15. https://www.katherinecadwell.com/harkness-method/

16. See, for instance, Alexander, R. (2004) *Towards Dialogic Teaching: Rethinking Classroom Talk*. London: Dialogos; and Alexander, R. (2006) *Education as Dialogue*. Hong Kong: Hong Kong Institute of Education and Dialogos.

17. See the research conducted by the Education Endowment Foundation on collaborative learning, including peer-mentoring, cooperative group work, and other examples. https://educationendowmentfoundation.org.uk

18. Knoll, M. (2014) "Project Method," in C. Phillips (ed.), *Encyclopedia of Educational Theory and Philosophy (Vol. 2)*. Thousand Oaks, CA: Sage, 665–669.

19. See the example of Madeley Court School's Personal Record of School Experience (www.hse.org.uk).

20. See chapter 7 of Gill and Thomson, *Human-Centred Education,* for other suggestions.

21. For example, across California, 34 high schools have formed a network, the California Performance Assessment Collaborative, to promote portfolio-based assessments.

22. Hauger, B., and Mæland, I. (2015) "Working with Youth at Risk: An Appreciative Approach," in T. Dragonas et al. (eds.), *Education as Social Construction: Contributions to Theory, Research and Practice*. Chagrin Falls, OH: Taos Institute Publications.

23. www.selfmanagedlearning.org

24. This is a variation of the learning agreement developed by students at the Self-Managed Learning Centre, East Sussex, UK.

25. Adapted from Cunningham I., and Bennett, B. (2000) *Self Managed Learning in Action: Putting SML Into Practice*. London: Routledge.

26. See the entry on learning journals in Moon, J. (2004) *A Handbook of Reflective and Experiential Learning*. London: Routledge; also see Langer, A. (2002). "Reflecting on practice: Using learning journals in higher and continuing education," *Teaching in Higher Education*, 7(3): 337–351.

27. Topping, K. J. (2018) *Using Peer Assessment to Inspire Reflection and Learning*. London: Routledge.

28. The research consisted of three parts: one-to-one mentoring, group-based exploration (reported here), and dedicated cognitive development.

6

Relational Approaches
to Evaluating Teaching

I do what I do every year. I teach the way I teach every year. My first
year I got pats on the back; my second year got me kicked in the
backside. And for year three, my students' scores were off the charts.
I got a huge bonus, and now I am in the top quartile of all the English
teachers. What did I do differently? I have no clue.

—American high school teacher[1]

Young people in our schools suffer from largely meaningless and ill-serving
tests for up to a dozen years of their lives. For those wishing to become
teachers, the engines of assessment will follow them into universities and beyond. "At last . . . ," the newly graduated teacher might exclaim, "I am free of
tests." Or so one might think. But no, the "ideology" of measurement swallows
all who enter in education—students, teachers, and administrators alike.

In this chapter, we challenge the prevailing practices of teacher appraisal
and performance management and open the discussion of more relationally
enriching horizons. We first scan the detrimental effects of the traditional
measurement-based approach to assessing teachers. It is not simply the personal well-being of teachers that is at stake, but their capacity to teach, participate in communities of learning, and develop as professionals. We then
introduce a relational approach to the evaluation of teaching practices in
which professional development is the primary purpose. This framework
sets the stage for exploring a range of emergent and innovative practices that
serve the ends of teachers' professional learning and holistic growth. These
practices are appreciatively sensitive to the importance of relational processes in teaching and learning. Through these illustrations, we see how the
evaluative process can not only respect and enhance the efforts of teachers,
but also contribute to the relational processes at the heart of education.

Beyond the Tyranny of Testing. Kenneth J. Gergen and Scherto R. Gill, Oxford University Press (2020). © Oxford
University Press. DOI: 10.1093/oso/9780190872762.001.0001.

Teachers' Appraisal in Question

Many of the problems plaguing the assessment of student performance apply to the appraisal of teachers.[2] As discussed in Chapters 1 and 2, these are variously problems with the validity of measurement; the narrowness of measurement criteria; the spawning of suspicion, alienation, and conflict within classrooms; and more. This is to say nothing of the glaring irony of using test scores to measure student performance and simultaneously relying on the same scores to assess their teachers. Rather than elaborating further on how these critiques apply to teacher evaluation, let us turn a new page.

Our concern begins with the foibles of collapsing teacher evaluation into the same manufacturing paradigm as traditional schooling. Under the factory model, teachers are assessed and appraised by measuring their effectiveness, which is defined by the National Comprehensive Center for Teacher Quality in terms of quantifiable student "outputs."[3] From such a perspective, as suggested by the Organisation for Economic Cooperation and Development (OECD), teacher assessment is aimed at improving teachers' performance. Thus, performance indicators are used almost exclusively to reward the effective and threaten or eliminate the weaker educators. There is virtually nothing in the process that enhances the teacher's professional growth. A further outcome of this performance management approach is that while teachers' practices are the focus of evaluation, teachers themselves are seldom involved in the processes. Those who know most about teaching are left mute with respect to such issues as target setting, improvement planning, or deciding how to go about the evaluation.[4] While teachers' appraisal systems have undergone significant changes over time, the fundamental concern remains constant: to measure teachers' efficiency and effectiveness in producing student performance.[5] This concern is at one with the gradual infiltration of business management language and practice into education. By using such terms as "performance appraisals," "target-setting," and "curriculum deliveries," there is a steady and systemic commodification of education.[6] The result is that teachers are increasingly working within a pre-defined curriculum framework, packaged and pipelined toward standardized and measurable outcomes. Assessment practices serve solely the demand for accountability. We have, then, an audit agenda rather than a feedback agenda aimed at supporting teachers' ongoing learning and professional development.[7] An audit agenda allows a cost–effect analysis based on teachers' productivity.[8] In effect, this performance management process closely resembles industrial or commercial product assessment for quality assurance.[9] This is a true intrusion of neoliberal ideals into education.[10]

The obsession with accountability also misconstrues responsibility. It assumes that the teacher is the only one who is responsible for the student's learning. This assumption fails to recognize the relational processes underlying both teaching and learning. As we have argued, responsibility for learning should never reside in the individual; it is a collective achievement. Thus, to define the quality of teachers' work in terms of student outcomes disregards the ways in which students are active participants in their own learning.[11] This is to say nothing of classroom relationships, family, economic conditions, and so on.

Adopting a management discourse is pernicious in many ways. It tends to emphasize the solely instrumental end of education aimed at manufacturing students as prepackaged "products." Within such a discourse, teaching is regarded as an act of "producing." When teachers become objects to be managed and shaped in the service of economizing,[12] they are alienated from the context of their relationships within schools.[13] They are turned into wage laborers, with the noble aspects of teaching downgraded to product-making. Their contributions to education are effectively reduced to participation in a "teaching machine." With their "outputs" measured by their students' test scores, it is possible to compare teachers' performance. This allows the system to apply a reward–punishment mechanism to improve teacher performance—rewarding "good" and "effective" teachers and punishing the "bad" and "ineffective" teachers. The teacher thus has no intrinsic value but acquires his or her worth only in terms of fulfilling a function.

When educational institutions align their aims with neoliberal ideals, the teacher is also conceptualized in unfortunate ways.[14] For one, the teacher is the "expert" or the "knower" whose mastery of a particular area of knowledge deems him or her suitable for the "job" of "molding" the "products"; for another, the teacher is the "provider" or the "executer" who is charged with the responsibility of implanting this knowledge in the minds of students. Both views tend to regard education as mostly a matter of *instructing*. Thus. teaching is mainly the practice of *transmitting* or delivering predefined knowledge and information, and learning is a process preparing for tests.

Such an orientation obscures two major issues, the first of which is the potential for teachers to be learners themselves. Teachers have lifelong learning needs and aspirations for betterment, and capacities to learn and develop personally and professionally. As we propose, teaching is essentially a process of co-creation. Optimally it involves dialogue, collaboration, mutual engagement, and reciprocal learning. A good teacher is a multi-being who can not only guide students' exploration and inquiries, but also function as a facilitator, mentor, collaborator, and co-inquirer in learning.[15] What is further left out is the importance of teachers' well-being in the vitality of school culture. Much research identifies the destructive impact on teachers' well-being of measuring their performance through student test scores.[16] When evaluative practices reduce teachers to cogs in machines and their work approximates an assembly line, their well-being is eroded.

Despite the burgeoning practices of mindfulness therapies and mental health support to de-stress teachers,[17] traditional teacher assessment continues to stifle the development of teachers and the culture of schools.[18] We should not be surprised that the pursuit of efficiency, effectiveness, and economic benefit has been met by teachers' resentment and resistance,[19] In many locales this discontent has led to a mass exodus of teachers from the profession.[20] The conditions could be otherwise. As we propose, by adopting relational approaches to evaluating teachers, we open a space for enhancing teachers' well-being and contributing to their professional learning and development.

Evaluation as Comprehensive Professional Development

Like most professionals, teachers wish to teach well and develop professionally. They care about their students' learning and growth; their relationships with students, colleagues, and parents; and the flourishing of the community. How can we set in motion practices of evaluation that speak to these concerns? More specifically, what are the potentials for relationally sensitive practices in the evaluation of teaching?

In response to this pivotal question, we propose an integrated approach to the evaluation of teaching. Among the specific aims is to enhance the teacher's professional development.[21] We call this approach *comprehensive* because we wish to place professional development in a much broader context than usually defined. To view teacher development in terms of boosting student performance is destructively narrow. We must think far more comprehensively about the teacher who is at once a guide, a facilitator, a mentor, and a learner. We should see the teacher as an active participant in the processes of teaching and learning. This means that the idea of professional development must be expanded to include the development and nurturing of the relational process—including relations between teachers, their students, and colleagues, as well as between parents and caretakers. Also important is aligning evaluative practice with teachers' holistic well-being, including their satisfaction with their teaching and learning activities and their lives and relationships in the school community.[22] To achieve these ends, we see four major avenues to comprehensively evaluating and supporting teachers' professional development.

Enhancing mutual learning within the professional community. The primary source of development should take place within the teaching community itself. The major repository of wisdom and knowledge about teaching lies within this community. In sharing stories, values, opinions, and practices, the participants in this community can support each other's development and stimulate a process of self-evaluation. In our view, professional development should move beyond the enhancement of the individual's capacities. Ideally dialogues within the community should include the aims of education, the school's ethos, curriculum design, pedagogical ideals, and overall strategies for improving teaching. The emphasis shifts in this case away from the individual and isolated teacher to the larger relational process of which teachers are a part.

Improving practices through collaboration with students. As pointed out, there is no teaching without the collaboration of learners. In relational approaches to evaluation, the teacher is no longer "the subject of assessment" but a co-inquirer with students. In-depth and constructive evaluation and dialogic reviews should be regarded as collaborative, with growth and development as their aim. Such collaboration should simultaneously enrich the relationship with students and among colleagues and invite appreciation of relational process, all geared toward mutual learning. By involving student voices in the evaluation of teaching, students can expand the teacher's consciousness of "what works best" within the learning process. Students can help to shape a vision of a maximally engaged learning process for the class as a whole: "How are *we* doing?," "How could *we* do it better?" In this way students participate in the educational processes and decision-making that shapes their lives.[23]

Inspiring engagement through affirmation. Professional development is often defined in terms of improving teacher performance. Yet skilled performance alone is insufficient. If teachers are not engaged and believe that their efforts are meaningful and rewarding, then schools become dreary places. Sustained and creative engagement in teaching is thus the third feature of professional development. A relational approach shifts the focus away from a deficit-oriented model of development, with its emphasis on identifying teacher weaknesses and problems as guides to improvement. Rather, it stresses the valuable aspects of a teacher's practices. It nurtures the teacher's strengths, talents, and potentials. In so doing so, confidence is bolstered, creativity encouraged, and zest is injected into one's professional activities. An appreciative approach offers a way of exploring what is meaningful in teaching and how shared educational dreams can be realized.[24]

Sustaining reflection through inquiry. Finally, it is important to establish processes and pathways for sustaining teachers' deep and continuing reflection on practice. Good teaching depends on many factors—in one's personal life, within the classroom, with the school community, and beyond. The challenge here is to sustain reflection on these issues, including the way the teaching process may transform life within these various domains.[25] Relational approaches thus invite active and ongoing inquiries about one's life as a teacher and the web of relations into which this life is woven.

Relational Practices in Evaluating Teaching

We are scarcely alone in our concern with alternatives to current practices of teacher evaluation. There are many innovative and relationally sensitive alternatives already in motion. We turn now to several of these inspiring bellwethers. While each of these practices serves multiple purposes, we focus on the way each realizes one of the objectives included in our vision for teachers' comprehensive professional development.

Enhancing Mutual Learning in the Professional Community

Traditional teacher appraisal is both hierarchical and individualistic. It is hierarchical because it entails a person of superior rank within the school—such as a department head or principal—assessing or judging teachers over whom they have control. It is individualistic because it defines each teacher as a separate unit, with his or her accomplishments judged accordingly. To break free from the talons of management mentality, the relational alternative starts with the recognition of teaching as a relational process with teachers already embedded in a professional learning community. Any inquiry into teaching should thus be rooted in collaborative mutual learning.[26] In turn, mutual learning can enrich the relationship among colleagues, strengthen the professional community, and move beyond the alienating effects of hierarchy and individualism.

To illustrate the potentials, consider the practices of Sunnybrook primary school.[27] Serving a diverse community, Sunnybrook has always found itself sitting in the intersection between the demand for accountability from educational authorities and the need to support children from different backgrounds. This tension is particularly pronounced when it comes to evaluating teachers' practices. To reconcile the conflict between the inescapable accountability agenda and the desire for teacher's professional development, the school created a system of mutual learning as an approach to teachers' professional development. The two major pathways to mutual learning are: (1) *mentoring* and (2) *peer evaluation*. Both mentoring and peer evaluation feature reflective dialogue on important questions concerning pedagogical practices, with the aim of fostering a deep engagement with processes of teaching and learning.

Mentoring is typically used when new or novice teachers are each paired with a more experienced or senior colleague as their mentor. The mentor observes, reflects, and reviews the work of the mentee and offers feedback and advice for the novice to gain deeper insight into the school's ethos, culture, and practices. The newcomer thus learns about school policies, pedagogical approaches, curriculum focus, and classroom practices. In principle, the mentor takes the responsibility of providing guidance, challenge, and support to the novice.

Sunnybrook expanded the traditional approaches to mentoring novice teachers with two additional but important emphases: the first is on improving the teacher's professional learning. This involves sharing a vision of what good teaching consists of and reflecting on the mentor and mentee's respective practices. The second emphasis is on collaborative learning through deep dialogue. Deep dialogue includes sharing life histories and personal aspirations. It helps to break down the otherwise hierarchical structure within the school and build nourishing relationships between mentors and mentees. This means that mentors are not considered as superior and may also review and reflect on their own practices during the dialogues.

Peer evaluation or peer feedback is likewise a well-researched practice and has been implemented by many schools.[28] In the traditional peer-evaluation process, teachers participate in a small group where they observe, review, and provide feedback on each other's practices. Based on their particular history, Sunnybrook decided to create their own model of peer evaluation. It involves four teachers as a team who take turns to visit each other's classes, with the aim of observing, reflecting, and learning from each other's work.[29] Following the visit and observation, there is usually an immediate debriefing dialogue. While the events are still fresh in mind, the observing teacher reflects on the teaching practices just observed, such as how the class has progressed from his or her perspective, what has been enjoyable and appreciated most, how the activities contributed to the children's learning experiences, and the quality of children's engagement. Then the observing teacher invites the observed to reflect on the classroom process; for instance, what worked particularly well, what was most pleasing and why, and what could have been done differently. This kind of debriefing feedback is informative for both the observer and the observed. In addition to debriefing, once every week or two, the teams of four come together for more extended conversation about each other's teaching, and learning.

Mentoring and peer-evaluation practices can be both illuminating and inspiring. They speak directly to teachers' desire to develop and grow professionally. However, they also present significant challenges. Three of these are particularly noteworthy. The first challenge is time. Being a busy school that caters to a large number of vulnerable children, teachers at Sunnybrook are already overstretched. As a state school, each teacher also has additional administrative duties. Mentoring and peer evaluation appear to be more time-consuming than traditional performance management. For example, when one teacher is mentoring or observing another teacher, someone else must cover his or her class. Most schools cannot afford additional teachers. To protect their program, Sunnybrook set aside specific time for evaluative dialogue. The school also enlisted support from the wider school community. For instance, on specific days community volunteers co-facilitate sports, arts, music, and other activities, allowing some teachers the time for much needed reflective conversations.

The second challenge is trust. Mutual learning should not threaten teachers with the fear of being judged, compared with others, or undermined by colleagues. Honest discussion requires time to mature. To develop this non-judgmental space, Sunnybrook's leaders invited the mentoring pairs and peer-evaluation teams to identify their own topics for learning and improvement. Here the leaders relinquished top-down control of the deliberations.

Biographical sharing became an integral part of the process, thus encouraging curiosity in each other's life history, personal values, and practices. Instead of an audit agenda, the school nurtured the teachers' relationships. Trust was further invited by emphasizing a common concern: the students' learning experiences. Replacing the tradition of judgment—whether one is a "good" or "bad" teacher—the question becomes: "How can we best enrich the learning lives of our students?" In this way, teacher evaluation is formative and nurturing and integral to learning, well-being, and professional development.

The third challenge is tenacity. It is about ensuring that both mentoring and peer evaluation can remain within a continuous flow of professional dialogue. Too often, feedback and evaluative comments can become monologic, as the observer simply addresses the observed: "It was good to see the children so engaged during the lesson" or "Clearly it wasn't possible for you to see in advance all the difficulties the children would experience, but you were aware of the situation and changed the task immediately. Well done." Such feedback, though meaningful, does not invite further exploration. As the teachers at Sunnybrook learned, the secret to sustaining professional dialogue lies in the art of crafting questions.[30]

Hence the teachers began to explore ways to integrate probing and challenging questions into mentoring and peer-evaluation sessions. For instance, between the mentor and the mentee, or among peers, questions would invite further elaboration on the intentions and features of the practices (e.g. "Could you say more about how you saw events unfolding in today's class?"). Questions might probe the teachers' thinking behind the class activity design and the steps taken to guide the students' learning (e.g. "I was impressed with the way you motivated the children. How did it come about?"). Further questions could encourage a *feedforward* (e.g. "If you were to do this again, how might you do it differently?" or "How might I support your future effort?").

Sunnybrook has now integrated these relationally rich approaches to evaluation into the official requirements for teacher appraisal. Indeed, Sunnybrook is representative of increasing numbers of schools that are relying on mentoring or coaching as a key to teachers' learning and development. Research continues to identify opportunities for teachers' reflection and mutual learning through these approaches.[31] Equally, peer evaluation is increasingly included in public schools that value teachers' continuing professional development. Exploration into these practices continues around

the globe—from Europe and Africa to the Americas and the Asia-Pacific—
and suggests that here is indeed a major means of uniting evaluation and
teachers' development.[32]

Enhancing Practice Through Collaboration with Students

Standardized performance ratings do little to enhance teachers'
understandings of their practice. Seldom does teacher assessment provide opportunities for reflecting on, for instance, "What are my students'
interests?" "Do they find the activities in my class interesting or meaningful?"
Or "How might I improve my practices?" Nor do test scores help teachers
understand students' needs, experiences, or level of engagement. Listening
to students' voices can accomplish these ends. Some schools do use student
surveys to tap students' perspectives in evaluating teachers.[33] However, there
remain the interminable questions of the survey's validity and reliability
and whether students' evaluation of their teachers may simply reflect their
grades. Thus, while the importance of students' evaluation of their teachers is
widely recognized, it also matters how students' perspectives are integrated
into teachers' professional development.

Without listening to students and understanding their hopes and
challenges, it is easy for a teacher to fall back on traditional and often deadening practices of transmitting content. In a broad sense, when student voices
do not count, the teacher's voice becomes impersonal and its content irrelevant. This is not only because relationships are the touchstone of meaningful
teaching and learning, but the monologic delivery of pre-packaged content is alienating, for both teachers and students. It is vital, then, to listen to
students, integrate their voices into teaching practices, and bring these voices
into dialogue. Through listening and dialogue, teachers can learn more about
students' interests, learning habits, past and present learning experiences,
and so forth. With such information and understanding, teachers can better
guide and facilitate students' ongoing progress, and together they can co-
create engaging learning experiences.

Forward-looking educators have long promoted dialogue as a way of
enhancing both teaching and learning. For instance, the idea of student participation in teacher development has been lauded as "a transformative notion of education at the heart of which lies the commitment to teaching and
learning as a genuinely shared responsibility."[34] It is against this background

that the Folk School, a large US middle school, began innovating.[35] The prospects of partnering with students to improve the qualities of teaching and learning inspired the school's leaders and teachers to seek ways of incorporating student feedback into the evaluation of teachers' practices. It was clear from the school's experience that teachers' classroom practices can make a huge difference to students' learning, and feedback from students can help teachers reflect on their practices and guide their professional learning. [36]

Based on these understandings, an administrative team, in consultation with teachers and students, developed a framework for program evaluation. The team was especially concerned with issues common to both teachers and students, including richness of learning experiences, motivation and responsibility, and well-being as persons. It was felt that student input on such issues would furnish a wealth of materials for reflection and action. After some experimentation the team proposed three formats enabling students to contribute insights relevant to evaluating teachers' practices.

The first is *process feedback*. This takes place during the lessons. For example, a teacher might pause during a teaching session and ask how the students feel about the activity: "Is the session is going well?" "What do you find most helpful?" Or "Are there ways we could help make this clearer or more useful?" It turns out that students are really enthusiastic in discussing such questions, especially when teachers are open to receiving constructive criticism. Classroom-based process feedback is thus helpful in speaking directly to students' needs and interests. In contrast to an accountability audit, learning now becomes a shared responsibility. Students can recognize their part in making the class more engaging and learning more interesting.

The second evaluation format is *end-of-semester feedback*, carried out formally at the end of each semester. All students are invited to respond anonymously to a survey questionnaire. The questionnaire includes both scaled questions on their learning, motivation, and well-being during the semester and on the teachers' practices. These are followed by open-ended questions to allow detailed feedback, comments, and anecdotes. The relevance of the questions to students' experiences means that most students want to take part and think carefully and deeply about how to respond. As the questionnaire is completed anonymously, power imbalances between the student and teacher are minimized. Students can feel free to provide constructive, frank, and even critical feedback to help teachers evaluate their practices.

The third format for generating meaningful feedback is *focus group conversation*. These conversations are held with five to seven student volunteers and are hosted at the semester's end by the school's administrative team. The conversations are open-ended and take place in a relaxing atmosphere. The questions focus once again on such topics as students' learning experiences, motivation, overall development, and well-being. They also discuss the specific aspects of teaching practices most enabling for students' learning and for teacher improvement. Because the dialogue is around practices, rather than making judgments about the teacher, the conversations can be candid and open. Most students feel their voices are heard. Hence the focus group conversations are usually lively, energetic, and rich in their yield of insights and ideas.

By engaging students in the evaluation of teaching practice, both teachers and students benefit. Teachers' professionalism and students' learning are simultaneously enriched, along with a sense of collaborative interdependence. Teachers recognize that students can be their professional learning partners and that they can trust the students to help expand their pedagogical horizons; students realize that they can shape their own learning by helping teachers to grow professionally. They feel they can truly make a difference in school and take increased responsibility for their education. Together, these processes nourish the relationships between teachers and students along with their well-being.

Inspiring Engagement Through Affirmation

Traditional teacher assessment threatens teachers' personhood and professionalism. In contrast, we ask how a relational approach to evaluation might nourish and inspire engagement in the profession. In this case we turn to the appreciative orientation to evaluation increasingly adopted by schools and learning institutions.[37] This echoes our earlier proposal for equating evaluation with valuing. When applying an appreciative perspective in evaluating teachers, we shift away from shortcomings and insufficiencies. Rather, we focus on teachers' strengths, talents, and potential. We direct attention to what has worked well in the past and what is working well now. We invite imagination and innovation in building from these assets.[38]

Take the Newton School's process as an example.[39] For a long time, this small primary school had relied on the standard model of performance management to evaluate teachers. As this model linked teachers' appraisal to their salary rates and promotions, a culture of competition and fear emerged.

Teachers made great efforts to prepare children to perform well on tests. The school was data-driven in its attempt to climb up the ranks of independent schools. The ranks, in turn, were linked to the school's economy. The overall atmosphere was stressful, with distrust among the teachers and between teachers and the school administrators.

When the new principal, Marianne, came to the school, she listened to the staff's frustrations and anxieties and noted teachers' defensiveness and weariness. Through further consultation, Marianne came to feel that the root of the discontent could be traced to the assessment framework. She thus decided to work with other senior leaders to seek change. As an immediate step, she moved to abandon the standard practice of measuring teacher efficacy by student test scores; she proposed instead to protect spaces for teachers to come together and reflect on their practices. For the 14 members of the staff, this seemed to be a great idea. However, the initial enthusiasm soon waned. There was a history of defensiveness and distrust among the teachers, and having a designated time for collective reflection was contemplated with apprehension and worry. Teachers didn't find it easy to evaluate each other's practices, let alone offer potentially critical feedback. Well-intended professional learning turned out to be superficial discussions. Power dynamics also interfered with open inquiry. Experienced teachers' comments were treated as more authoritative than those of the novices, resulting in the silencing of some teachers.

In this situation, Marianne proposed a process encouraged by her familiarity with *appreciative inquiry*.[40] The process was described as an effort to support the teachers' professional learning with a special emphasis on appreciating some of their existing practices. The event was carried out during a 2-day in-service professional development session and consisted of the following steps:

Life histories of the school. First, Marianne invited the staff to create a storyboard of the school's histories. Along the school's "journey," each member of the team added their personal stories and their place in the school's overall development. The narrative process helped the teachers recognize each other's educational values and visions, as well as conceptions of learning, thus building their solidarity as a team.

Life-giving features. The staff were then invited to map out the life-giving features of the school, based on their sharing of stories about a time when they had been especially inspired by activities at the school. They discussed why these features were so nourishing and how they were achieved. Through this step, the team became aware that the school's life-giving features were also what brought each member the greatest joy and delight in teaching and learning.

Strengths, talents, and potential. Each member of the staff was then invited to map out their own strengths, talents, and potentials as they contributed to the school's accomplishments. This was complemented by group work, with three or four colleagues discussing each other's qualities. The result was professional affirmation for all and positive relations among the teachers.

Envisioning a shared future. With all the staff member feeling energized, the team imagined the school's future development. While the preceding activities emphasized personal skills and potentials, this phase was dedicated to building a collective dream for the school and to exploring avenues to its realization. The additional hope was to foster awareness of how much the school's future depends on teachers' professional development and their relationships.

Taking these steps together, the team realized that questions and inquiries about personal and collective strengths, values, hopes, and dreams were transformative.[41] A distinct shift in the relationships among teachers could be detected. With the focus on appreciation of their work, defensiveness gave way to more open reflection on routes to improvement. Teachers were less fearful of making mistakes and more willing to take risks in innovation. The appreciative lens was thus empowering, with teachers feeling they could learn and develop professionally from strength to strength. The innovations in the teachers' development program were subsequently incorporated into the school's overall development plan—a strategic blueprint, revised every 3 years. Teachers could now feel that their professional development was at one with the school's strategic planning.

Many schools have adopted an appreciative approach to the evaluation of teachers' practices.[42] Instead of seeing teachers and their practices as problems to be solved and managed, the appreciative approach regards teaching practice with curiosity and openness and launches an inquiry to explore the life-giving opportunities for teachers' professional learning and development. This approach to evaluating teaching can further strengthen relationships among teachers within a learning community.

Sustaining Reflection Through Action Inquiry

The fourth aim of a comprehensive program for teacher development is that of sustaining in-depth reflection over time. Teachers recognize that reflection on their practices can be central to their development.[43] Yet traditional teacher assessment seldom provides opportunities for sustained inquiry into one's teaching practice. Teachers know that conversations with colleagues and students can be helpful, but they are also aware that such conversations don't always provide the depth and detail that is needed. How can schools provide platforms for such exploration?

We are drawn in this case to research practices available to teachers for focused and in-depth illumination. However, when it comes to doing research into one's own teaching, a dilemma often emerges. Teachers don't always see how traditional empirical research, with its emphasis on measurement, control groups, and statistics, is either feasible or relevant.[44] This dilemma can be dissolved through *action-based research*.[45] Teachers' action research can generate significant reflection on educational values, beliefs, and meanings. [46] It can encourage experimenting with new ideas in teaching and learning and help to integrate theory and practice.[47] Collaborative action research is playing a significantly increasing role in schools today.[48] We see it as a pivotal form of relational evaluation in the service of teachers' professional development. Indeed, many schools have provided time and resources for teachers to carry out research into their pedagogy, relationships, values, dreams, and more.

Given the potentials and promises of action research, many schools attempt to make it an integral part of their program, one especially relevant to evaluating teachers' practices.[49] In addition to the need for time and resources, it can also be challenging to connect action research to teachers' professional development.[50] And, too, a systematic approach to action research's reflective cycle—starting with questions and moving to continuing inquiry and improved practices—is often lacking.[51]

Here we bring together teachers' experiences in several secondary schools to illustrate an effective way forward.[52] Although many teachers have a research-oriented background, these schools saw increased potentials in establishing a partnership with local universities. Thus, professional researchers were invited to the school and worked alongside teachers in exploring ways to integrate research into their development. The collaboration led to a systematic approach that could be used by all the teachers—the *What?—So What?—Now What?* model for professional development.[53] The "3Ws" framework was most helpful in dividing the research into specific and interrelated phases and was easily explained to participants.

In the investigative step of the "What?" phase, teachers focused on an aspect of their teaching that could benefit from concerted attention and systematic inquiry. In the case of Anne, a Finnish history teacher, the focus was on her supervision of student projects. She thus invited her students into a collaborative inquiry and found them most eager to participate. She began with investigative questions, such as: "How was I doing in supervising your project work?" "Was my guidance clear enough?" "Were you able to act on my written feedback on your project?" Anne listened attentively to her students' comments, probed some of them, and carefully made notes on points that she would like to consider more or follow up on later.

During the more reflective "So What?" phase, the group of teachers came together to reflect on their various investigations. Each made a presentation on their exploration, including their particular classroom concerns, students' comments on their practices, and their own thoughts about these comments. The presentations in turn invited further questioning and reflection from their peers. In Anne's case, her colleagues asked: "What assumptions were you making in the way you were supervising the projects?" "What did you most value in your efforts?" And "What did you anticipate in terms of students' learning?" Re-reading and reflecting on her notes with peers, Anne realized that her supervision was too much focused on the end-products of the student projects (i.e., the final report and presentation and the marks her students would receive). Reflecting further, she could see that this focus was also connected to her desire to see the newly arrived immigrant students in her class succeed. "I wanted them to show the world that they can be successful in our society," she said. As the "So What" discussions continued, Anne could begin to see her teaching as a form of political activism. As a history teacher, she mused, her project supervision should primarily be about nurturing her students' learning process.

The "Now What?" phase shifts from investigation and reflection to action. Here teachers return to their students for further conversations. Anne thus asked her class, "What should I/we do to improve my supervision?," "What resources do I/we need to make these improvements?" and "What could we hope for from these changes?" After extended conversations, Anne and her students decided that while the outcome was important to them, they learned most from process-related questions, for example, how to collect and interpret historical evidence.

Over time, teachers were more able to generate different kinds of meaningful inquiry into diverse aspects of practice. The presence of professional researchers from the local university provided needed confidence in the action research cycles and the rigor of teachers' inquiries. School administrators learned that the systematic nature of the inquiry was immensely helpful in bringing about specific improvements in practice and in teachers' professional development. Hence they continued to ensure that time, space, and resources were available to support teachers' research. The participating teachers realized that by embedding action research in their classroom practice, in collaborating with students and colleagues, and by applying a reflective lens to their teaching processes, the resulting fruits were meaningful and substantial. The action research cycles also had ripple effects: students' learning and well-being were enriched.

It is well acknowledged that teachers' action research can sustain their professional learning and development and inspire transformation in teaching.[54] The promise of action research lies not only in the fact that it is a teacher-led approach to professional learning, but that it also fosters collaborative relationships. Invited is multidimensional dialogue and partnership with students, colleagues, the community, and other schools. Every classroom is a potential site for action research, every teacher a researcher, every colleague a co-inquirer, every student a research collaborator, and every school a community of inquiry.

From Teachers' Appraisal to Professional Learning

In approaching teacher evaluation from a relational perspective, we find myriad opportunities for nourishing the holistic growth of teachers and supporting their professional development. We thus shift the focus from measuring, judging, rewarding, and punishing to inquiry, reflection, dialogue, and continuous learning.[55] In the practices just described, evaluation of teaching is not something done *to* the teacher; instead, it is carried out *with* teachers and their colleagues, students, and other stakeholders.[56]

Good teaching reflects our shared communal existence, where multitudes of relationships are played out dynamically in classroom life and beyond. The evaluation of teaching not only draws resources from such communal resources but can further enrich the relational processes of which the teacher is a part.

Notes

1. Amrein-Beardsley, A., and Collins, C. (2012) *The SAS Education Value-added Assessment System (EVAAS): Its Intended and Unintended Effects in a Major Urban School System.* Tempe, AZ: Arizona State University.
2. We take the term "appraisal: from OECD (2009) *Creating Effective Teaching and Learning Environments: First Results from TALIS.* Paris: OECD.
3. Goe, L., Bell, C., and Little, O. (2008) *Approaches to Evaluating Teacher Effectiveness: A Research Synthesis.* Washington, DC: National Comprehensive Centre for Teacher Quality.
4. Green, T., and Allen, M. (2015) "Professional development urban schools: What do teachers say?," *Journal of Inquiry and Action in Education*, 6(2): 53–79; Kane, T., Kerr, K., and Pianta, R. (2014) *Designing Teacher Evaluation Systems: New Guidance from the Measures of Effective Teaching Project.* New York: John Wiley & Sons.
5. Ibid.
6. Spring, J. (2015) *Economization of Education: Human Capital, Global Corporations, Skills-Based Schooling.* London: Routledge.
7. Goe, L., and Holdheide, L. (2011) *Measuring Teachers' Contributions to Student Learning Growth for Nontested Grades and Subjects.* Nashville, TN: National Comprehensive Center for Teacher Quality.
8. Skourdoumbis, A. (2017) "Assessing the productivity of schools through two 'what works' inputs, teacher quality and teacher effectiveness," *Education Research Policy Practice*, 16: 205–217.
9. Hebson, G., Earnshaw, J., and Marchington, L. (2007) "Too emotional to be capable? The changing nature of emotion work in definitions of 'capable teaching,'" *Journal of Education Policy*, 22: 675–694.
10. Mather, K., and Seifert, R. (2011) "Teacher, lecturer or labourer? Performance management issues in education," *Management in Education*, 25(1): 26–31.
11. Gill, S. and Thomson, G. (2012). *Rethinking Secondary Education: A Human-Centred Education*, London: Pearson Education.
12. Evans, L. (2011) "The 'shape' of teacher professionalism in England: professional standards, performance management, professional development and the changes proposed in the 2010 White Paper," *British Educational Research Journal*, 37(5): 851–70.
13. The mode of life is a Foucauldian concept and the form of life a Wittgensteinian notion. Gergen, K. (2009) *An Invitation to Social Construction* (2nd ed.). Thousand Oaks, CA: Sage. See Gergen, K. (1982) *Toward Transformation in Social Knowledge.* New York: Springer-Verlag.
14. Smyth, J., and Shacklock, G. (1998) *Re-Making Teaching: Ideology, Policy and Practice.* London: Routledge; Fielding, M., and McGregor, J. (2005) "Deconstructing student voice: New spaces for dialogue or new opportunities for surveillance?" Paper given at the Annual Meeting of the American Educational Research Association, May 2005, Montreal, Canada.

15. Gill, S. (2015) "'Holding oneself open in a conversation': Gadamer's philosophical hermeneutics and the ethics of dialogue," *Journal of Dialogue Studies*, 3(1): 9–28.
16. See, for example, Davidson, K. (2009) "Challenges contributing to teacher stress and burnout," *Southeastern Teacher Education Journal*, 2(2): 47–56; Gonzalez, A., Peters, M., Orange, A., and Grigsby, B. (2016) "The influence of high-stakes testing on teacher self-efficacy and job-related stress," *Cambridge Journal of Education*, 47(4): 513–31; Richards, J. (2012) "Teacher stress and coping strategies: a national snapshot," *Educational Forum*, 76: 299–316.
17. Kolbe, L. J., and Tirozzi, G. N. (2011) *School Employee Wellness: A Guide for Protecting the Assets of our Nation's Schools*. Atlanta, GA: Centers for Disease Control.
18. See, for example, Dibben, P., Wood, G., Roper, I., and James, P. (2007) *Modernising Work in Public Services: Redefining Roles and Relationships in Britain's Changing Workplace*. Basingstoke: Palgrave Macmillan.
19. Mather and Seifert, "Teacher, lecturer or labourer?"
20. Richardson, H. (2019) *Four Out of 10 Teachers Plan To Quit, Survey Suggests*. BBC, April 16, 2019. https://www.bbc.co.uk/news/education-47936211
21. Hill, H., and Grossman, P. (2013) "Learning from teacher observations: Challenges and opportunities posed by new teacher evaluation systems," *Harvard Educational Review*, 83: 371–84.
22. See: Thomson, G., and Gill, S. (Forthcoming) *Happiness, Flourishing and the Good Life: A Transformative Vision of Human Well-Being*, London: Routledge.
23. Fielding, M. (2001) "Students as radical agents of change," *Journal of Educational Change*, 2(2): 123–141.
24. Gergen, M., and Gergen, K. (2003) *Social Construction: A Reader*. London: Sage.
25. Freire, P. (1972) *Pedagogy of the Oppressed*. Harmondsworth, UK: Penguin.
26. See also Hargreaves, A., and O'Connor, M. T. (2018) *Collaborative professionalism: When Teaching Together Means Learning for All*. Thousand Oaks, CA: Corwin.
27. Sunnybrook School represents a composite set of practices from three British primary schools.
28. Wilkins, E., and Shin, E. (2011) "Peer feedback: Who, what, when, why, and how," *Education Digest*, 76(6), 49–53.
29. Chism, N. (2007) *Peer Review of Teaching: A Sourcebook* (2nd ed.). Bolton, MA: Anker Publishing.
30. Spec, M., and Knipe, C. (2005) *Why Can't We Get It Right? Designing High-Quality Professional Development for Standards-Based Schools*. Thousand Oaks, CA: Corwin Press.
31. Wall, H., and Palmer, M. (2015) "Courage to love: Coaching dialogically toward teacher empowerment," *The Reading Teacher*, 68(8): 627–635; Carr, M., Holmes, W., and Flynn, K. (2017) "Using mentoring, coaching, and self-mentoring to support public school educators," *The Clearing House*, 90(4):116–124; Robbins, P. (2017) *How to Plan and Implement a Peer Coaching Program*. New York: ASCD; Asanok, M., and Chookhampaeng, C. (2016) "Coaching and mentoring model based on teachers' professional development for enhancing their teaching competency in schools (Thailand) using video tape," *Educational Research and Reviews*, 11(4): 134–140.

32. Pham, K., and Heinemann, A. (2014) "Partners with a purpose: District and teachers union create an evaluation system that nurtures professional growth," *Journal of Staff Development*, 35(6): 40–47; Msila, V. (2009) "Peer evaluation: Teachers evaluating one another for an effective practice," *International Journal of Learning*, 6(6): 541–557; Darling-Hammond, L. (2013) "When teachers support & evaluate their peers," *Educational Leadership*, 71(2): 24–29.

33. Peterson, K. Wahlquist, C., and Bone, K. (2000) "Student surveys for school teacher evaluation," *Journal of Personnel Evaluation in Education*, 14(2), 135–153; Ferguson, R. F. (2012) "Can student surveys measure teaching quality?" *Phi Delta Kappan*, 94(3), 24–28; Downer, J. T., Stuhlman, M., Schweig, J., Martínez, J. F., and Ruzek, E. (2015) "measuring effective teacher-student interactions from a student perspective: A multi-level analysis." *The Journal of Early Adolescence*, 35(5–6): 722–758.

34. Fielding, "Students as radical agents of change," 137.

35. This case is a composite of several forward-thinking US schools.

36. Fielding, M. (2008) "Interrogating student voice: Pre-occupations, purposes and Possibilities," *Critical Perspectives in Education*, Summer.

37. For example, Preskill, H., and Catsambas, T. (2006) *Reframing Evaluation Through Appreciative Inquiry*. Thousand Oaks, CA: Sage Publications; and Gergen, *An Invitation to Social Construction*.

38. Cooperrider, D., and Whitney, D. (2005) *Appreciative Inquiry: A Positive Revolution in Change*. San Francisco: Berrett-Koehler.

39. Newton School is the pseudonym of a British community school located in Kent.

40. For an introduction to Appreciative Inquiry, see https://appreciativeinquiry.champlain.edu/learn/appreciative-inquiry-introduction/

41. Whitney, D., and Trosten-Bloom, A. (2003) *The Power of Appreciative Inquiry*. San Francisco, CA: Berrett-Koehler.

42. Kozik, P., Cooney, B., Vinciguerra, S., Gradel, K., and Black, J. (2009) "Promoting inclusion in secondary schools through appreciative inquiry," *American Secondary Education*, 38(1): 77–91; Shuayb, M. (2014) "Appreciative inquiry as a method for participatory change in secondary schools in Lebanon," *Journal of Mixed Methods Research*, 8(3): 299–307; Steyn, G. (2012) "Reframing professional development for South African Schools: An appreciative inquiry approach," *Education and Urban Society*, 44(3): 318–341.

43. Schön, D. (1983) *The Reflective Practitioner: How Professionals Think In Action*. New York: Basis Books; Moon, J. (2008) *Reflection in Learning & Professional Development*. Abingdon, UK: RoutledgeFalmer.

44. Elliott, J. (1981) "Foreword," in J. Nixon (ed.), *A Teacher's Guide to Action Research, Evaluation, Enquiry and Development in the Classroom*. London: Grant McIntyre; Bennett, C. (1993) "Teacher-researchers: All dressed up and no place to go," *Educational Leadership*, 51(2): 69–70.

45. Altrichter, H., Posch, P., and Somekh, B. (2007) *Teachers Investigate Their Work: An Introduction to Action Research Across the Professions* (2nd ed.). Routledge: London; Stringer, E. (2008) *Action Research in Education* (2nd ed.). London: Pearson Education; Gilles, C., Wilson, J., and Eias, M. (2010) "Sustaining teachers' growth and

renewal through action research, introduction programs, and collaboration," *Teacher Education Quarterly*, 37(1): 91–108.

46. Clauset, K., Lick, D., and Murphy, C. (2008) *Schoolwide Action Research for Professional Learning Communities: Improving Student Learning Through the Whole-Faculty Study Groups Approach*. Thousand Oaks, CA: Corwin; Mills, G. (2011) *Action Research: A Guide for the Teacher Researcher* (4th ed.). Boston: Pearson; Burns, A. (2010) "Action research: What's in it for teachers and institutions?," *International House Journal of Education and Development*, 29, 3–6.

47. Mertier, C. A. (2016) *Action Research: Improving Schools and Empowering Educators* (5th ed.). Thousand Oaks, CA: Sage; Mills, G. E. (2016) *Action Research: A Guide for the Teacher Researcher* (6th ed.). Philadelphia, PA: Pearson; Gill and Thomson, *Rethinking Secondary Education*; Gill, S., and Thomson, G. (2016) *Human-Centred Education: A Handbook and Practical Guide*. London: Routledge.

48. Schneller, L., and Butler, D. (2014) "Collaborative Inquiry: Empowering Teachers in Their Professional Development," Education Canada, 42-44; Cammarota, J., and Fine, M. (Eds.). (2008) *Revolutionizing Education: Youth Participatory Action Research in Motion*. New York: Routledge.

49. Hong, C., and Lawrence, S. (2011) "Action research in teacher education: Classroom inquiry, data-driven decision making," *Journal of Inquiry and Action in Education*, 4(2): 1–17; Avalos, B. (2011) "Teacher professional development in teaching and teacher education over ten years," *Teaching and Teacher Education*, 27(1): 10–20; Hughes, S. (2016) "Joining the game: Living and learning as an action researcher," *The Canadian Journal of Action Research*, 17(1): 3–19.

50. Cain, T., and Harris, R. (2013) "Teachers' action research in a culture of performativity," *Educational Action Research*, 21(3): 343–358.

51. Hine, G. (2013) "The importance of action research in teacher education programs," *Issues in Educational Research*, 23(2): 151–163.

52. The following account is a composite case drawing together practices in schools from both Finland and the United Kingdom.

53. Rolfe, G., Freshwater, D., and Jasper, M. (2001) *Critical Reflection in Nursing and the Helping Professions: A User's Guide*. Basingstoke: Palgrave Macmillan.

54. Rogers, D., Noblit, G., and Ferrell, P. (1990) "Action research as an agent for developing teachers' communicative competence," *Theory Into Practice*, 29(3): 179–184; Altrichter, Posch, and Somekh, *Teachers Investigate Their Work*; Roulston, K., Legette, R., Deloach, M., and Pitman, C. B. (2005) "What is 'research' for teacher-researcher?," *Educational Action Research*, 13(2): 169–189.

55. Guba, E., and Lincoln, Y. (1989) *Fourth Generation Evaluation*. Newbury Park, CA: Sage.

56. Danielson, C. (2012) "Observing classroom practice," *Educational Leadership*, 70: 32–37.

7

Relational Approaches
to School Evaluation

The evidence is clear. If you rely on prescription, testing and external
control over schools, they are not likely to improve.
—Pasi Sahlberg, Education Ministry, Finland

We live in an age of assessment. We commonly believe that measuring the
world is a major step toward controlling it. The logic has been reasonably
successful in medicine, chemistry, biology, and the like. As the argument
goes, surely it should apply to education. Through measurement we thus try
to gain control over the vast and complex process of education. We want to
be certain that all the money, time, and effort invested in our educational
institutions yield results. We measure students, teachers, administrators—
and of course, the searchlight must also fall on schools themselves. Yet, given
all we have said about the myriad flaws in assessing students and teachers,
why should we expect that assessing schools would make a contribution to
learning? Is it possible that testing schools indeed undermines both learning
and the well-being of the school community itself?

In this chapter we open discussion on a relational orientation to school
evaluation. We first scan major problems in traditional models of school
assessment. This prepares the way for exploring the potentials of relational
practices in evaluating the work of schools. How can the life of the school
community be nourished through relationally sensitive practices of evaluation? Two cases will be used to illustrate these possibilities, the first an in-
ternally directed practice undertaken by the school itself and the second an
attempt to combine external with internal evaluation. Finally, we gather the
threads of these explorations to offer an integrating framework for school
evaluation.

Beyond the Tyranny of Testing. Kenneth J. Gergen and Scherto R. Gill, Oxford University Press (2020). © Oxford
University Press. DOI: 10.1093/oso/9780190872762.001.0001.

The Perils of School Accountability

What is a "good school," and what measures would one use to make such a judgment? As an analogue, one might ask, what is a "good person" and what assessments would help one identify and compare one person against another? Let's say the government decided to measure "good personhood" in the following ways: (1) church attendance to assess spiritual goodness, (2) size of the biceps to measure physical goodness, (3) the number of friends on Facebook to ascertain of social goodness, and (4) vocabulary size to determine intellectual goodness. Absurd, we might respond; the measures are irrelevant, unfair, and arbitrary. Yet we approach just such absurdity in our current attempts to assess schools.

Governing bodies from regional to national levels typically rely on standardized measures as the primary means of assessing the "goodness" of schools. The advantages are many, with simplicity and economy as immediate benefits. Such measures ensure that all schools are treated equally and make it possible to compare outcomes across schools and across time. With the availability of international tests, such as the Organisation for Economic Cooperation and Development's (OECD) Programme for International Student Assessment (PISA), school comparisons can now be made around the world. Such data also permit statistical analyses from which significant differences can be detected and predictions drawn.

Most importantly, it is reasoned, such data can be used to improve the level of educational attainment. Poor schools may be punished in various ways, including the firing of administrators and teachers, turning the school over to for-profit proprietors, or elimination. Likewise, improvement is motivated through competition—between schools, regions, and even nations.[1] Average schools should strive to increase their ranking, while poorly performing schools would be pressured by parents wanting "good" schools for their children. For governing bodies, such data not only provide a means of holding schools accountable, but also of satisfying various stakeholders on whose behalf that these governing bodies are exercising their responsibilities.

This orientation to evaluation is most dramatically represented in national government programs such as the "No Child Left Behind" and "Every Child Succeeds" programs in the United States and "Every Child Matters" in the United Kingdom. Nobly conceived, these programs mandate annual standardized testing of both primary and secondary students, in the United States between the third and eighth grades. In the United Kingdom, students take national exams at the ages of 16 to attain the General Certificate of Secondary Education (GCSE) and at 18 for the General Certificate of Education at an Advanced Level (A-Levels).[2]

The reader will be quick to surmise that it is just such high-stakes testing programs that have been subject to the biting critiques discussed in Chapter 1. To refresh, consider some fallacies of measurement. It is not simply that existing measures are exceedingly narrow, but it is unclear what is actually measured. Children from broken homes, with little social support, hungry, sleep-deprived, living in fear, and lacking role models are not likely to perform well on standardized tests—regardless of the skills and dedication of their teachers and school administrators. To fault the schools responsible for educating these disadvantaged children is akin to finding a scapegoat for an irresponsible society.

Such tests also fail to reflect the many forms of knowledge and capability that are meaningful for children and young people in various contexts. Nor do they reflect the schools' wider aims and the cultural ethos in which they reside. Above all, they fail to capture those crucial but less easily measurable qualities of education, such as mutual care, curiosity, engagement, interest, creativity, and participation.

Nor is it clear that such programs, modeled on a carrot-and-stick market strategy, have more than modest success in achieving their narrow goals of performance improvement.[3] The effort is enormously costly for taxpayers, as discussed in Chapter 1, and there is little to show of any value. While they do little to fulfill their assigned goals, their collateral impact is enormous. "Teaching to the test" is only one of the corrosive effects. As discussed in the preceding chapter, for example, when teacher assessment is gauged in terms of student performance, teachers are alienated from their students, from each other, and from their profession. When school leaders pressure their teachers to "produce data" and "improve test scores," their relationships also become distant, and unsympathetic. Such pressures are then transferred to students whose poor performance leads them to believe they are de facto failures. They become disaffected, and further disconnected from their personal development, from learning, and from education.

The face-to-face exchanges permitted by evaluation committee visits to schools are little improvement. For instance, school inspection in the United Kingdom starts with each school completing a self-evaluation form. The questions represent criteria that administrators believe are important to school performance. School inspection thus defines students and teachers through a narrow view created by the metric: students and teachers are effectively converted to data points. When the inspectors finally arrive, they ask the stakeholders to complete questionnaires which are once again turned into metrics. Dialogues between visitors and school staff are suffused with power dynamics, fear, and suspicion. Alienation often prevails, as discussions focus on the capacity of the schools to jump through the hoops established by outside authorities. What could be a collective inquiry into quality takes the form of an impersonal audit.

There are also more subtle effects. Critics argue that data-driven assessment tends to privilege political power over school autonomy. It is a form of top-down control.[4] In requiring accountability by a governmental authority, a relationship of distrust is established. When schools must prove their worth to an outside authority, school leaders become fearful and authorities become suspicious. Furthermore, when schools must dance to the tune of the authorities, schools relinquish reflection, imagination, and responsibility for education.[5] When education becomes an instrument of public management, its deeper human significance dissolves. Matters such as human value, compassion and understanding, individual and community well-being, and peace and justice, move to the margins.[6] Standardized school assessment is not like a meat thermometer that tells us whether the turkey is properly cooked; rather, it cooks the turkey.

From Resistance to Reconstruction

With the damaging consequences of traditional school evaluation, we should not be surprised at the enormous pushback. The frustration of teachers and administrators is pervasive.[7] However, there are also glimmers of hope. School inspections are being reformed, and slowly the test scores are being decoupled from inquiry into the quality of education offered by schools.[8] It is heartening to focus on two specific cases that provide direction and support for active resistance. This will set the stage for considering relationally sensitive alternatives.

In the first case, the Little London Community Primary School in the inner city of Leeds was among the few schools in England to opt out of Standard Attainment Tests (SATs) in 2017. This decision was supported by teachers, parents, and others in the community and particularly welcomed by the students. The school serves an extremely diverse community. Almost

90 different languages are spoken among the children, the majority of whom are virtually condemned to failure on their SATs. Refusing to allow these children to be stamped with this identity, the school leaders boycotted the SATs on the ground that testing is damaging the children's learning.

When the Office of Standards in Education (OFSTED) team arrived on the day of SATs in May 2017, the school's leaders and governors stood by their decision.[9] They argued that when teaching to the test, teachers are not able to meet the children's learning needs and support their progress. Instead of being stressed-out by SAT scores, the school now devotes time to developing a richer curriculum, including collaborative projects, outdoor activities, and the arts. The school does apply a rigorous system of self-evaluation, including teachers' evaluations and student's self and peer evaluations. The school thus feels it is able to support children to learn in richer and more meaningful ways, to develop their individual skills and interests, and to encourage them to appreciate learning as an end in itself. The school now invites other schools to join them in common reflection on multicultural education and tailored evaluation.

A second form of resistance takes the form of a major policy change. At the end of 2017, New Zealand's Education Minister, Chris Hopkins, announced that schools across the country would not be required to report the 2017 results of the traditional standardized tests to the Ministry. More dramatically, the requirement would be abandoned from then onward. According to the Minister, New Zealand wanted teachers to focus "less on testing and more on teaching because that's the way we're going to improve students' progress."[10] New Zealand thus became the first economically developed country in the world to abolish the system of national standardization.[11] To be sure, the new policy continues to spark active debate. Without standardization and testing, it is asked, how do we know whether our children are making progress? How can we reconstruct the process of evaluation to yield better understanding without sacrificing the well-being of the schools themselves?

The demand for evidenced-based programs is everywhere in motion. What stands as evidence, however, that a school is performing well, that one school is superior to another, or that an innovation is effective? As we have seen, defining evidence solely in terms of standardized measures and statistical comparisons is both misleading and deeply damaging. We have also touched on the potential of qualitative data to expand understanding. How do students (and teachers) describe their experiences, their hopes, and their achievements? Yet even such qualitative evidence is replete with methodological problems. In writing about their experiences, for example, there will be differences in the willingness of respondents to reveal, in their capacities for narration, in what they remember at the time, and so on. One may also learn about a school through face-to-face dialogue with its participants. However, such dialogue is also limited as *evidence* by the selection of the participants, their particular differences, power relations, and the like. All that counts as evidence, then, is colored by assumptions, generated under particular conditions, and the results can be multiply interpreted.

From a relational standpoint, school evaluation should be viewed as a *process of inquiring, valuing, and co-constructing meaning*. All forms of evidence may contribute to this process, but none should provide grounds for definitive conclusions. Traditional forms of standardized evidence can surely make a contribution. For instance, it may be useful to know whether a given class of students demonstrates progress over the years in language or math. Such evidence can help teachers and students to reflect on how they are engaged in teaching and learning over time and explore how the teacher and the class have contributed to such outcomes. Qualitative evidence can more easily facilitate discussion on motivation, the components of success, and the quality of relationships. Anecdotes, stories, and vivid illustrations add a human face to abstract numbers and offer a forum for negotiating values and actions. The challenge for relational approaches to school evaluation is thus to generate multiple sources of information and different kinds of data for stoking the fires of deep reflection and holistic analysis. To be sure, ambiguity will prevail, but in a world of multiple perspectives and rapid change, clarity is a seductive illusion.

Relational Alternatives to School Evaluation

From a relational perspective, there is no objective assessment of how well or poorly a school is working. Rather, there are multiple and shifting perspectives, each saturated with values and interests. Teachers' views of the school will differ from those of administrators, and these will differ from the perspectives of students, parents, and governmental agencies. Some will value performance on traditional subject matters, others will prioritize students' well-being, with others emphasizing the flowering of individual talents, and so on. Most participants will also have multiple and conflicting values, and these will change across time and circumstance. When a single, uniform set of standards is imposed, all nuances are lost; and when multiple voices and values are silenced, democratic education is in decay. As we have proposed, it is when we bring the multiple voices and values together in mutually attentive and caring ways that learning flourishes and a community thrives.

In this light, our aim is not to abandon school evaluation but to locate means of energizing the relational processes at the core of a school's flourishing. New spaces must be created and fostered for collaborative reflection, deep dialogue, and co-inquiry into the values and activities within our schools. Within dialogic spaces, school administrators, teachers, students, parents, and other stakeholders can explore how the school is doing on multiple levels. They can address the ways that the community is working together to support students' learning and teachers' professional development. All stakeholders can be encouraged to take an interest in learning processes and assume responsibility for overall growth and well-being. Sensitively conducted, participants can achieve a deeper understanding and better insight into the diverse, unfolding needs and values at play. The aim would not be a final fixing of "*the* route to excellence" but an attempt to continuously interweave the multiple pathways.

Are these just idle dreams? We have already seen how schools and governments have resisted the forces of top-down assessment and standardization. Many forward-thinking teachers, principals, school governors, and policy makers now join in exploring educationally meaningful and relationally sensitive innovations in school evaluation. Here we share two significant practices, the first featuring the potentials of internal evaluation and the second illustrating an integration of internal and external evaluation.

Internal Evaluation: Locally Crafting Excellence

Consider a guild of craftsmen, a circle of women quilters, or boys playing a pick-up game of basketball. In each case there is a concern with *excellence*. Participants observe each other, talk together about what they are doing, commend and correct each other in their styles and tactics, and entertain ideas about future directions to improve the 'art'. No outside authority is necessary to direct or judge. Indeed, without understanding the group from the inside, an outside authority would find it difficult to make meaningful judgments. Now let us consider the potentials of school evaluation as a process of bringing together stakeholders for in-depth reflection on qualities of teaching, experiences of learning, principles of leading, and the overall richness of school life. Here the school constitutes itself as a learning community with inquiry centered around its future betterment. To illustrate, in this excerpt. an 8-year-old boy is taking part in the New School's annual evaluation. He is responding confidently to questions posed by a parent volunteer:

PARENT VOLUNTEER: "What do like about your school?"
STUDENT: "I like my school because of my friends."
PARENT VOLUNTEER: "What can you tell me about you and your friends?"
STUDENT: "My friends and I talk a lot, and we do things together at school. Um, I like being with my friends so much, I want to be with them all the time. Holidays are boring because they are not there."
PARENT VOLUNTEER: "Wow. It must feel so good to have such friends."
STUDENT: "My friends help me with my work too."
PARENT VOLUNTEER: "Who else helps you with your work at school?"
STUDENT: "My teacher of course. She is very nice. I like my teacher."

The New School is an elementary school in a small Sussex town in England, catering to 80 students aged 3–12. Founded 20 years ago by local parents and educators, there is pervasive appreciation of the centrality of relationships in their work. Since its inception, the school has annually conducted what they call a *whole-school inquiry*. Included in the inquiry are all major stakeholders: children, members of the staff (school governors, the principal, deputy principal, teachers, teaching assistants, volunteers), and parents. The inquiry is structured around traditional evaluation themes, such as (1) qualities of teaching, (2) progress in learning, (3) community engagement, and (4) governance.

Over the years, the school has continued to improve the evaluative process and structure, and it now consists of three major components. First is the *evaluative questionnaire*, which features thematized questions directly relevant to specific stakeholder groups. Within each theme, participants respond on a 5-point scale to a series of statements tapping into their experiences. To illustrate, under the theme of *learning*, the children may be asked to what extent they like being in the school, feel safe, enjoy taking part in activities, find their work interesting, have friends, and can help others in school. For the younger children, the questionnaire is completed with the support of parents and trained community volunteers. Under the same theme, parents may be asked to what extent they feel their children are engaged, curious, interested, motivated to learn, developing appropriately, receiving emotional support, and encouraged to contribute to others' learning. Similarly, teachers might be questioned on the extent to which their students are motivated to learn, asking good questions, making progress according to their needs and capabilities, working collaboratively, willing to take risks in project work, and are mindful of others' interests and needs. Participants are also invited to add details or stories in their own words, thus adding a human face to the numbers. The questionnaire responses provide a wealth of information for subsequent discussion.

Supplementing the questionnaires, the second major component of the process consists of *in-depth interviewing*. Participants are asked if they are willing to be interviewed by trained professionals on behalf of the school governors. The interviews focus on experiences and perspectives related to different aspects of school life. Typically, five volunteers are randomly selected from each group (e.g., students, administrators, teachers, teaching assistants, parents). The interview is semi-structured around the four main themes of evaluation. As illustrated by the extract at the beginning of this section, the hope is that the interviews will foster a more nuanced understanding of the school's practices and their effects on the community's learning and well-being.

Focus-group dialogues serve as the third component of the evaluative process. The dialogues are open-ended, inviting participants to reflect on the results of the two preceding inquiries. The purpose is to seek insights into what the school has learned from the evaluative process, what the school community might need to change or improve, and how. The dialogues are informed by appreciative inquiry practices and are facilitated at different levels. At the *classroom level* students join with administrators and teachers. At the *school level* administrators and teachers can focus on their own special concerns. Finally, at the *community level*, administrators, teachers, parents, and stakeholders within the community come together. Group size is limited to roughly 12–15 to invite conversational depth.

To illustrate in more detail, we include here some sample questions from the focus group conversation.

What have we/I learned from the inquiry so far?
    What has stood out as three high points in my/our schools experiences in the present?

How are the children and adults engaged in learning and life of the community?

Which valuable aspects of my/our practices continue to nourish and sustain the community well-being?

Which are the most promising areas to expand on to make our school a thriving community?

Who will take responsibility for the effort?

What will an ideal collaboration look and feel like?

Of special note are the ways in which the questions direct the inquiry toward appreciating the personal and collective strengths and potentials of the school community. They also help identify possible pathways and steps to bring about positive change. The participants are even invited to suggest groups and committees who could share the responsibilities in effecting the necessary changes. Following the focus group dialogue, the school brings data, narratives, and multiple insights together for an *integrative analysis*. The analysis is conducted by a school evaluation committee and includes administrators, teachers and parents. This small team works with professionals to draw more general conclusions and to make plans for the next year.

This multivocal inquiry stands in sharp contrast to standardized testing. It is also a vast improvement over outside inspectors visiting for 2 days, making impersonal assessments of a school, and then holding the principal accountable for shortcomings. Instead of measurements, comparisons, and judgments, a relational approach can inspire the community's curiosity about its own processes and experiences of learning and drive inquiry toward shared understanding and responsibility for innovation. Policies and practices are no longer limited to the decisions of the school administrators; all participants take part in co-creating the educational process. As the headteacher of the New School says, "There is no better way to know the school than having everyone come together and share *our* stories of learning."

Blending Internal and External Voices

As argued, using standardized tests to judge schools from the outside can be perilous. Much the same can be said about the audit orientation of outside evaluation committees. School inspection can be as oppressive as standardized testing.[12] At the same time, a strong case can be made for bringing national and regional values to bear in evaluating local school systems. This is not only because of the threat of a fragmented society, but also because there are needs and values essential to the life of the society of which local schools are a part. If a democracy is to thrive, for example, a shared understanding of democratic practices is essential to education. The challenge, then, is to develop practices in which both internal and external voices may be brought together in the process of evaluation.

In this context we are drawn to a program developed by the New Zealand Educational Review Office (ERO). Although Anglo/European culture prevails, the country hosts more than 200 ethnic minorities, with a significant body of indigenous Maori. Caring attention is given, then, to the values of both unity and diversity. All schools are expected to take part in an "ongoing, cyclical process of evaluation and inquiry for improvement."[13] The process places an emphasis on students' learning and achievement, the schools' priorities or goals for progress, and actions for innovation and improvement. Most saliently, the program integrates national indicators with the school's self-review and stresses both participatory and collaborative processes. Furthermore, the practice respects the specific needs of individual school communities. The sensitivity to relational process is evident.

The ERO evaluation employs two types of indicators: *outcome indicators*, which reflect student achievement, progress, and related goals; and *process indicators*, which are sensitive to the practices and processes relevant to students' learning and the school's improvement. Outcome indicators are quantitative, but going beyond the limited focus on academic performance alone, they include measures of students' confidence, well-being, and participation in learning. Process indicators use qualitative data from the school and focus on such factors as leadership, effective teaching, learning opportunities, curriculum relevance, and innovation. As reasoned,

> Where evaluation against the outcome indicators indicates poor performance, the process indicators can be used as a tool for investigating the school conditions that are contributing to this poor performance. Where evaluation against the outcome indicators indicates excellent performance, the process indicators can be used as a tool for analyzing which school processes and activities have contributed to this excellent performance.[14]

Yet these outside indicators are not used to make summative judgments of the school or to impose policy. Rather, they are provided to the schools as primary sources for local dialogue and planning. Furthermore, the ERO offers the schools a framework for discussion that centers on school conditions contributing to qualities of students' experience, or the so-called learner outcomes. The framework emphasizes six major conditions, including (1) stewardship; (2) leadership for equity and excellence; (3) educationally powerful connections and relationships; (4) responsive curriculum, effective teaching, and opportunity to learn; (5) professional capability and collective capacity; and (6) evaluation, inquiry, and knowledge-building for improvement and innovation.[15] Interestingly, in their desire for *culturally responsive schooling*, ERO has taken care to link each of these conditions with Maori cultural values, including, for example, mutual responsibility, teachers' authority rooted in care for students' holistic well-being, and solidarity in the learning community toward common purposes. By following these values, ERO affirms the centrality of extended family-like relationships in schooling, recognizing rights and responsibilities, commitments and obligations, and supports as fundamental to communal life.

The evaluative process begins with an ERO team visiting the school for a discussion of goals, procedures, and indicators. This discussion also launches a within-school process of evaluation consisting of four phases.[16] It begins with *noticing* (e.g., paying attention to the students' experiences and achievements). Here outcome indicators are applied to assist the community in mapping out the context of students' learning and identifying what matters most in terms of students' development: "What does the information tell us about the extent to which students are learning and in what context?" This review will attend to indicators such as self-confidence, language and culture, well-being, achievement and progress, and participation. Equally, it will identify those students who are not doing as well and why.

Inquiry then moves into a phase of *investigating*. Here process indicators assist the team as it draws from the six domains of influence to explore where to focus the evaluation. Focal questions might include: "How do we know what has contributed to students' achievements and learning experiences as such?" "What else do we need to know and how?" "What further information do we need?" "How might we find out?" "What questions do we need to answer/focus on?"

Following the investigation, the evaluation enters a process of *collaborative sense making*. At this phase, conversations tend to explore what counts as effective and meaningful practices to meet the school community's specific aspirations. By drawing on the indicators and other sources, collaborative meaning-making contributes to the next step: *prioritizing to take action*. Here conversation is aimed at identifying needed improvements and selecting the most important actions to take. Resources are also identified to help ensure the success of these actions.

As the plans are put into motion and the results become available, further efforts are made to *monitor and evaluate the impact*. Here the cyclic process is completed by returning to its starting point. Once again, outcome indicators are applied to evaluate and review the impact of the actions taken within the school community. Discussion returns to the aims of education and whether the school community's practices are indeed providing opportunities for all to learn, progress, and achieve. In other words, the cyclic process stays focused on the range of values and priorities identified by the community but with national interests taken into account.

The ERO approach especially draws out the relational potentials of working together with schools. As the evaluative dialogues take place in the schools, the indicators and domains of inquiry provide a common language for conversations. Such language builds a foundation for evaluative thinking, reasoning, and decision-making within the schools.[17] As the community's capacities to reflect, review, and evaluate are enhanced, so is dialogue between schools and ERO representatives enriched. Hence the school evaluation process serves as a learning opportunity for the school and the system of education as a whole.

Relationally Centered Resources for School Evaluation
The efforts of the New School and the ERO are scarcely isolated in the attempt to replace top-down school assessment with locally and relationally centered practices of evaluation. Other schools have increasingly sought ways to resist dancing to the tune of standardization and imposed control. These initiatives provide useful and inspiring resources for schools more generally. We touch here on several of the most relevant:

In the United Sates, one of the most widely known assessment alternatives is *empowerment evaluation*.[18] Although developed for the purposes of community organizing, the practice has specific applicability to school systems. Rather than testing school systems with standardized performance indicators, the site of evaluation is shifted to the local participants. This enables the learning community to become self-directing, to deliberate on its activities against the goals set for itself, and to take necessary actions for further progress or improvement. The evaluators in this case serve as coaches or facilitators and help the learning community to build ongoing practices of self-evaluation. Over time educational communities are enabled to chart their future, evaluate their progress, and transform plans and programs on a continuing basis. However, similar to the ERO program, the use of standardized assessments is not precluded. Instead, such performance indicators are intended to provide useful inputs into dialogues about local progress. Rather than dictating policy, test scores become adjuncts to local school development.[19]

Practices of school-based evaluation may vary considerably from one community to another, but a typical empowerment procedure might take place in several stages, including (1) a process of "taking stock" in which all members of the school community participate in dialogue to identify shared educational aims and to survey available resources to support these aims, (2) broad and inclusive discussion of an ideal or dream school to which the community might aspire, (3) the establishment of cadres that develop specific plans for moving toward the ideal, and (4) setting up administrative committees that implement proposed changes. The various groups engaged in implementation also establish yardsticks by which they can evaluate their progress. Over time educational communities are enabled to chart their future, evaluate their progress, and alter plans and programs on a continuing basis.

Many schools find inspiration in *dialogic evaluation*.[20] In brief, such evaluation tends to emphasize equality and justice, to recognize multicultural intelligences, and to prioritize qualitative analysis as opposed to quantification—all with an eye to broad-scale social transformation. Dialogic evaluation is engaged, inclusive, and respectful of the values, perspectives, experiences, and aspirations of the many stakeholders.[21] Going beyond the flawed percentile scores on national tests, dialogic evaluation weaves together multiple opinions and indicators of efficacy—which may or not include test scores.[22] Dialogic and collaborative approaches such as illustrated here can be enormously effective in mobilizing community care and support of the school.

Appreciative evaluation practices have emerged largely in the context of program evaluation and assessing development in large-scale organizations. However, for many, the relevance to school evaluation is clearly apparent. Drawing from social constructionist theory, practitioners find that when dialogue focuses on *problems*—such as the poor performance of students, teachers, or school systems—it tends to solidify the reality of the problems. It is to look at the glass half-empty. When problems are the central reality, discussions will often lead to mutual blame, alienation, distrust, lowered motivation, and more. These are scarcely the grounds for productive discussion or enthusiastic planning for the future. By contrast, the appreciative approach centers discussion on what is valued or prized by the participants.[23]

Similar to the whole-school inquiry, narratives of positive experiences are first shared in dyads or small groups. Mutual appreciation and a sense of positive potential often follow. These narratives are then collected, thus allowing the larger group to explore the common values represented in the stories. Reflection on values then moves to the means of building futures in which these values would be most fully instantiated. What concrete steps would be promising? What resources would be needed? Who might be the most appropriate person to help move the community forward? Groups are then established to monitor progress toward the shared goals. On a broader scale, an entire school system might participate in what is called an appreciative inquiry "summit."[24]

In the United States, an innovative relational process called *lifescaping*[25] integrates dialogic and appreciative practices into an action research format. The emphasis is on multi-voiced participation in identifying desired goals, an ongoing gathering of relevant data, reflection on what is learned, and the shaping of relevant action. Lifescaping practices can be applied effectively to school evaluation. Like whole-school inquiry, lifescaping would welcome all stakeholders in the school community—including staff, parents, and students—into a continuous collective inquiry.[26] Lifescaping gives voice to the values and visions of the stakeholders, rather than to outside authorities imposing their policies on them. Applying lifescaping action research to evaluate the work of the learning community stresses the importance of *with-ness*, bringing together time, context, and relationships in the conversations. Here we move toward relationally rich ecologies.[27]

Practices such as these resonate with similar initiatives in many parts of the world. They all point to the possibility of a more democratic, inclusive, and discerning orientation to evaluating schools. They foster a more equal distribution of power, and urge us to explore how all participants in a learning community can be empowered to act as dialogue partners.[28] They invite us to think of school evaluation as a *whole community* endeavor, with no principled border to what counts as community.

Toward an Integrated Framework

We find in these various practices a deep valuing of the relational processes that can animate and inspire teaching and learning. They avoid the oppressive and debilitating imposition of a singular voice, whether represented in standardized test scores or rigid school inspection criteria. Rather, they celebrate dialogic and collaborative inquiry, strive for listening and inclusion of all voices, are sensitive to community contexts, and approach evaluation as a formative as opposed to summative process.[29]

Is it possible, then that the many insights offered by such practices could be integrated into an overarching framework for realizing school evaluation in a relational key? What would a comprehensive framework for school evaluation look like as a process of *acting with* the teachers, students, and others in the community rather than *acting on* them? More importantly, how could the evaluation of schools be itself a process of reflection, appreciation, and learning? Finally, how might the school evaluation further enrich the relational processes active in schools and bring forward improvement and innovation?

There is much to be said on these issues and our attempt at this point is simply to open the dialogue. Here we draw not only from existing practices, but also from various elements of relational theory and practices discussed in preceding chapters. Our chief concern is with identifying major domains of school evaluation. To what issues should evaluation be directed? What kinds of criteria are important? We then touch on the process of evaluation, emphasizing how interactive practices of evaluation may become generative for all concerned. Drawing together the multiple voices of theory and practice, we see six domains of inquiry as central to holistic school evaluation.

Teaching and Learning

In the factory tradition of assessment, school evaluation primarily focuses on the product: namely, student performance. In turn, it is reasoned that student performance is dependent on teacher efficacy. Teachers are responsible for ensuring that students know more when they finish their education than when they begin. By contrast, from a relational standpoint, teaching and learning cannot be separated. A teacher is not skilled in communication, for example, unless there are students who are open to the teacher's ways of communicating. This orientation suggests three focal points of evaluation: teacher preparation, student preparation, and the dialogic relational process of teaching and learning together. Here again is reason for a more dialogic and continuously relational orientation to evaluation. Thus, in the case of teachers, it is important to reflect on issues such as whether there are means for their keeping abreast of their fields and developments in pedagogy, open pathways to innovation, and means for enhancing capacities to communicate in meaningful and effective ways. In the case of students, we should be concerned with such issues as students' engagement in school, their progress in developing skills and abilities, and their capacities for collaboration. Finally, evaluative dialogue should center on the relational qualities of the pedagogical process. These may be subsumed in the second domain of inquiry.

Relational Well-Being

If relationships are not only the foundational source of learning and well-being, then the quality of these relationships must be a central focus of school evaluation. This should include relationships among all stakeholders: teachers, students, school leaders, parents, and community members. For example, is there mutual respect and caring in the classroom, on playgrounds, after school, at home, and so on? Are students free to ask meaningful questions in class? Is there an openness to dialogue and collaboration and a sharing of responsibilities? Are there congenial contexts for developing colleagueship, friendships, and family relationships with parents and others within the community? The well-being of relationships will also be reflected in the well-being of students and staff themselves. Do they feel safe, supported, enlivened, and nourished? Ideally, this focus on relational well-being should include relationships with the broader world, both within and beyond one's community, nation, or one's traditions. Where in our classrooms, one might ask, are the portholes for developing mutual understanding across the globe?

Learning Environments

The school's physical and cultural environments play a significant role in both the learning process and the well-being of the school community. The physical features of the school—both inside and out—along with the surrounding environment make a difference in one's sense of security, belonging, optimism, participation, and pleasure. If classrooms are ill-lit, furnishings are shabby, hallways are dark, paint is peeling, or the classroom temperature is too low or too high, school becomes a dreary and forbidding place. Are there computers, is there equipment for play, are there spaces for interaction, are students properly fed, are there adequate supplies? Is there green space and attention to environmental aesthetics? All contribute to the learning process and the well-being of students and staff.

There are also the more ineffable qualities of the cultural environment to consider. Most immediate is the question of safety, both *private* and *public*. In the private world, do students feel safe emotionally? Do they feel they are the subjects of bullying, prejudice, or discrimination? Do they feel included despite being different, physically, racially, culturally, or in terms of capabilities? Regarding public safety, are students safe within the school and in their travels to and from it? Are staff, students, and families affected by community violent conflict, drug abuse, unemployment rates, support services, and public transportation? To be sure, schools cannot be held responsible for the quality of community life, but evaluations of one's school should take such factors into account. In some cases, schools may even play an active political role in bringing about change.

Leadership and Governance

The main objective of leadership and governance is to ensure that the educational processes, teaching practices, school culture, and the environment all align well with the vision and objectives of the school. Unfortunately, the idea of leadership is traditionally linked to the factory model of education, with school leaders (and their staff) acting as managers overseeing school functioning. As we have argued, this tradition not only breeds a culture of surveillance and distrust, but it also undermines the motivation for teachers and students to share responsibility for learning. The governance process should ideally contribute to the full and zestful engagement of all stakeholders in the educational process. This sensitivity to education as a relational process is now manifest in numerous works on school governance variously emphasizing distributed leadership, collaborative leadership, and relational leading.[30] Such works almost invariably emphasize dialogue and collaboration and the necessity of nurturing of the responsibility of all members of the community. Relationally sensitive leadership shows respect for the voices of the staff, students, parents, and community. Listening is an essential preliminary to decision-making.

In this context, attention might be given to questions such as the following:. How do leaders enable everyone to contribute to the objectives of the school? How do they ensure the well-being of students, teachers, and the community? How do they encourage students and teachers to be pro-active in pursuing learning and contributing to the flourishing community? How do they engender a culture of relationship, dialogue, and collaboration within the school? How do they attend to the relationships, structures, and processes to facilitate dialogue, create space for pedagogical conversations, and draw insights from the community's lived experiences? Concern may also extend to the process of governance itself. For example, does the governance process encourage the community to join in the collaborative effort to develop and improve the school? To what extent does the practice of governance prioritize cohesiveness, collaboration, and co-creation? Are there spaces for listening and dialogue so that diverse voices are integrated into decision-making? How do the school's policies and practices mutually support each other? Inquiry into such issues can contribute to the cultivation of a full community of learning.

Community Engagement

Learning thrives through relationship, not only within the school but also with parents and community members. School evaluation should thus take into account the participation of parents and other community stakeholders in school life. Stakeholder participation can vitally enrich and enhance the learning and flourishing of the school. School evaluation can fruitfully be directed to such questions as whether there are opportunities for community members to become involved with the school, for example, in volunteering, hosting field trips, contributing to school events, speaking to classes, and so on. Are there ways the community can look inward to appreciate the school's work and to explore what is working well for the students and teachers? Are there means to see how the school's work supports and contributes to the wider community? Are there opportunities for the community to contribute ideas and insights for developing the school? And most importantly: What might we do more *together*?

Innovation and Transformation

The final domain of evaluation concerns the school's capacity for innovation and transformation. This is especially important in the light of the rapid developments in communication technology. For example, how does leadership encourage the staff to explore innovative practices in teaching and learning? What are the opportunities provided by the school for nurturing teachers' capacities for research and inquiry, along with their continuous professional learning? How is change observed and discussed, and how does such discussion foster innovation? And how does the school community assume responsibility for implementing creative and novel ideas to advance the school's vision? Because creativity is born through the mixing of ideas, attention should also be directed to how partnerships and collaboration across boundaries are facilitated. Is there support for collaborative initiatives for meaningful changes?

Evaluation as a Generative Process

How might these issues be explored in action? We have consistently stressed the importance of listening, dialogue, and collaboration in this volume. From a relational standpoint, these processes should play a key role in school evaluation. Yet, while focal in their significance, the devil resides in the subtle details of relating. Even the best intentions of school inspectors for productive dialogue with teachers will confront the challenge of power relations. Community meetings to discuss school policies can become antagonistic shouting matches. When parents visit schools, they often enter the discussion with blame for teacher shortcomings. We are all too prepared to find fault in others, to avoid blame, to justify their actions, to defend their rights, to find flaws in others' arguments, and to claim the moral high ground.

This is not the place for exploring the practical details essential for generative dialogues. In earlier chapters, we suggested some major ingredients. We pointed to conditions in which power relations are minimized, collective responsibility is emphasized, and all voices may be heard. We stressed the importance of sympathetic listening, a focus on strengths, and an appreciative orientation to inquiry. There are many additional resources for building generative dialogues.[31] But the major point is that the participants in school evaluation must pay continuing attention to the *how* of the practices of inquiry and reflection.

To conclude, traditional approaches to school evaluation are not designed for complex and evolving educational challenges. To escape the limitations of the assessment tradition, we have proposed a shift to relational process. Here evaluative practices can maximally sensitize participants to the fruits of their actions while simultaneously supporting the processes of teaching and learning, enriching relationships, and enhancing the broader community of learning. Such evaluative processes are based on a transformative conception of evaluation, one that respects the voices and values of all, is sensitive to the community's cultural context, and cherishes the human relationships at the core of learning and well-being.

Notes

1. Hargreaves, D. (1990) "Making schools more effective: the challenge to policy practice and research," *Scottish Educational Review*, 22(1): 5–14.
2. The argument for national testing is often couched in terms of its contribution to equal education and opportunity. As critics point out, however, testing has succeeded in reinforcing the dominance of the elite. See Leman, N. (1999) *The Big Test: The Secret History of American Meritocracy*. New York: Farrar, Straus and Giroux; and Guinier, L. (2015) *The Tyranny of the Meritocracy*. Boston: Beacon.
3. See Wrigley, T. (2013) "Rethinking school effectiveness and improvement: a question of paradigms," *Discourse: Studies in the Cultural Politics of Education*, 34: 31–47; and page 55 in Brown, S. (1994) "School effectiveness research and the evaluation of schools," *Evaluation and Research in Education*, 8(1–2): 55–68.
4. Harris, A., and Chrispeels, J. (eds.) (2009) *Improving Schools and Educational Systems*. London: Routledge.
5. West, J. (2017) "Data, democracy and school accountability: controversy over school evaluation in the case of DeVasco High School," *Big Data and Society*, January–June: 1–16.
6. Fullan, M., and Hargreaves, A. (1992) *What's Worth Fighting For in Your School? Working Together for Improvement*. Buckingham: Open University Press.
7. For instance, in Greene, P. (2019). "It's a new school year. What should be the big education policy issues?" *Forbes*, August 14, 2019, the author sites a range of US states in which alternative routes to high-stakes standardized testing are taking place.
8. For instance, in the United Kingdom, from 2019, the Office for Standards in Education (OFSTED) will look beyond standardized testing scores in school inspection. In fact, the framework aims to focus the evaluation conversations on educational practices and processes themselves rather than on data. See OFSTED (2019) *The Education Inspection Framework*. London: Office for Standards in Education.
9. See   https://www.yorkshireeveningpost.co.uk/news/leeds-headteacher-bans-ridiculous-sats-tests-1-8550659
10. Gerritsen, J. (2017) "National standards ditched by government," Radio New Zealand, December 13, https://www.radionz.co.nz/news/national/346011/national-standards-ditched-by-government
11. Finland has no mandated standardized tests, with the exception of a single exam at the end of students' senior year in high school.
12. See critiques on external inspection system in the UK and other parts of Europe. Terhart, E. (2013). "Teacher resistance against school reform: reflecting an inconvenient truth," *School Leadership and Management*, 33(5): 486–500.

13. See page 6, in Education Review Office (ERO) (2016) *School Evaluation Indicators: Effective Practice for Improvement and Learner Success*. New Zealand: Education Review Office.

14. Ibid, 12.

15. Ibid.

16. Education Review Office (ERO) (2016). *Effective School Evaluation: How to Do and Use Internal Evaluation for Improvement*. New Zealand: Education Review Office.

17. Education Review Office (ERO), *School Evaluation Indicators*, 8.

18. See Fetterman, D. M., and Wandersman, A. (eds.) (2004). *Empowerment Evaluation, Principles in Practice*. New York: Guilford; and Fetterman, D. M., and Wandersman, A. (2007) "Empowerment evaluation, yesterday, today, and tomorrow," *American Journal of Evaluation*, 28: 179–198. See also O'Sullivan, R. G. (2004) *Practicing Evaluation: A Collaborative Approach*. Thousand Oaks, CA: Sage; and Stake, R. E. (ed.) (2006) *Standards-Based and Responsive Evaluation*. Thousand Oaks, CA: Sage.

19. For an in-depth account, see Schneider, J. (2017) *Beyond Test Scores: A Better Way to Ensure School Quality*. Cambridge, MA: Harvard University Press.

20. Ryan, K., and Destefano, L. (2004) "Disentangling dialogue: Issues from practice," *New Directions for Evaluation*, 85:63–76; Schwandt, T. A. (2005). "The centrality of practice to evaluation," *American Journal of Evaluation*, 26(1): 95–105.

21. Greene, J. C. (2001) "Dialogue in evaluation: A relational perspective," *Evaluation*, 7(2): 181–187.

22. See also Cousins, J. B., and Whitmore, E. (1998) "Framing participatory evaluation," *New Directions in Evaluation*, 80: 5–23.

23. see Preskill, H., and Catsambas, T. T. (2003) "An overview of appreciative inquiry in evaluation," *New Directions for Evaluation*. Winter: 100; Preskill, H., and Catsambas, T. T. (2006) *Reframing Evaluation Through Appreciative Inquiry*. Thousand Oaks: CA: Sage.

24. See Gergen, K. (2009). *Relational Being: Beyond Self and Community*. New York: Oxford University Press.

25. Lewis, R. E., and Winkelman, P. (2017). *Lifescaping Practices in School Communities: Implementing Action Research and Appreciative Inquiry*. New York: Routledge. Zhang, X. (2015) School principals: Problem solvers and appreciative leaders, in Dragonas, T. et al. (eds.) *Education as Social Construction*. Chagrin Falls, OH: Taos Institute.

26. Ibid.

27. Lewis, R., Herb, C., Mundy-Mccook, E., and Capps-Jenner, N. (2018) "Lifescaping action research pedagogy," *Educational Action Research*, 1–17.

28. Ryan, K. E., and L. DeStefano (eds.) (2000) *Evaluation as a Democratic Process: Promoting Inclusion, Dialogue, and Deliberation. New Directions for Evaluation*. San Francisco, CA: Jossey-Bass, 85.

29. As can be seen, relationally rich practices of evaluation walk hand in hand with the responsive evaluation movement. See Greene, J. C., and Abma, T. A. (2002) *Responsive Evaluation: New Directions in Evaluation*. San Francisco, CA: Jossey-Bass. See also, Greenstein, L. M. (2017). *Restorative Assessment: Strength-Based Practices That Support All Learners*, Thousand Oaks, CA: Corwin.

30. Giles, D. (2018) *Relational Leadership in Education*. London: Routledge; Deflaminis, J. A. (2016) *Distributed Leadership in Schools*. New York: Routledge; Muhammad,

A. (2017) *Transforming School Culture: How to Overcome Staff Division* (2nd. ed.). Bloomington, IN: Solution Tree Press.

31. See, for example, Lipmanowicz, H., and Mccandleuss, K. (2014) *The Surprising Power of Liberating Structures*. Seattle, WA: Liberating Structures Press; Patterson, K., Grenny, J., McMilan, R., and Switzler, A. (2011) *Crucial Conversations: Tools for Talking When Stakes Are High* (2nd ed.). New York: McGraw Hill; Juzwick, M., et al. (2011) *Inspiring Dialogue: Talking to Learn in the English Classroom*. New York: Teachers College Press.

8

Relational Evaluation and Educational Transformation

> If we teach today's students as we taught yesterday's, we rob them of tomorrow.
>
> —John Dewey, *Democracy and Education*

Discontent with the factory model of education is both widespread and intensifying. As we have outlined, such discontent is represented not only in the many trenchant critiques of assessment, but also in the flowering of relationally sensitive practices of evaluation. At the same time, increasing numbers of innovators—teachers, school leaders, scholars—have bravely moved on to generate alternatives to old-style practices of teaching, organizing curricula, designing classrooms, relating schools to communities, and crafting school communities. With practices, values, concepts, and enthusiasm now at the ready, educators everywhere are poised for a unified transformation.

It is with this aim in mind that the present chapter first explores the relationships among what are often viewed as the three pillars of education, namely pedagogy, curriculum design and evaluation. Of particular concern are the mutually fortifying relationships among innovations in flexible curricula design, dialogic and collaborative pedagogies, and relational. evaluation. Unless we replace traditional assessment practices with a relational orientation, these innovations will be shackled. By liberating evaluation, the way is open to the flowering of interlocking and conceptually related practices.

We then turn to the major barrier to unified transformation, namely the longstanding and normalized "rituals" of assessment. If a relational approach to evaluation is key to educational transformation, we must respond to the major objections. For example, where in a teacher's already crowded day is

Beyond the Tyranny of Testing. Kenneth J. Gergen and Scherto R. Gill, Oxford University Press (2020). © Oxford University Press. DOI: 10.1093/oso/9780190872762.001.0001.

there time for dialogic practices of evaluation? How well can administrators and policy-makers function without comparative measures and statistical safeguards? And how can universities or employers make selections among teeming numbers of candidates without cost-effective and time-efficient use of grades and test scores? These are among the challenges that must be addressed.

Major transformations in educational systems seldom occur in a cultural vacuum. There are myriad stakeholders and broad support is essential. We thus complete the chapter with an exploration of two significant trends in cultural life, one obstructing the path to relationally enriched transformation and the other rendering it necessary. The former is represented in what we call *control creep*, that is, the subtle forces toward the ordering of society and its institutions. The common demands for evidence-based decisions are but one manifestation; educational assessment is another. At the same time, however, there is a countermanding cultural force at work, one that increasingly disrupts these impetus toward order. It is a force emerging from burgeoning developments in communication technology—computers, smartphones, social media, and the like. As these technologies transform the patterns of cultural life, so too do they rupture the traditions of education. These changes add significant weight to the need for relational transformation in education. Ultimately, they will ensure its embrace.

Shaking the Pillars of Education

We are not alone in the ideals that underpin our vision of education, nor in the innovative impulses set in motion. Such ideals and impulses have been driving forces for innovation around the world.[1] As we have pointed out, there are striking similarities in core values shared across this spectrum, with significant affinity to the relational orientation we have set out. It is just here that we also confront the potentials for a broad-scale transformation in education. While the main focus of this work is on educational evaluation, the implications are far more profound. Practices of evaluation are closely intertwined in school life more generally, both within the classroom and without. So far, we have emphasized the ways in which evaluative practices can affect both learning and relationships. This is a limited focus. A shift in evaluative practices is an invitation to major transformation.

Educators often speak of three major domains of school practice: pedagogy, curriculum, and evaluation.[2] While these are characterized as "pillars of education," the domains are scarcely independent. Change in one domain will affect the others. A formalized curriculum, for example, will lend itself to the kind of top-down teaching that ensures curriculum coverage; if students were given the opportunity to co-create their own curricula, lectures might be replaced by collaborative classrooms. Thus, a fundamental shift in practices of evaluation has far-reaching implications. As mentioned, the vast share of the emerging innovations in pedagogy and curricula are harmonious with the relational orientation put forward in this book. Opening the door to relational evaluation will welcome these innovations into full flowering. Here we glimpse the possibility for profound transformation. Let us explore.

Toward Emergent and Inquiry-Based Curricula

There are many arguments favoring standardized curricula. Such curricula permit the teacher to rely on "packages of knowledge" consistent with delivery-based pedagogy. These curricula aim to ensure equality in education, lend themselves to the continuity of knowledge and cultural legacies, and provide promise of preparation for many occupations and professions. As already explored, all these presumptions are open to question. This is especially so in the light of major intensification in the global flows of people, ideas, and innovations. Standardized curricula homogenize a nation's people in a world that requires increased diversity, flexibility, creativity, and collaborative capacity.[3] Failure to attend to the corrosive effects of standardized curricula on our students' well-being and the wellness of our world is tragic. Still, standardized curricula and national testing are inseparable bedfellows, and, together with school comparisons, they are among our targets. Not only are they insensitive to the enormous variations in needs, wants, interests and talents of those who are affected, they also sap the relational process of vitality. The teacher's part in education is reduced to that of an assembly line foreman making sure the machine is efficiently functioning. Likewise, the student becomes a mere object to be shaped and molded. Whether there is generative relations, mutual caring, sensitivity, delight, or curiosity is largely irrelevant or interfering.

However, if we replace traditional assessment with relational approaches to evaluation, we also lock arms with significant innovations in education.

We begin to think of a curriculum more as a "guide" or "compass" to accompany learning journeys,[4] as opposed to a "marching order." Opportunities for multiple and flexible trajectories are thus invited. One of the most prominent innovations in curriculum development is presaged by schools that practice *emergent and inquiry-based curricula.* Early interest in such curricula blossomed especially in the era of child-centered education.[5] The continuing attempt is to link the curriculum to student interests, curiosity, and enthusiasms, as opposed to a set of predetermined goals. Thus, curricula are not preplanned, but emerge over time.[6] Decisions are contextual, open-ended, and dialogically based.[7] This also means that a different learning trajectory can be generated for each student, with pedagogical styles tailored to his or her needs. Typical here is the work in many primary schools across the globe drawing inspiration from Reggio Emilia approaches to education.[8] In a caring environment, children converse with teachers, parents, and other stakeholders in the community about what would be fascinating and important to explore.

Many would agree that co-created curricula are appropriate for primary schools but would dispute their applicability at secondary and high school levels. According to conventional wisdom, the principal task of primary schools is to lay broad foundations, while later schooling should be more focused on mastery of content. As often argued, if students are left to follow their own interests, they will learn little that can be of use, and will be unprepared for the world of work. To such objections, we would argue that, on the contrary, when the curriculum becomes relevant to their interests and passion, there is no end to their learning. As to the relevance of schooling for work life, there is broad criticism of the relevance of existing curricula to the demands of the times. And, when guided and supported by teachers, those who follow their passions will be more willing to meet the variegated demands of the workplace.

Consider, for example, the highly developed network of High Tech high schools in the United States.[9] Featuring inquiry-based curricula, students are directly involved in co-creating and generating contents specifically relevant to their emergent interests. There is a major emphasis on student projects to ensure learning that is rigorous and engaging. Also inspiring in their approaches are the Youth Invest schools in Norway (see Chapter 5), the Evangelical School Berlin Centre, and the phenomenon-based learning programs in Finland. In all these cases, students have a major voice in shaping their curricula; there is little lecture-style instruction, and no standardized testing. In the Agora Schools in the Netherlands, not only are standardized curricula abandoned, there are no age-based cohorts.[10] With the assistance of a carefully selected faculty, students may follow their own learning journey. In each case there are strong signals of success, both in relevant learning and secure passage into the working world.

One may justifiably question these innovations in terms of their avoiding the issue of *essential knowledge*; that is, knowledge that every educated citizen should have. Shouldn't public schools ensure that every individual has a basic command of the common language and a fundamental grasp of biology, history, geography, mathematics, civics, and the like? How do these laissez-faire curricula serve these public needs? The question of what constitutes essential knowledge will always be controversial. In general, the greater the circumscribing of what students *must* learn, the more deadening the effect on learning. Ask most upper-level students why they take most of their courses and the typical answer will be "because they are required."[11] If pressed, many will respond that they need the courses to get into college or university.[12] Only occasionally they will murmur that it is good to know these things. This is not because students care little for learning; it is the compulsory mastery of the predetermined contents that is most off-putting.

Yet, even with agreement about certain essentials, there is no need to govern, determine, or standardize the curriculum. In many schools experimenting with emergent curricula, there is a minimal number of required or core courses. General knowledge can be offered, and specialized knowledge can be developed through personal interest and project work. If a student is working on a project on climate change, for example, he or she may seek knowledge in meteorology. Here the core courses might not be required but simply recommended for those clearly in need. In still other cases, teachers are highly cognizant of the essentials, and as they guide students' inquiry, they help them to integrate the essentials into their pursuits. Evaluative reflection can be inserted into such a process, to supply them with an indication of areas in which they might need further work. We return to this point in a later discussion of standards.

Toward Dialogic and Collaborative Pedagogies

As we see, standardized curricula walk hand in hand with traditional assessment practices. At the same time, this pair requires a partner in pedagogy. In particular they place strong demands on the teacher to transmit a core body of knowledge to students. It is the teacher's responsibility to ensure student mastery, which means controlling how, when, and where knowledge transmission takes place. The most obvious means of fulfilling this responsibility is through systematic checks on comprehension and retention. In effect, a top-down pedagogy, with a teacher at the front of the class—leading, lecturing, and directing the class—is "just natural." If students were given the opportunity to follow their interests, the teacher would be in danger of losing control. Test performance would suffer, which would suggest that both teaching and learning are deficient. By contrast, in shifting from traditional assessment to relational approaches of evaluation, the floodgates of possibility open wide. Relational practice prioritizes tailored learning experiences, both feeding student enthusiasm and supporting those whose curiosities extend beyond an ill-fitting curriculum. Teachers have the opportunity to tailor pedagogies to students' diverse and developing needs in the local circumstances.

It is just here that we find relational approaches to evaluation working harmoniously with a family of innovations already under way in education. Here we have in mind developments in collaborative learning, dialogical learning, connections-based learning, group project learning, cooperative learning, and unison reading, among others.[13] All these practices serve many of the same relational objectives we are advancing. They may, for example, effectively reduce the distance between teacher and students, casting them as co-participants and partners in teaching and learning. Through dialogue, leadership and power in the classroom can be shared.[14] Individual accountability can be shifted to a relational responsibility in which the classroom becomes a community of learners.

More generally, these pedagogical practices prepare students to participate generatively in relational process itself. They can enhance the art of listening, the appreciation of multiple values and opinions, the building of skills in co-creating new ideas, competencies in comparing and synthesizing, the tolerance of ambiguity, and skills in working productively with conflict. Ultimately these pedagogies invest value in the relational process itself, a process central to the global future. In the coming world conditions, we collaborate or perish!

Toward Schools as Learning Communities

Relational approaches to evaluation are at one with transformative movements in both pedagogy and curriculum. Together they replace the deadening effects of standardization and assessment with potentials for active engagement in learning, the enrichment of educational outcomes, and the nurturing of the relational process at the heart of education. Students, teachers, and administrators work *with* each other toward the aims of learning and well-being. They are not in competition, not under surveillance, not fearing grades and ranking, but working together toward valued futures. Here we can see the potentials for schools to shut the doors of the factory model and open themselves to becoming learning communities.

The notion of a learning community finds its roots in Dewey's thinking and continues to inspire scholars to explore ways in which learning is ignited within communities.[15] As advanced throughout this book, learning is rooted in relational participation. When relationships prosper, we learn from each other—not only in terms of content but in how to participate meaningfully in the community itself. The idea of a learning community also expands learning to beyond students, teachers, and administrators. Parents, caretakers, neighbors, businesses, local government, and other stakeholders are invited in as learning partners. Schools as learning communities seek to involve everyone in the process of teaching and learning.[16] Mutual trust issues from the collaborative efforts of all. We thus shift away from the dehumanizing mechanism of current mass schooling toward schools as dynamic centers of activity, engaged in a collective search for ways of being, learning and flourishing together.

Get Real! Relational Evaluation in Question

Given the range of detrimental effects and the lack of convincing gains, the New Zealand government abolished national exams. As might be anticipated, the decision did not meet with unanimous approval. The critics were many. Transformation invariably encounters questions and objections, and these require sensitive attention. Multiple goods are at stake. Where do our proposals for relational evaluation fall short, and what ideals are endangered? Aren't there very real and very serious impediments to change? Yes, to be sure. Let us consider some of the most important objections.

Where Is the Time?

Practices of relational evaluation will be attractive to many teachers and school administrators. After all, there is little joy in functioning as an assessor, overseeing impersonal exams, watching for cheaters, and assigning grades. The pleasure of teaching usually derives from engaging relations with students as they advance in their learning. Yet the enthusiasm for relational approaches may quickly fall away with the question: "Where will I find the time?" Teachers' days are jam-packed—hours of teaching, class preparation, meetings, grading, other administrative tasks, playground duties, and so on. Many relational practices of evaluation appear to be time-intensive. How can teachers find time for dialogue, mutual exploration, the collaborative reviewing of plans and progress, and the like?

This is a legitimate question and speaks as well to the enormous responsibilities placed on the shoulders of contemporary teachers. One might counter with the observation that relational evaluation would mean a reduction in the arduous challenges of developing tests, ensuring against cheating, marking papers, and dealing with disgruntled students and parents. However, the implications for demands on time are broader. The critique of "no available time" also presumes that relational practices of evaluation would simply replace tests and exams, with all else in the classroom practice and culture remaining in place. In the preceding section, we challenged this assumption. Relational approaches to evaluation invite transformation in both pedagogy and curriculum. These can significantly reduce the demands on teacher time.

First consider pedagogy. A shift to collaborative classrooms, project-based learning, and dialogic teaching will typically reduce the amount of class preparation time. A teacher doesn't have to carefully preplan every minute of instruction, ensure memorization of key points, think of ways to sustain attention, discipline the inattentive, and so on. The direction of the day will be less regimented, with students joining in shaping the trajectory. The classroom is not dominated by the teacher's authority (and therefore the teacher's lone accountability), and the quality of learning becomes a shared responsibility.

There are further gains when we turn to developments in curricula. With emergent and inquiry-based curriculum, for example, teachers would no longer be saddled with delivering predetermined and externally imposed packages of knowledge. This would free time for them to work with students as co-inquirers into the myriad ways of knowing and learning, and thus as co-creators of curricula. Such curricula also tend to be more personalized and engaging for the students involved. This would also mean time saved from disciplining recalcitrant students, dealing with stress and anxiety, and working with students who are disaffected and disenfranchised. As we take up in the next chapter, this emphasis on co-inquiry, also favors inviting the participation of the broader community. With testing and grading out of the way, parents, caretakers, and other local stakeholders can join in supporting and enriching students' learning. Again, demands on teacher time are reduced.

Without Grades, Where Is the Rigor?

The possibility of education without grades is shocking to many. Grades and periodic summaries or report cards are simply basic to school life. Yet, as we have tried to demonstrate, grades reflect little of a student's learning experience, provide little guidance on future planning, and primarily function as control devices with injurious effects on relationships. The issue of grading students has a long history of controversy[17] and has spawned equal interest in meaningful alternatives.[18] As we have proposed, through relationally sensitive practices of evaluation, students do receive useful feedback, and once the threat of judgment is removed they can be inspired in their learning. Of special importance, students are not identified in terms of their relative superiority or inferiority with respect to arbitrary and poorly reasoned standards. With a shift to more emergent and personalized curricula, as just discussed, practices of evaluating students by comparing them with each other are largely discarded. Students' learning experiences may indeed be evaluated, but these evaluations are largely tied to their own individual progress. We may thus welcome the broad, international movement to abandon grading in schools.[19] While this movement is especially pronounced in primary schools, it is moving into secondary schools as well. The future should see its full flowering.

One of the strongest arguments against this movement concerns rigor. Many ask, "Where is the rigor in practices of relational evaluation?" "How do we know anything is actually being learned?" This objection is primarily born out of suspicion: relational practices of evaluation seem to depend on the teacher's subjective intuitions, and, given the emphasis on student–teacher relationships, the room for bias is enormous. This is in comparison to what is viewed as the objective or value-neutral precision of tests However, as we have tried to show, tests are never value-neutral. They will always favor certain groups over others, and the biases here are systemic; they imperceptibly favor a hierarchical social structure.

At the same time, there is a legitimate space in the present analysis for performance testing: that is, standardized tests of skills or knowledge in a given area of study. At various points in time a student may wish to know how he or she has progressed in mastering a given content area. "In my field of interest, where am I in terms of knowing what is essential?" Closely related, in many secondary schools there has been increasing reliance on *standards-based learning*.[20] Rather than a lock-step curriculum with frequent grading, students are liberated to learn in many different ways and at differing speeds. However, they are guided by the fact that they will ultimately be assessed in terms of a common performance standard. There are wide variations in how standards-based learning programs are realized. Where standards govern across the course curriculum and performance is graded, such programs approximate assessment in the factory tradition. However, standards-based learning can be restricted to those particular content areas—such as reading and biology—where equality in education is essential. Competitive grading can be eliminated in favor of personalized feedback on performance. In this context there will be spaces for thriving relationships. We return to these issues shortly.

Without Measurement, Where Is Accountability?

It is often said that exams and testing have important instructive value for teachers, administrators, and policy-makers. As commonly argued, standardized assessment devices give teachers information on how well their classes are absorbing the curricula content, they provide administrators information on teacher efficacy, and they inform policy-makers on how school systems are functioning. In each case, it is argued, those in charge need information so they can do a better job. In this light, relational practices of evaluation might seem deficient in furnishing sound facts for effective decision-making. Let us examine this critique more carefully.

At the outset, there are all the problems with measurement discussed in preceding chapters—problems of validity, insensitivity, effects on the learning process, class biases, and so on. Let us ask further about what we actually learn from test scores. For example, to revisit an earlier point, what does a teacher learn from knowing his or her class average for a national test? As pointed out, students differ in their abilities, interests, personalities, socioeconomic backgrounds, and so on. What does it mean, then, if the class average is below the national standard on a given test? Is it the particular composition of the class, the teaching methods, the weather on the day in which the test was given, the particular subject topic, or something else? What if the class does exceedingly well, how is one to interpret this success? Now contrast these problems with what the teacher can gauge about students' learning through relational approaches to feedback and learning review. Here the teacher can acquire intimate knowledge of each student's interests, levels of thinking and articulation, personal qualities, family circumstances, and so on. Such information can be truly helpful for the teacher in adjusting to the individual student's needs and learning trajectory.

School principals and local school administrators are confronted with the same ambiguity in knowing how to interpret overall test scores for a teacher's class or for the school as a whole. If one cannot determine what precisely is measured, then the very idea of a valid measure evaporates. There is also the question of comparison: To what should such scores be compared? Should the scores be compared with those in the preceding year? This is scarcely appropriate given multiple fluctuations from year to year. And if one compares a given year with a pattern across time, is this reflecting a shift in the ethnic or class composition of the class, national trends, or other factors? And how many years constitute a significant pattern?

One may raise similar questions about comparisons across schools. Administrators wish to know how a school is performing in comparison to others. But what others? Even nearby schools will differ in students' cultural composition, socioeconomic status, and so forth. Test scores will be affected accordingly. What about regional or national comparisons? The same challenge repeats itself: public schools tend to have strikingly different characteristics—inner-city schools, small suburban schools, village schools. What would count as a fair comparison? Of course, the local problem of interpreting differences is duplicated at the regional and national levels. And there is the closely related question of judging a meaningful difference. In comparing schools, how many test points may constitute "a difference that makes a difference?" In effect, test scores scarcely provide the kinds of facts essential for effective decision-making. Evidence-based decisions of this kind provide only the illusion of rational policy-making.

We must finally question the very idea that policymakers and leaders should be judging the efforts of schools. Presumed here is a form of hierarchical decision making with its roots in the factory metaphor of education. Relying on test scores to make judgements of others' performance reinforces the hierarchy and maintains top-down control. At the same time, it sews the seeds of alienation and distrust. Consider that different realities and rationalities are co-created by those within different levels of the hierarchy. The realities in which teachers live are not the same as those of the administrators, the local government leaders, or senior policymakers. For those at the lower levels, the policies of those on high may seem ill-formed or oppressive; those on high may be suspicious of those below. "What are they really up to?". It is just this kind of alienated relationship that has led school administrators and teachers to falsify student performance indicators.[21] In sum, the ethos of hierarchy and control is toxic. It is at this point that our proposal for relational evaluation speaks to the very organization of educational systems.

How, then, might we restructure the process of decision-making so that relational well-being is in the forefront of our concerns? We are scarcely alone in asking such a question. Already there is an ample literature on shared or distributed leadership in schools,[22] and many schools now see the possibility of replacing top-down leadership with collaborative teams.[23] The extensive literature on relational leading in organizations is also germane.[24] Here the chief emphasis is on leadership that emerges from and sustains generative relations. Leadership is not located within persons but within the relational process. Here, organizational studies have illustrated the rich potentials of collaborative decision-making.[25] When decisions reflect multiple perspectives, they gain in sophistication and strength. Theories and practices of collaborative governance are also making their way into public services.[26] All work in concert with relational practices of evaluation. All move us toward replacing the traditional organizational structure—in schools and in society at large—with processes of relational coordination.

What About National Standards?

There is active discussion both within countries and across nations concerning educational standards. "Are our standards high enough?" "Are our schools failing to meet national standards?" "How might we raise our standards to compete with other countries?" The concerns with educational "standards" may seem reasonable at first glance. It has been a major source of educational reforms on the both sides of the Atlantic, and a key stimulus in the Organization for Economic Cooperation and Development's (OECD) creation of an international program for student assessment (PISA). By definition, a *standard* is a reference point against which other things can be evaluated. It is here that significant questions follow. First, why should any administrative group set standards for schools without engaging those for whom the requirements are life-changing? Why should there be a single standard—for example, in math or reading—without first discussing the rationale, the need, and the ramifications with those who must meet this benchmark? There is also the question of the logic by which such standards are determined. The issues are enormously complex, involving employment needs, the economy, cultural history, cultural composition, technology, global relations, imagined futures, and more. How, then, are decisions derived? Why are the rationales not more transparent and open to public discussion?

Of further importance is the way in which established standards restrict the range of subjects. As the range of subject matters is decreased, so do we close down on what we may know. As the range of our knowledge is restricted, so are our capacities for deliberation and innovation. When verbal literacy serves as the standard, for example, we shut down potentials in digital literacy and visual literacy. Ultimately, the well-being of the society suffers. It is through multiple approaches, resources, and strengths that we survive and thrive. Particularly in the context of the climate emergency and rapid global change, a premium must be placed on diverse learning experiences and learning in all forms.

These arguments do not at all reject the abiding concern that all citizens acquire sufficient knowledge and skills for meaningful participation in society. As rightfully argued, social equality depends on equal-quality education for all. As we have seen, standardized curricula and tests favor the affluent, and in this sense perpetuate inequality. It may also be useful for certain students at certain times to know how well they have mastered a particular subject matter. However, in such instances, test scores would function formatively, providing a convenient yardstick. Here practices of standards-based learning may be applicable. With general standards of mastery established, students could volunteer to take the relevant tests at any point they felt equipped. Music performance is such an example. The question would not be how well they performed in comparison to others, but rather, where do they stand with respect to standards of mastery (knowledge and skills) within a particular field of study. If dissatisfied, they might re-take the test at a later date. Multiple attempts would be possible, with the view of reaching a level that is rewarding.

What About the Plight of Higher Education?

A major hurdle standing in the way of transformation in evaluation is the *problem of selection to institutions of higher learning*. Because of fierce competition for entrance, most students submit applications to multiple schools. Colleges, universities, and professional schools are thus deluged with applications, and reviewing them is a momentous task. One major way of lifting the weight—reducing the countless hours of subjective deliberation— is reliance on performance measures. Standardized test scores are the most obvious resources. In this case all applicants are evaluated along a continuum, and an efficient presorting is accomplished. Efficiency in making judgments is often assisted by student's course grades: grade point averages (GPAs) in the United States; A-levels, Business and Technology Education Council (BTEC), or General National Vocational Qualification (GNVQ) grades in the United Kingdom; the baccalauréat (BAC) in France; Gao-Kao grades in China;[27] and so on. For many students, parents, and institutions, the GPA or its equivalent serves as a numerical indicator of "mental merit" and a critical signal of the student's future. Indeed, colleges and universities often take pride in announcing the GPAs of their incoming students. Similar practices are applicable in most countries in the world.

So long as institutions of higher learning continue to insist on numerical scores, secondary and high schools will continue using traditional assessment devices. They would do so even if there were no national tests. Why? Because students and parents alike would insist on it. They are caught up in the "race to the top," and to remove the performance indicators would leave them floundering. Good scores signify superiority and the promise of future success. For the same reasons, parents pay large sums of money so their children can attend private schools, or move their residences so their children can enter better schools.[28] Yet, this reliance on grades and test scores for admission to higher education is a massive force in impoverishing education.

Putting aside the thorny issues of mis-measurement, what are the alternatives? This is becoming a serious question for institutions of higher education. In our view the task of evaluating students for advanced and higher learning should fall on the shoulders of these institutions themselves. Secondary and high school education should not be hostage to their needs. Rather, such institutions should create their own specialized forms of evaluation. There is ample reason for moving in this direction.

First, admissions boards are themselves uncomfortable with relying on tests and grades in judging student qualifications. They are well aware of the biases in test scores discussed in Chapter 1. It is partly for this reason that universities are increasingly opting out of relying on national tests such as the SATs. They are also aware that schools differ markedly in their demands on students. Identical grades from different schools mean different things. It is also difficult to discern what lies behind the "good" grades—a slavish devotion, a reliance on extra tutoring, perseverance in drilling for exams, class background, basic brilliance? There is little means of knowing.

In addition to the ambiguity of grades, colleges and universities differ in their emphases, cultural ethos, visions of an ideal student body, and so on. They may variously desire an international mix of students or distributions in religious, ethnic, socioeconomic background, interests, talents, skills, and so on. Summary scores on measures of remote relevance to these particular needs are of little value. If institutions of higher education must rely on quick and easy summaries, it would be far better if such scores were tied to their specific institutional needs.[29]

If universities and vocational or professional institutions did develop their own scanning and admissions methods, then secondary and high schools could furnish them with rich and detailed information on the work of individual students. Here we have in mind precisely the kind of information issuing from relational approaches to evaluation. Consider the personal record of school experience described in Chapter 5. In Medeley Court School in the United Kingdom, the student learning records are kept until the end of secondary education. The records can then be made available to specified universities. The Waring School in Massachusetts generates a narrative transcript charting the applicant's intellectual curiosity, academic strengths, and interests as a lifelong learner, along with evaluative comments from referees who truly know the candidate. The Waldorf schools also provide informative portfolio certificates. Personalized documents such as these can add rich dimension to more focused scanning and admissions methods. By relying on these more institutionally relevant selection practices, public education would be liberated.

Cultural Tensions and Educational Transformation

We have made a concerted case for relational process as the fundamental basis of successful education. To this end, practices of relationally sensitive evaluation can deepen learning, energize engagement, and enrich relationships. As proposed in this chapter, by incorporating such practices into school life we open the door to the full flowering of emerging innovations in relationally sensitive curriculum design, and pedagogy. These are precisely the shifts in education that are required for the challenges of a world of increasingly rapid and complex change. Yet, while this vision may be inspiring, its realization depends importantly on surrounding cultural conditions. Do such conditions stand in the way of transformation or place wind in the sails? Two of these cultural forces demand particular attention, not only because of their sweeping significance in the contemporary world, but because they are largely antithetical to each other. While the first buttresses and extends the scope of standardization and measurement, the second holds promise for an inevitable transformation.

Control Creep: Public Management and the Subjugation of Society

The cry for *evidence-based* practices is omnipresent. As we have characterized the rationale, reliable and accurate performance measures are essential to judging and improving the efficacy of our educational system. Sound evidence is needed to assess student mastery, teachers' effectiveness, school leadership, and more. Coupled with this cry for evidence is the need to economize. With limited funds for public education, the demand is to maximize performance at minimum cost. Increasingly, then, we are sucked into a world of tests, reports, questionnaires, and inspections. Ironically, as the demands have intensified, so have learning and well-being deteriorated.

Yet, education is scarcely the only domain in which the coupled cries for evidence and economizing are dominant. As many analysts see it, this demand is only one symptom of an increasingly expanding cultural movement. The quandary of our schools finds parallels in our corporations, public services, hospitals, communities, and more. In each case we seem headed for increasing controls, surveillance, and measurement in the service of economically efficient productivity. Much like the decay in education, life within these institutions has suffered. We are creating social worlds that are becoming unlivable for their denizens. A brief sketch of this development is useful in thinking through its consequences and alternatives.

Often characterized as the Enlightenment (or Age of Reason) the 17th and 18th centuries in the West gave birth to a scientific orientation to understanding and decision-making. Reliance on religious doctrine gave way to a trust in systematic observation and logic. Thus began the slow undermining of religious belief and its influence in shaping society. This was coupled with a slow expansion in the power of civil governance and, with it, public planning, bureaucracy, and public education. By the twentieth century, spurred by powerful advances in physics, chemistry, biology, and engineering, science emerged as a major cultural force.

It is important in the present context to note two significant features of this movement: first is its *emphasis on control*, and second the *absence of concern with ethics or values*. Scientific research is primarily devoted to revealing reliable patterns in nature, The ultimate goal is the capacity to explain and predict, primarily for purposes of control. It is not in the business of telling people what they *ought* to do. As commonly reasoned, if we understand the causes of an illness, we may control their effects; if we understand the factors that influence the growth of crops, we can ensure a better harvest. Over the course of the twentieth century, this logic was increasingly applied to patterns of human behavior. There is obvious utility, for example, in charting demographic changes, crime rates, illiteracy, and poverty. With good measures in hand, we feel that we may gain control over the future.

However, in the applications of science to human affairs, the scientific worldview rapidly began to infiltrate everyday life. One of the most prominent examples is the advent of *Taylorism in the industrial world of the 1930's*. With its emphasis on time-motion measurements of worker proficiency, there emerged an orientation to management that remains with us today. The common practice of performance evaluation in the corporate world is but one outcome. Such assessments enable management to use subtle forms of reward and punishment to affect productivity. Performance evaluation also influences who will rise or fall within the organization. The emphasis on control and assessment is also reflected in the institutions of public administration. The idea of public administration emerged in the Enlightenment, with its alliance to the scientific orientation rapidly expanding in the nineteenth century. By the twentieth century, administrative bureaucracies were flourishing, with reliance increasingly placed on data gathering and statistics. As commonly understood today, the central pillars in public administration include economy, efficiency, and effectiveness.

As the scientific worldview has increasingly insinuated itself into cultural life, there is an associated loss of concern with human values. Science is said to be impartially objective in its accounts of the world. Human values (other than those built into science itself) thus represent threats to scientific objectivity. There is only one world, according to this view, and scientific reports on this world should not be influenced by one's religion, political views, personal desires, and the like. Increasingly, then, we come to see values are "merely subjective" or "matters of taste." As the social sciences blossomed in the twentieth century, the philosophy of ethics was dwarfed by the philosophy of science.

Here we also glimpse a major reason for public education's largely antiseptic treatment of value issues. Public education should teach the facts, it is said, and not proselytize. Classroom discussions of pressing social issues, for example, the right to bear weapons, immigration, gender fluidity, or racial discrimination, must proceed with caution, if they are allowed at all. Schools provide few opportunities for ethical and moral reflection or for participation in productive dialogues where values clash.[30]

At the same time, this empty space of value deliberation has provided an opening for an unquestioned good: material wealth. If we are human beings living in a material world, as science suggests, then no philosophy is needed to justify the desire for material well-being. Material wealth (as symbolized by money) is by definition valuable; to acquire money is to achieve the good.[31] Other values—such as honesty, justice, generosity, or beauty—are peripheral.

At the same time, one's accumulation of wealth is coupled with capacities for control. To possess wealth is to have the means of hiring or influencing the needy or less wealthy. The capacity of large corporations to purchase the decisions of those who govern is but one example. The drive to enhance power through wealth is furthered by competition. Darwin's writing on the survival of the species prepares the way. As commonly understood, we are fundamentally locked in a competition,[32] and survival depends on superiority. Because wealth stands as the major means of control, the Darwinian perspective has become closely allied with free-market capitalism. Corporate profits distinguish between the strong and the weak, between the good and the undesirable. For much of the West, these visions of the world are now entrenched in the political landscape. The goal of governing the society became increasingly linked to economic growth and competition. As we touched on at the beginning of this book, the term *neoliberal* has come to signify a movement—especially in the United States and the United Kingdom—in which government policies give license to corporations to seek their own good: that is, to compete successfully. Free enterprise, it is argued, will ultimately favor the common good. The riches accumulated at the top, it is promised, will "trickle down" to all. This has meant removing restrictions from the operation of corporations, banks, and other economic enterprises. Such values as equality, justice, and compassion are largely discarded in favor of a posture of "anything goes, so long as you can afford a top defense lawyer."

In sum, we confront a condition in which control, measurement, economic gain, and competition now form a dangerously potent combination.[33] When those in power are armed with surveillance devices and united by the pursuit of economic gain, there is little to deter their growth and prosperity. Policies can be determined by those in power, assessment practices assure their implementation, and all can be justified in the name of economic competition. To have power and wealth increases one's power and wealth. In the United States, for example, one percent of the population now owns more than 30 percent of the nation's wealth. We may characterize these developments as *control creep*, a cultural process in which "just acting logically"—making money, making sure things are functioning efficiently, and beating the competition—are creating generalized misery. Human beings are readily redefined as commodities, data points, percentiles, profiles, target audiences, and customers. The process functions like a mold that slowly and stealthily robs a house of its capacity for human inhabitation.[34] And this drift has increasingly shifted toward the public sector. Coupled with the concept of "new public management," it has become attractive to convert hospitals, prisons, public transportation, and universities to economic enterprises. With the metaphor of schools as factories, the groundwork was already prepared for the invasion of public education.

In this book, we point the way to an internal revolution in education, a revolution set against the force of creeping control. Working from the ground up, teachers, school administrators, parents, and other stakeholders may implement and support educational practices that can enrich both learning and the relationships on which it relies. Here lie the well-springs for restructuring practices of policy-making in such a way that top-down control, surveillance, efficiency, and economy cease to be dominant. When the well-being of relationships is valued, there is no *center* of power; decisions emerge from relational process. In the cultural context of control creep, is such a transformation possible? A second cultural movement provides hope.

The Technology Tempest: Disorder and Its Consequences

Simultaneous to this creeping urge to order is a contravening cultural force: technology. Most focally, we have in mind the massive development and dissemination of information communication technology (ICT). Within the past three decades we have come to live in a world of instantaneous, global, and around-the-clock connection. These technologies function as a continuous, dynamic source of new knowledge, multiple opinions, updated information, innovative ideas, inspirations, ideals, social movements, and political unrest. As a result, they challenge all attempts to stabilize, structure, standardize, or universalize. Such technologies are rapidly making their way into educational institutions, affecting the ways we conceptualize learning and teaching along with meaning of schooling itself.

One might justifiably argue that such transformation began from the bottom up rather than top down—that is, within the student population as opposed to the teaching profession. Because of their increasingly sophisticated use of such technology, many young people know more about environmental topics, gender issues, food health, technology, music, sports, fashion, space travel, and prehistoric animals than their parents or teachers. Outside the classroom walls, they also acquire new ranges of know-how, for example to compose electronic music, generate films, create online games, and even build their own personal computers. Many children have already embarked on courses of personalized learning by the time they enter primary school. To be sure, the tech industries have long seen the economic potentials of the educational market. Computers and electronic notebooks are now commonplace, with cell phones becoming instruments of learning, and virtual reality technology and 3-D printing in the offing. Technological innovation and student enthusiasms converge.

Numerous educators have added both theoretical and practical dimensions to these movements.[35] In terms of our preceding discussion, their challenging deliberations conjoin with the enthusiasms of students and the tech industry. Together they work toward transforming the major pillars of education: curriculum, pedagogy, and assessment/evaluation. Many of these transformations invite precisely the forms we are advocating. Consider the matter of curricula.

The traditional view of a fixed curriculum, pegged to specific age groups and common across school systems, is slowly becoming fossilized. The reasons are several: in a stable world, fixed and relevant curricula may be useful. In the digital world, one cannot predict what students will need to know in the future. As a graduation speaker at Harvard Business School reputedly announced, "Everything you have learned here is now irrelevant." In effect, it is not mastering "what is known" that is essential, but how to engage in continuous learning and creative improvisation. The unpredictable character of emerging demands requires a population with highly varied potentials. Diversity is a major ally to a flourishing society; standardization is its enemy. We are now at risk of educating students for a world of the past, where little that they learn is relevant to the challenges ahead. Finally, curricula structured around separate disciplines create silos. One learns and practices within the reality of the silos. However, the infinitely complex problems of the future—often called "wicked problems"—require dialogue, integration of perspectives, and innovation. The current trend toward inter- and transdisciplinary initiatives in higher education is a barometer of what is to come.

Turning to pedagogy, the Digital Revolution also means that the teacher ceases to be the primary source of knowing.[36] Students will have advanced knowledge and opinions in many subjects about which the teacher is ignorant. Equally, their interest in these domains can be intense. The teacher's role subtly shifts, then, toward facilitating, guiding, counseling, creating opportunities, setting limits, and serving in other ways that enable students to navigate the learning processes. As described earlier, the teacher becomes a learning partner, or co-inquirer. This opening to individualized learning is also coupled with a widespread movement toward blended learning (integrating digital with face-to-face) and computerized classrooms. Here, ICT also facilitates dialogic and collaborative learning. As quickly surmised, the walls of the classroom are slowly dissolved. Students learn how to engage effectively with the global flow of information, opinion, values, and innovation.

In terms of assessment, technology has long been used to improve the efficiency of scoring standardized tests. However, with increased sophistication in ICT, it is now possible to gear evaluation to the specific learning trajectories of the individual student. Already in place are means of providing students with continuous feedback as they attempt—as in computer games—to enhance their skills in subjects such as math and second-language learning.[37] Through ICT it is also possible for students to report on their learning experiences, states of well-being, and class dynamics on a continuous basis. Review of students' classwork can also be done digitally: learning journals, portfolios, and records of progress can all be stored digitally and reviewed online. Such technologies supply a further answer to the earlier question of the time cost for teachers' evaluative dialogue with students. In all these ways, developments in technology support a movement toward relational dimensions of evaluation.

Beyond Order and Chaos: Co-Creation

In a broad sense, the forces for both order and disorder are inherent in our social existence. We strive to achieve and sustain what is good in our lives, and the ordering that results is simultaneously constraining. In today's world, both counterforces are mobilized as never before, with each intensifying the activity of the other. As we hone the devices of control, so do we impassion the quest for freedom; as the technologies of communication release constraints, greater surveillance is required. Organizational theorists have long been concerned with these conflicting tendencies, especially as the demands for organizational proficiency confront increasingly rapid and uncontrollable disruptions. One of the most evocative concepts to emerge from these discussions is that of the *chaordic* organization. How, it is asked, can we develop organizations that recognize the value of order and the demands for change? How can these otherwise conflicting forces be integrated into the organization, just possibly adding to its vitality?

These are indeed rich questions for the future of education. How do we integrate the needs and traditions of society with technology's invitations to everywhere? To be sure, the major thrust of the present work has leaned toward liberation. Placed in question are tests, grades, standardized measures, and other accouterments of control. Embraced are dialogic processes in which growth, creativity, and plural worlds are in the forefront. However, it would be major mistake to conclude that we thus advocate an "anything goes" orientation to education. We are quite willing to replace the factory orientation to education with a vision of schools as sites for enriching the ongoing process of co-creating meaning. However, as proposed in Chapter 2, a major purpose of education is to enhance the potentials of the young for participating in society's spheres of social process. Because cultural life carries with it traditions of enormous significance, these must figure importantly in the educational process. Language is a good case in point. Meaningful participation in society is vitally dependent on skills in language. At the same time, such languages have often been forged by centuries of co-creative exchange.

To speak intelligibly is to carry the voices of a cultural past. To be skilled in a language is to be skilled in a tradition.

While honoring cultural traditions, including those of the professional worlds, it is also imperative that such traditions are not frozen in place. All our traditions have emerged through a co-creative process—people coordinating words and actions within particular times and circumstance. To systematize and regulate these traditions is to cripple the very process from which they emerged. It is to fossilize tradition, rendering it progressively irrelevant to contemporary conditions and to addressing the future. It is thus that educational institutions should place the co-creative process toward the center of its concerns. As proposed, this process should be nourished and sustained in pedagogy, curriculum, and evaluation. It is through this process that traditions may be taken up as resources for actively and imaginatively creating viable futures.

Notes

1. Note should also be taken of the expanding enrollments in private schools concerned with student well-being and the quality of relating. Here we include such classic models of innovation as the Waldorf, Montessori, Reggio Emilia, and Society of Friends schools, along with charter and magnet schools in the United States, the United World Colleges, and the human-centered and democratic movements in education.
2. Here we employ Bernstein's concept of three interrelated aspects of education: curriculum, pedagogy, and assessment. Bernstein, B. (1977) *Class Codes and Control: Towards a Theory of Educational Transmissions*. London: Routledge and Keegan Paul.
3. See also Robinson, K. (2001) *Out of Our Minds: Learning to Be Creative*. Chichester, UK: Capstone; Wagner, T. (2012) *Creating Innovators: The Making of Young People Who Will Change the World*. New York: Scribner; Wagner, T., and Dintersmith, T. (2016) *Most Likely to Succeed: Preparing Our Kids for the Innovation Era*. New York: Scribner; and Clapp, E. P. (2016) *Participatory Creativity: Introducing Access and Equality to the Creative Classroom*. New York: Routledge.
4. See Gill, S., and Thomson, G. (2012) *Rethinking Secondary Education: A Human-Centred Approach*. London: Pearson Education.
5. Darling, J. (1993) *Child-Centred Education and Its Critics*. London: Sage Publications.
6. Malaguzzi, L. (1996) *The Hundred Languages of Children: The Reggio Emilia Approach to Early Childhood Education*. New Jersey: Ablex Publishing; Hart, S., Dixon, S., Drummond, M., and McIntyre, D. (2004) *Learning Without Limits*. London: Open University Press; Stacey, S. (2009) *Emergent Curriculum in Early Education*

Settings: From Theory to Practice. St Paul, MN: Redleaf Press; Wein, C. (ed.) (2008) *Emergent Curriculum in the Primary Classroom: Interpreting the Reggio Emilia Approach in Schools*. New York/Washington, DC: Teachers College Press/National Association for the Education of Young Children.

7. See Dewey, J. (1938) *Logic: The Theory of Inquiry*. New York: Holt, Rinehart, and Winston.

8. For an outline of Reggio Emilia's educational philosophy and pedagogical features, see Malaguzzi, *The Hundred Languages of Children*, or visit the Reggio Emilia website: https://www.reggiochildren.it/identita/reggio-emilia-approach/?lang=en

9. More details about the HTH Schools, visit their website: www.hightechhigh.org

10. See more about Agora Schools at their website: https://niekee.nl/agora-vmbo-havo-vwo

11. See interviews with students captured in Gill and Thomson, *Rethinking Secondary Education*.

12. Ibid.

13. See, for example, Skidmore, D., and Murakami, K. (eds.) (2017) *Dialogic Pedagogy: The Importance of Dialogue in Teaching and Learning*. Bristol, UK: Multilingual Matters Press; Matusov, E. (2009) *Journey into Dialogic Pedagogy*. Haupaugge, NY: Nova Science; Littleton, K., and Mercer, N. (2013) *Interthinking: Putting Talk to Work*. London: Routledge; Barkley, E., Cross, K., and Major, C. (2005) *Collaborative Learning Techniques*. San Francisco: Wiley; McAllister, C. (2011) *Unison Reading: Socially Inclusive Group Instruction for Equity and Achievement*. Thousand Oaks, CA: Corwin; Pack, B. (2019) *The Cooperative Classroom*. Independently published; van den Linden, J., and Renshaw, P. (2004) *Dialogic Learning: Shifting Perspectives to Learning, Instruction and Teaching*. New York: Springer; and Mercer, N., et al. (eds.) (2019) *The Routledge International Handbook of Research on Dialogic Education*. New York: Routledge.

14. Freire, P. (1970) *Pedagogy of the Oppressed*. New York: Continuum.

15. See Dewey, J. (1916) *Democracy and Education*. New York: Macmillan; Dewey, J. (1938) *Experience and Education*. New York: Collier; Lave, J., and Wenger, E. (1991) *Situated Learning: Legitimate Peripheral Participation*. Cambridge: Cambridge University Press; and Wenger, E. (1999) *Communities of Practice. Learning, Meaning and Identity*. Cambridge: Cambridge University Press.

16. Gill, S., and Thomson, G. (2016) *Human-Centred Education: A Handbook and Practical Guide*. London: Routledge.

17. See, for example, Barnes, M. (2015) *Assessment 3.0: Throw Out Your Grade Book and Inspire Learning*. Thousand Oaks, CA: Corwin; Dueck, M. (2014) *Grading Smarter, Not Harder: Assessment Strategies That Motivate Kids and Help Them Learn*. Alexandria, VA: Association for Supervision and Curriculum Development; Sackstein, S. (2015) *Hacking Assessment: 10 Ways to Go Graceless in a Traditional Grades School*. Cleveland, OH: Times10 Publications.

18. Berdik, C. (2018). "What's school without grade levels?" The Hechinger Report. *Future of Learning*, July 30, 2018 https://hechingerreport.org/whats-school-without-grade-levels/

19. Examples are found in many parts of the world, including project-based learning at Warren New Tech in rural North Carolina; the "No Grades No Grades" approach to learning in Pittsfield School District in rural New Hampshire; and the competency-based learning approach, where students receive credits for learning at their own pace in 40 schools in New York City, as documented in Spencer, K. (2017) "A new kind of classroom: No grades, no failing, no hurry," *The New York Times*, August 11, 2017.

20. A challenging movement is now taking place within private secondary schools in the United States to replace traditional transcripts with more particularized competency-based documentation. Colleges and universities would not be supplied with an applicant's list of courses and grades, but instead evidence of the level of mastery achieved by a student over a wide range of competencies. See Jaschik, S. (2017) "A plan to kill high school transcript . . . and transform admissions," *Inside Higher Education,* May 10.

21. See, for example, www.publicschoolreview.com/blog/when-teachers-cheat-the-standardized-test-controversies

22. Lave, J., and Wenger, E. (1991) *Situated Learning: Legitimate Peripheral Participation.* Cambridge: Cambridge University Press; MacBeath, J. (1998) *Effective Leadership in a Time of Change.* London: Paul Chapman Publishing; Spillane, J., Halverson, R., and Diamond, J. (2001) "Investigating school leadership practice: a distributed perspective," *Educational Researcher*, 30(3): 23–28; and Spillane, J. (2006) *Distributed Leadership*. San Francisco, CA: Jossey-Bass.

23. For example, Rubin, H. (2009) *Collaborative Leadership: Developing Effective Partnerships for Communities and Schools.* Thousand Oaks, CA: Corwin.

24. See, for example, Cooperrider, D., and Whitney, D. (1999) *Appreciative Inquiry.* San Francisco, CA: Berrett-Koehler; Gergen, K. (2009) *An Invitation to Social Construction* (2nd ed.). London: Sage; Gergen, K. (2010) *Relational Being.* New York: Oxford University Press; and Pearce, C., and Conger, J. (2003) *Shared Leadership: Reframing the Hows and Whys of Leadership.* Thousand Oaks, CA: Sage.

25. Brazer, S., Rich, W., and Ross, S. (2010) "Collaborative strategic decision making in school districts," *Journal of Educational Administration*, 48(2): 196–217; Cranston, N. (2001) "Collaborative decision-making and school-based management: challenges, rhetoric and reality," *Journal of Educational Enquiry*, 2(2): 1–24; Supovitz, J., and Tognatta, N. (2013) "The impact of distributed leadership on collaborative team decision making," *Leadership and Policy in Schools*, 12(2): 101–121.

26. For example, Grandori, A. (2009) "Innovation, uncertainty and relational governance," *Industry and Innovation*, 13(2): 127–133; and Ansell, C., and Gash, A. (2007) "Collaborative governance in theory and practice," *Journal of Public Administration Research and Theory*, 18: 543–571. See also https://relationalwelfare.wordpress.com

27. Gao-Kao refers to the national college or university entrance exam in China.

28. Green, F., Anders, J., Henderson, M., and Henseke, G. (2017) "Who chooses private schooling in Britain and why?" LLAKES Research Paper 62. London: Centre for Learning and Life Chances in Knowledge Economies and Societies.

29. Wagner and Dintersmith, *Most Likely to Succeed.*

30. For a discussion of the restoration of ethics in public education, see Gill, S. & Thomson, G. (eds.). (in press). *Ethical Education: Towards an Ecology of Human Development.* Cambridge: Cambridge University Press.

31. It is informative to consult an online source for synonyms for the word "value." In a recent search, we were supplied with the following: *merit, worth, usefulness, use, utility, practicality, advantage, desirability, benefit, gain, profit, good, effectiveness, efficacy, importance, significance, point,* and *sense.* All carry echoes of a world in which value and acquiring money are closely related. The only entries that suggested a more humane domain of value were *help, helpfulness,* and *assistance.*

32. See for instance, Thomas Hobbes's argument on human nature in his 1651 book, 'Leviathan', and Charles Darwin's theory of evolution.

33. Peters, M. A. (2011). *Neoliberalism and After?: Education, Social Policy, and the Crisis of Western Capitalism.* New York: Peter Lang.

34. See also Dahler-Larsen, P. (2011). *The Evaluation Society.* Palo Alto, CA: Stanford Business School Press.

35. See, for example, Wegerif, R. (2014) *Dialogic: Education for the Internet Age.* London: Routledge; Collins, A., and Halverson, R. (2009). *Rethinking Education in the Age of Technology.* New York: Teachers College Press; U.S. Department of Education (2017) *Reimagining the Role of Technology in Education: 2017 National Education Technology Plan Update.* Washington DC: Office of Educational Technology; and Sullivan, F. R. (2017) *Creativity, Technology, and Learning.* New York: Routledge. Also see www.watchknowlearn.org/; www.edutopia.org/videos.

36. See, for instance, the Khan Academy offerings to students worldwide: https://halcyonschool.com

37. See, for example, the personalized learning practices of the High-Tech high schools in San Diego, California: https://www.hightechhigh.org/about-us/

9

Toward Systemic Transformation in Education

> We are tied together in the single garment of destiny, caught in an inescapable network of mutuality. And whatever affects one directly affects all indirectly.
>
> —Martin Luther King Jr.

There were times when we could view exams, tests, and other forms of educational assessment as aids to learning. We hoped they might guide students, teachers, and schools toward enriching the process of learning. Yet these aids to learning are now becoming the primary goals of education. Far from reflecting the capacities or celebrating the accomplishments of students, teachers, or institutions, the assessments now define what is good and what is less so. The measures are blind to almost all that is central to the lives of the participants and they undermine the process of learning itself. Such laments have long been voiced, and while there is a resounding harmony among many who seek alternatives, sweeping change has not resulted. The major resistance to change, as we see it, lies in the long-standing vision of education as a system of production. As discussed in Chapter 1, like factories, schools have been viewed as rationally designed assembly lines whose aim is to manufacture standardized products. So long as this factory metaphor remains in place, there is little room for significant change.

Our hope in this work is, first of all, to furnish an alternative vision of the educational process. As put forward in Chapter 2, schools are not structures to be managed, but are more akin to conversations in motion. Students, teachers, administrators, and staff all participate in an ongoing process of co-creating meaning. The walls of the school are artificial boundary markers with conversations crossing the threshold in both directions. Because these

Beyond the Tyranny of Testing. Kenneth J. Gergen and Scherto R. Gill, Oxford University Press (2020). © Oxford University Press. DOI: 10.1093/oso/9780190872762.001.0001.

conversations take place fluidly across multiple sites—merging, shifting, and conflicting in novel ways—we may begin to see the school as an active, living process of relating. Whether learning is inspiring or deadening, classrooms are exciting or boring, school activities are absorbing or frustrating, playgrounds are bubbling or frightening, homework is energizing or annoying—all depend on relational process. The character of this relational process affects whether teachers and administrators are fulfilled or emptied in their efforts, parents are supportive or punitive with their children, and community members are engaged or alienated from their local schools. Traditional assessment practices are deeply flawed, but their greatest damage is to the generative potentials of the relationships.

With relational process in the foreground, a new space is opened for thinking about how evaluation can contribute positively to education. In Chapter 3, we thus explored the rationale and potentials of evaluation in a relational key. Avoiding the term "assessment"—with its emphasis on measurement-based judgment—we were drawn to the notion of evaluation as a processes of *valuing*. Here, evaluation holds the potential for recognizing the centrality of care and caring in education and, therefore, in relationships. In this context, we proposed that relational evaluation should serve three major goals. First, evaluative practices should breathe life into the learning processes. With proper care, evaluation should excite students' interest in subject matter and build relevant capacities and skills. Second, relational approaches to evaluation should inspire students' continued engagement in the learning process. Here we highlighted the potential of evaluation to invite continuing curiosity and build the courage to explore. Finally, such evaluation should contribute to the quality of relationships. Here we stressed the ways in which evaluation might foster trust and mutual caring along with an appreciation of the relational process in itself.

While these objectives might seem idealistic, we turned in Chapter 4 to ways in which many primary schools have already set ground-breaking practices in motion. Here we distinguished between evaluation taking place within the process of ongoing interchange and evaluation reserved for periodic intervals of reflection. In the former case, crafted questions, peer collaboration, and appreciative feedback can all serve an evaluative function. In the place of periodic exams, we pointed to the use of learning reviews, portfolios, and formative feedback. All can be invaluable sources for inspiring and sustaining the learning process. Contributing particularly to generative relations, we centered on such practices as circle time reflection, dialogic inquiry, and project exhibition. These practices illustrate the multiple ways in which sensitive and caring evaluation can take place without reliance on tests and grades.

In Chapter 5, we explored practices of relational evaluation in secondary schools. Here we placed special importance on the contribution of dialogue to in-process evaluation. When carefully facilitated, dialogue contributes in multiple ways to evaluation. As alternatives to examinations, we illustrated the evaluative potentials of collaborative reflections and personal records to enhance learning. In their capacity to sustain engagement in learning, we pointed to the effects of learning journals and learning agreements. In their potential to build positive relations, we singled out the evaluative process occurring in learning groups.

A relational approach to evaluation also extends to teaching. Current assessment practices provide little useful information to help teachers develop. Using student performance to judge teachers can also undermine confidence and foster alienation. As we find, relationally enriched practices of evaluation can inject creative energy into the teaching process, while simultaneously supporting teachers' growth and learning. The process of evaluation, as we see it, should be integral to teachers' professional development. In Chapter 6, we outlined a fourfold framework for such development. Emphasized were practices of mutual learning among teachers, inviting students as learning partners, emphasizing teacher strengths and talents, and developing teachers' research into their practices.

Our existing approaches to assessments of schools suffer largely many of the same shortcomings as judging students and teachers. Especially important is the insensitivity of school inspections and standardized measures to local school needs and circumstances. In Chapter 7, we explored the potentials of two relationally sensitive alternatives to traditional school assessment. In the first, an Austrian school developed a way of carrying out its own evaluation. This process of whole-school evaluation is especially interesting in its attempt to draw the surrounding community into the process. A second illustration explored how New Zealand has implemented a form of school evaluation in which school evaluators work collaboratively with stakeholders of the school community in the evaluation processes. This is especially meaningful in the rich multicultural context of the country, where it is important to attend to both national and local concerns.

Thus we find relationally rich innovations in evaluation functioning at every level—from primary to secondary classrooms, to the professional development of teachers, and to the improvement of entire schools. As explored in the preceding chapter, a shift to relational evaluation has profound implications for education, because of its simultaneous alliance with active and wide-ranging developments in both pedagogy and curriculum planning. Pedagogies emphasizing dialogue, collaboration, and cooperation, for example, all appreciate the potentials of relational process to enrich learning. Similarly, the increasing reliance on emergent curricula provides a space for multiple learning trajectories. The full-flowering of these practices is stifled by traditional practices of assessment. In contrast, by replacing assessment practices with relational approaches to evaluation, we open the way to a major transformation in education.

Yet to replace the factory orientation with a relational vision of schooling, extended efforts are needed to support and sustain. If transformation is to flower, action is required on many fronts. Innovation in practices of evaluation, pedagogy, and curriculum are critical. But if generative relations lie at the heart of education, an active expansion in such relations may be a central ingredient of large-scale change.[1] We thus end this book with proposals for relation-enriching actions in the classroom, the whole school, the community, and in institutions of higher education.

Relational Practices in the Classroom

The primary site for developing relational well-being is the classroom, with teachers holding the most significant keys to reform. Thinking beyond relational practices of evaluation, what are the most promising courses of action? Throughout this book, we have championed the use of dialogue in the classroom, collaborative decision-making, and participatory projects. We have also had much to say about honoring multiple voices, appreciation, and caring interchange. These various discussions all point to a more general challenge: fostering *generative coordination*. As discussed in Chapter 2, such coordination contributes to the well-being of the participants as well as the strength of the relational process itself. Such relational processes are marked, for example, by mutual appreciation, insight, and creativity; they are constituted in dialogues where participants may reach new and significant understandings of themselves and the world around them. This is in contrast to *conventional* coordination, the unremarkable patterns of everyday interchange, and *degenerative* coordination, in which irritation, distrust, alienation, and anger are invited.

The significance of acquiring skills in generative coordination far exceeds its contribution to learning and school life. In many ways the global future depends on people's capacities for such forms of relating. As the world's peoples are increasingly on the move—both physically and virtually—we increasingly confront our differences. As problems with the environment, economies, human rights, social justice, advances in weaponry, lethal viruses, and so on are compounded, so is the speed at which their repercussions travel the world. These are conditions in which generative forms of relating are essential. Without skills in listening, understanding, appreciating, collaborating, and co-creating we are endangered.

At present, however, human skills in generative coordination are impoverished. We are well practiced in developing and defending our own interests, but positive coordination with others—and especially those who differ—is largely absent from our vocabularies of relating. In part we may trace such incapacity to our educational systems. For most schools, the focus is on the performance of the individual student. It is the "mental performance" of the individual that is focal. Broad programs to increase student self-esteem, along with practices of testing and grading, are among the byproducts of this view. Relationships *among* students are of little concern except that they might interfere with individual performance. The individual is trained to "think" alone but not to collaborate with others. Assignments may enhance the individual's capacity for monologue, but capacities for dialogue go unnoticed. As we shift the emphasis from individuals to relationships, we move toward more promising world futures.

What might this mean for common classroom activities? Such a question begs continuing conversation. There are no singular and solid routes to generative coordination. Patterns of relationship are always in motion, and we never participate in the same conversation twice. A phrase may be repeated, but its repetition may lack the significance as the original—simply because it is a repetition. Thus, we must view generative coordination as an art as opposed to a subject to be mastered. It is a way of being open, sensitive, and flexible. Here we focus on four arts of relational flourishing in the classroom.

The Art of Inquiring

Classroom inquiry is typically built around a question of some kind. Yet there are many ways to ask a question, and how such questions are crafted is all important to the quality of the relations that follow. To ask, "Who can give me the *right* answer to . . . ?" lends itself to a hierarchy of alienated relationships. Similarly, to query, "Who knows the *best* way to think about this problem . . . ?" may invite students to find fault with each other's ideas. To ask a group, "How would *you* like to carry this out . . . ?" will typically yield conflicting opinions and ultimate losers. In contrast, asking a class, "How many ways could *we* imagine X could happen . . . ?" invites everyone into the conversation. The question suggests the value of multiple voices and reinforces the sense of *we*-ness.

One of the most important challenges in many classrooms is crossing cultural and value divides. How can teachers facilitate questioning that invites participation into each other's realities with a sense of understanding? The finely crafted question can again play a role. Asking a teenager "What was it like to come here from X country?" not only defines the student as the "other," but may also leave the student grappling with how such a story will be judged by the surrounding class. In contrast, asking students to each come prepared to tell a story about a "time when I was really grateful for someone's help" can invite both curiosity and learning. Learning to pose meaningful questions can cultivate mutual care.

The Art of Listening

Central to relational processes is the art of listening. By listening, in this case, we do not mean the simple registering of incoming information, but rather a pro-active participation in other's offerings. Listening in this sense is an expression of respect and forms the ground for mutual care. In listening recognition is given to otherwise alien values and perspectives. Invited are humility and openness to the diversity of the lived realities within the classroom and beyond.[2] In listening, the traditional boundaries between teacher and student are softened as each absorbs the realities and values of the other. The more listening that occurs, the more the classroom becomes a site for openness and collaboration.

There are many ways that teachers can invite students into this form of listening. Some are subtle, such as arranging the seating in the classroom. When teachers and students sit in a circle facing each other, everyone is invited to listen. As ideas and experiences are expressed, their worth is acknowledged through others' attentiveness. This is in contrast to sitting in rows in front of the teacher, where others are not in view or only seen from the rear. Because the circle invites listening, it injects value into relationships. The art of listening may also be cultivated by creating spaces throughout the day for collective conversation. Learning circle activities (Chapter 4) are but one example. A class of children might also listen to music or a story together, or read aloud to each other. Indeed, they might be invited to sit in silence to listen to their own (silent) voices.

The Art of Appreciating

As reasoned earlier, one cannot make meaning alone. Every word or gesture, every piece of clothing, every styling of the hair, comes into meaning through others' acknowledgment. Most important in sustaining our ways of being are positive acts of recognition—a nod, a smile, or words of agreement. Or, to put it another way, we come alive as persons through others' appreciation. The power of appreciation is scarcely a surprise; long acknowledged are the enlivening effects of compliments, praise, commendations, positive feedback, and the like. As evident in previous chapters, appreciation is an integral part of many relational evaluation practices. It also plays a major role in the emergence of strengths-based teaching practices. Appreciative inquiry as a practice has been widely integrated into schools worldwide, with special application to whole-school transformation.[3]

However, expressing appreciation is also an art. There is first the fact that such expressions can be interpreted in many ways. For example: "is this flattery?," "she says this to everybody," "he is just trying to manipulate me." Further, when a teacher expresses appreciation selectively to students in a class, a space is opened for jealousy and conflict. The art of appreciation requires sensitivity, reflection, and innovation. There are many pathways for teachers wishing to practice this art. For example, teachers can invite students to share the high points of their day, to reflect on what has contributed positively to their learning, or to speak about what they have most appreciated about each other.[4] Likewise, students can provide appreciative feedback on the teacher's activities or reflect on aspects of the lesson that they have valued most. Especially important is developing forms of appreciation that value the relational process itself. Questions such as "What have *we* done well?" or "What do we most appreciate about our group?" are illustrative.

The Art of Disagreeing

In a world of multiple realities and values, disagreement is inevitable. Whether disagreement proves illuminating or destructive, however, depends on skills in the art of disagreeing. A relational perspective is particularly helpful here, as one realizes that all points of view, value commitments, political perspectives, and so on are byproducts of relationships. They only acquire meaning and significance within these relationships. To understand this is to foster a certain form of humility about one's own realities and values. This does not make one's realities and values less significant, but it encourages one to recognize that those who disagree are mirror images of oneself. Each of us only makes sense within a particular social tradition.

Disagreement is itself a form of relating. Unfortunately, the trajectory of disagreement is often degenerative, with each side resisting or attacking the opposition. We learn very well the practice of arguing, but argument is often war by other means. Its symbolic intent is to annihilate the other, even if verbally. In contemporary education, students may become quite skilled in developing a position and arguing against all who disagree. How can we expand the vocabulary of disagreement, and avoid the invitation into a degenerative slide into alienation? How can express differences with more positive potential?

There are many ways in which the arts of generative disagreement may be fostered. The use of personal stories as a means of expressing one's position does not have the polarizing effects of defending a principle. To speak of one's suffering as opposed to blaming the other for racism, for example, invites the otherwise racist into the experience. Asking students to explore doubts in their positions can add a touch of humility to the conversation. In having students seek areas of agreement on "what we would like to accomplish *together*," the focus on irresolvable difference can be replaced with an optimistic solidarity. In innovative classrooms, students might even role-play each other's positions. In each of these practices, alienation and antagonism are avoided and dialogue may move toward relational well-being.

We may also gain insight from educational practices in contexts of conflict. For example, educators in Greece have engaged in a long-term program to integrate otherwise alienated Muslim and Christian youth in the province of Thrace.[5] In this case workshops were developed in collaboration with participants from both communities. Common activities were created, and an outreach program established to bring the community into the process. A major emphasis was placed on building skills of relating.

Relations in the Whole School

Here we shift the focus from enriching the relational life of the classroom to that of the whole school. In addition to efforts within the classroom, teachers and administrators can mobilize initiatives that vitally contribute to a relationally rewarding environment. Here we point to two such opportunities.

Collaborative and Participatory Decision-Making

Dialogue within classrooms can reduce the distance between teachers and students and define them as partners in teaching and learning. Leadership and power are thus shared in the learning processes, and responsibilities for learning become collaborative. With the active contribution of school administrators, the same logic can be applied at the whole-school level. Dialogic and collaborative decision-making in this context provide a fertile alternative to the corrosive logics of command and control and silo-like structuring favored by the factory metaphor. No longer would teachers and students be defined as *governed* or *led*, but instead be positioned as active participants in the governance process. With a voice in forming the future, governance becomes dialogue.

Inspiration for such a transformation can be drawn from the whole-school evaluation practices discussed in Chapter 8. There it was possible to bring together administrators and staff, along with parents and students themselves, in deliberating on the community's well-being.[6] In terms of cultivating students as future participants in society, the implications are substantial. The school becomes a learning laboratory for young citizens, enhancing their capacities for contributing to democratic processes. In learning how to collaborate more fully and effectively, students can recognize that differences in perspectives and values and ways of life can enrich and strengthen society. Education can thus contribute to participatory governance and, ultimately, a more harmonious and peaceful world.

Cultures of Inquiry in Schools

All evaluation—whether traditional tests or sensitive dialogue—reflects the assumptions and values of the evaluators. Partly for this reason we have emphasized the advantages of continuous multi-party dialogue. This reasoning also applies to whole-school culture. One major means of stimulating multi-party dialogue is through collective inquiry. In Chapter 7, for example, we discussed how teachers learned to carry out collective research into their own practices. They formed a small enclave of inquiry within the school from which illumination and mutual appreciation resulted. In our view, the entire school can reap such benefits. With the imaginative efforts of teachers and administrators, schools can become thriving cultures of inquiry.

Movement in this direction would be facilitated by ensuring that the school staff acquires skills in action-based inquiry. In turn, such inquiry would become a building block for project-based learning within the class. In effect, students would become reflective researchers.[7] Ultimately, such inquiry could usefully be directed to the whole school itself. Consider the outcome of collective inquiry into such questions as "What counts as good learning?" "How can we work together to enhance the learning experience?" "What are the purposes and values of education?" and "How should the school be evaluated?" From a relational standpoint, the answers to such questions should be not be imposed from outside but be matters of central community concern.

Relations in the Wider Community

We have consistently emphasized the ways in which relational evaluation lends itself to the development of schools as learning communities. As also proposed, the learning community should ideally extend beyond the walls of the school. Actively pursuing relationships with the surrounding community is thus invited. In this process all may flourish. Here we touch on two significant avenues to community connection.

Parents as Full Collaborators

Traditional assessment practices often drive a wedge between the young and their parents. As pointed out in Chapter 2, exam-related stress, anxiety, and depression are commonly linked to parental expectations and demands for high grades. In contrast, relational evaluation shifts the parental role from critic to collaborator in the child's education. This shift in roles can be significantly facilitated by teachers and school administrators. As discussed in Chapters 4 and 5, by inviting parents to sit in on project presentations, portfolio discussions, and learning reviews, they become partners in their children's education. In taking part in these activities, they demonstrate support of their children. They are encouraged to take an interest in their children's assignments, lend their enthusiasm, and offer advice.

We see such practices as steps toward a larger vision, one in which parents become partners in teaching and learning. Many schools already make use of parents as adjuncts to teaching. They share their professional experiences with interested classes. Such initiatives can be accelerated by systematically asking parents what they might wish to contribute to the educational program, whether in their children's classes or otherwise. Organizations such as the National Parent Teachers Association in the United States offer a range of resources for expanding these connections. However, we also see parents as becoming co-learners, thereby contributing not only to their children's learning and to the school, but to their own understanding as well. In German educational systems the concept of *Bildung*—emphasizing the shaping of the full person—plays a key role. With parents invited into the learning process, such shaping now expands into adulthood. With engaged parents, learning becomes a continuous activity of transformation.[8]

In turn, as parents become full collaborators in the educational system, they may become a significant force in its transformation. As illustrated in Chapter 4, parents may join together to successfully resist national policies they view as detrimental to their children. Similarly, parents can serve as important partners in driving policy change through, for instance, lobbying, joining social media campaigns, and supporting candidates in local elections.[9] Here they become co-creators of the future.

Neighborhood Institutions as Collaborators

The major stakeholders in our schools are undoubtedly the students, teachers, school administrators, and parents. At the same time, many neighboring institutions have a stake in what takes place in their schools. These may include businesses, religious institutions, police departments, social welfare systems, health centers, and performance arts groups. These stakeholders can contribute significantly to a school's thriving, thus enabling the school to enhance the well-being of the community. The potentials for collaboration are rich indeed.

Such reciprocal relationships are already practiced in many parts of the world. There are extended service-learning programs in the United States and apprenticeship programs in the United Kingdom. Equally, the creative arts have long offered opportunities for children and young people to participate and develop. Active programs in many inner cities have benefitted from the voluntary efforts of elder citizens to share their skills and wisdom with the young.[10] In Chicago, civic change agent Bliss Brown has brought together multiple institutions to enable underprivileged schools to flourish.[11] There are also informal learning programs in African countries where children participate in community gardens, wildlife centers, and peace building initiatives.[12]

Here is an open door for teachers and school administrators to invite collaboration with neighboring institutions. Such institutions might even be invited to join discussions evaluating the school's work and participate in generating its vision. For example, "To what extent can the school's work contribute to the well-being of the community?" Such evaluation might go both ways, further asking, "How have various organizations enhanced the educational potential of the school?" In the same way that it takes a village to raise a child, organizations may come to appreciate their role in "raising" their local schools.

Educational innovators have seen this challenge very clearly. Especially inspiring is the *Cities of Learning* initiative, started in Chicago and now spreading to the United Kingdom and beyond.[13] By tapping into the resources of the community, and by participating in the lived realities within the community, students acquire independent credit. They not only augment their skills, but they further learn about the meaning and relevance of their learning to the world of work Thus they bridge the arbitrary division between education and life in the world.[14] Such programs are indispensable in helping young people think about, pursue, and develop their interests in the context of the wider community.

Relationships with Higher Education

Final attention is directed to expanding relationships with institutions of higher education. In the preceding chapter, we discussed the problem of relying on grades and tests in selecting applicants and the need for such institutions to develop and tailor entrance tests to reflect their specific needs However, further attention is needed to the relationship between secondary schools and institutions of higher education. The potentials are far broader than the issue of assessment alone. Here we touch on two significant directions for enriching these relationships.

Toward Unlimited Learning

Our earlier arguments for emergent curricula point to the possibility of *unlimited learning*, by which we mean encouraging and stimulating young people to learn in multiple ways and regardless of timing. Universities can be a valuable adjunct. At present, universities are seldom involved with the education of secondary school students, other than offering "advanced placement" courses. Too often, these offerings are simply used by students to increase the likelihood of being accepted by a "good school." However, if universities are to serve the purpose of learning, they should open their doors to younger learners. Students should be encouraged to attend lectures, workshops, and discussions and to participate in other learning activities. For example, the Oxford University Summer School offers a program for school children aged 12–18, during which young learners enjoy a range of university-styled courses. Students may be introduced to a variety of subjects from architecture, history, or art to the natural sciences and engineering. Also exciting is the Schools-University Partnerships Initiative (SUPI) that functions across the United Kingdom.[15] The initiative supports collaborations between schools and universities in developing programs to inspire young learners from diverse backgrounds. Similarly, Queen's University, Belfast, and local secondary schools in Northern Ireland offer creative programs at the university. A program in creative technologies may include learning in robotics, virtual reality, and computer game design. Other programs center around environmental sustainability, creative arts, and health. All activities are interactive, experiential, and ungraded.

Building Links for Teachers' Inquiry and Professional Development

To support full transformation, schools and universities should also become partners in teachers' inquiry and professional development. There are cases in which university researchers involve school teachers and their students in ongoing research. Such practices should be encouraged and extended. Earlier we described the significance of teacher sophistication in action research (Chapter 6). University research teams could also come to schools and facilitate learning about research. They could help teachers and students develop research aptitudes and enhance their capabilities for collaborative research projects.[16] Especially welcome are the many coalitions between university researchers and school teachers aimed at experimenting with educational innovations. Schools play an invaluable role in piloting new practices, and collaborating with universities in creating and evaluating these practices can be invaluable.

Universities can also play a significant role in supporting the professional development of teachers and administrators. Universities have always played an important part in educating teachers and school leaders. However, we see universities as sustaining this role in supporting continued professional development. An ideal example is a program in which Beijing Normal University collaborated with a school system in Jiangsu Province in China.[17] A collaborative leadership model was introduced to school principals from primary and secondary schools that emphasized collaborative processes within the school and between the school and the community. Teachers were invited into appreciative discussion of their practices, thus enabling them to share and develop further. We also see a place for schools of education to initiate dialogues with local schools about critical issues of concern. Exploring such issues as the purpose of education, the arts of pedagogical engagement, the nature of learning, and the place of ethics in education should be unceasing.

Toward a New Narrative of Educational Life

We began this book with a story about education buckling in the face of growing numbers of disenfranchised and disinterested students, unprecedented levels of stress and depression, deteriorating interest in the profession of teaching, increasing bureaucratic control, and irrelevance to the times. And all of this despite waves of reform to boost education. Our primary purpose in this book has been to lay the groundwork for a new narrative. Relational process is the driving force in this narrative, with evaluative practices as a major pathway to realizing its potential. It is a pathway along which educators from around the world are now traveling, not only in practices of evaluation but in relationally rich innovations in pedagogy, curriculum, and leadership. When a narrative is truly inspiring, it can become a way of life. Indeed, an entire vision of education is in the making. Herein lies an invitation to join a global exploration of our potentials for human becoming.

Notes

1. This investment in broad-scale cultural change is amplified in the care-based ethic of program evaluation. See especially Visse, M., and Abma, T. A. (eds.). (2018) *Evaluating for a Caring Society*. Charlotte, NC: Information Age.
2. Siry, C., Brendel, M., and Frisch, R. (2016) "Radical listening and dialogue in educational research," *International Journey of Critical Pedagogy*, 7(3): 119–135.
3. See, for example, Dole, D., Godwin, L., and Moehle, M. (2014) *Exceeding Expectations: An Anthology of Appreciative Inquiry Stories from Around the World*. Chagrin Falls, OH: WorldShare Books.
4. In the Youth Invest school in Drammen, Norway, following a student presentation to the class, classmates can give the student cards that express what they feel were the strengths in the presentation. See Hauger, B., and Maeland, I. (2015) "Working with Youth at Risk: An Appreciative Approach," in T. Dragonas, K. J. Gergen, S. McNamee, and E. Tseliou (eds.), *Education as Social Construction* (pp. 92–107). Chagrin Falls, OH: WorldShare Books.
5. Vassiliou, A., and Dragonas, T. (2015) "Sowing Seeds of Synergy: Creative Youth Workshops in a Multi-Cultural Context," in Dragonas et al. (eds.), *Education as Social Construction* (pp. 192–212).
6. Dutch educator Loek Schoenmaker reports on a successful project to change a nationwide orientation to education in Surinam through a collaborative process involving students, community, and government. See Schoenmaker, L. (2014) *Happily Different: Sustainable Educational Change, a Relational Approach*. www.worldsharebooks.net
7. Fielding, M., and Bragg, S. (2003). *Students as Researchers: Making a Difference*. Swindon: Economic Social Research Council.
8. Gadamer, H-G. (1976) *Philosophical Hermeneutics*. Berkeley, CA: University of California Press.
9. Hartney, M. (2014). *Education Reform from the Grassroots: How and When Parents Can Shape Policy*. Washington DC: American Enterprise Institute.
10. See, for example, www.intergenerationalschools.org/the-intergenerational-school
11. See imaginechicago.squarespace.com. Brown's book can be downloaded at https://imaginechicago.squarespace.com
12. Avoseh, M. (2007). "The symmetrical relationship between learning and communities in traditional Africa," *Proceedings of SCUTREA*, The Queen's University of Belfast, Northern Ireland, 33–40.

13. See www.citiesoflearning.eu

14. For more discussion about the importance of work as constituted in our well-being, see Thomson, G., and Gill, S. (forthcoming) *Happiness, Flourishing and the Good Life: A Transformative Vision of Human Well-Being.* London: Routledge.

15. See www.publicengagement.ac.uk/nccpe-projects-and-services/completed-projects/school-university-partnerships-initiative

16. For instance, the University of Bristol has provided a joint bid for research funding that would bring university researchers and school teachers and students into collaboration.

17. Zhang, X. (2015). "School Principals: Problem Solvers and Appreciative Leaders," in Dragonas et al. (eds.), *Education as Social Construction.*

Author Index

For the benefit of digital users, indexed terms that span two pages (e.g., 52–53) may, on occasion, appear on only one of those pages.

Subject Index

For the benefit of digital users, indexed terms that span two pages (e.g., 52–53) may, on occasion, appear on only one of those pages.